W9-AEF-022

Confluences

Postcolonialism,

African American Literary Studies,

and the Black Atlantic

Confluences

JOHN CULLEN GRUESSER

The University of Georgia Press
Athens and London

Designed by Sandra Hudson

Set in 10 on 13 Minion by Wordstop Technologies (P) Ltd., Chennai, India

Printed and bound by Maple-Vail

The paper in this book meets the guidelines for permanence
and durability of the Committee on Production Guidelines
for Book Longevity of the Council on Library Resources.

Printed in the United States of America

09 08 07 06 05 C 5 4 3 2 1

Library of Congress Cataloging-in-Publication Data

Gruesser, John Cullen, 1959–

Confluences : Postcolonialism, African American literary studies, and
the Black Atlantic / John Cullen Gruesser.

    p. cm.

Includes bibliographical references and index.

ISBN 0-8203-2603-8 (alk. paper)

1. American literature—African American authors—History and
criticism—Theory, etc. 2. African Americans—Intellectual life—20th
century. 3. Literature, Comparative—American and English.
4. Literature, Comparative—English and American. 5. Atlantic Ocean
Region—Intellectual life. 6. Postcolonialism—Atlantic Ocean Region.
7. Gates, Henry Louis. Signifying monkey. 8. Atlantic Ocean Region—In
literature. 9. Gilroy, Paul. Black Atlantic. 10. African Americans in literature.
11. Postcolonialism in literature. I. Title.

PS153.N5G78 2005

810.9'896073—dc22

2004028321

British Library Cataloging-in-Publication Data available

A portion of chapter 3 is reproduced by permission of Routledge/Taylor
& Francis Books, Inc. Copyright © 1999, from John Cullen Gruesser, "An
Un-Easy Relationship: Walter Mosley's Signifyin(g) Detective and the Black
Community," *Multicultural Detective Fiction: Murder from the "Other" Side*,
ed. Adrienne Johnson Gosselin. A portion of chapter 2 is reprinted from
John Cullen Gruesser, "Say Die and I Will Die," with the permission of the
founder and editor, *Journal of Caribbean Literatures* 3.3 (2003): 99–109.

This book is dedicated to my parents,
Eileen Cullen Gruesser and John Anthony Gruesser,
in honor of their fiftieth wedding anniversary,
June 26, 2004

Contents

My soul has grown deep like the rivers.

LANGSTON HUGHES

Preface

We learn, unlearn, and relearn things throughout our lives. Relatives, friends, neighbors, teachers, mentors, and colleagues serve as our instructors. I'd like to take the time here to acknowledge some of those people who have taught and continue to teach me. I have to begin with my first teachers, my parents, from whom I am still learning. My wife Susan continues to teach me how lucky I am. As they enter new stages in their lives, my children, Jack and Sarah, provide me with insight into my own. And, particularly recently, I have learned what a remarkable person my sister Jenny is. Although their lives have diverged from mine and we longer see each other very often, longtime friends Mike Herrmann, Phil Johnson, Joe Murphy, and Tim Ungs have the ability to teach me new tricks. From high school through graduate school I was blessed with some extraordinary teachers who still inspire me, including Father John Crowley, John Horlivy, Joseph Duffy, and Craig Werner. I have learned a lot about teaching—and many other things—from colleagues in the English and other departments at Kean University (my "old" friend and neighbor Bert Wailoo among them). People I have come to know through professional organizations, such as the New Jersey

College English Association, the Poe Studies Association, and the Collegium for African American Research, have enriched my life. One of the benefits of being a college professor is that it makes it possible for me to learn from my students, several of whom have been or have gone on to become teachers themselves. Two students who taught me about courage and generosity and who died far too young were Tony Howard and Andrea Burris.

Through the miracle of books, I have been able to learn from people I have never met. One of them was the late Edward Said, whom I had the pleasure to hear speak a couple of times but did not know personally. Nevertheless, he has profoundly influenced my teaching and my scholarship. Much of my own early work, written before the term "postcolonialism" became prevalent, is indebted directly and indirectly to him. My first published essay, "'Ligeia' and Orientalism" (1989), applies his ideas to Edgar Allan Poe's 1836 story, and my dissertation, written between 1987 and 1989 and published in revised form as *White on Black* (1992), analyzes what Christopher L. Miller, in his effort to extend Said's concept of Orientalist discourse to texts about Africa, calls Africanist discourse.

Early versions of the readings of postcolonialism, Paul Gilroy, Salman Rushdie, Jean Rhys, Pauline Hopkins, Harriet Jacobs, Alice Walker, Walter Mosley, and Toni Morrison that appear in this book were presented at British Commonwealth and Postcolonial Studies conferences, New Jersey College English Association conferences, and scholarly meetings sponsored by the American Literature Association. Chapter sections on postcolonialism, Rhys, V. S. Naipaul, Mosley, Hopkins, Morrison, Harry Dean, Jacobs, and Walker have appeared in different form in *CEA Critic; The Journal of Caribbean Literatures; White on Black: Contemporary Writing about Africa,* published by the University of Illinois Press; *Multicultural Detective Fiction: Murder from the "Other" Side,* edited by Adrienne J. Gosselin and published by Taylor and Francis; *The Unruly Voice: Rediscovering Pauline Elizabeth Hopkins,* published by the University of Illinois Press; the Scholar's Forum of the Hawthorne in Salem Web site, http://www.hawthorneinsalem.org; *The Journal of African Travel-Writing* and *Black on Black: Twentieth-Century African American Writing about Africa,* published by the University Press of Kentucky; *College English Notes;* and *The Journal of Graduate Liberal Studies.* I thank the editors of these publications for allowing me to print this material in revised form here.

I am indebted to the following people for the advice and assistance they provided me on specific chapter sections—Sandra Adell, Elizabeth Ammons,

Kelly Anspaugh, Jana Argersinger, John Burger, Dean Casale, Paul Cyr, Carole Doreski, Mary Lou Emery, Styrk Fjose, Jason Haslam, Richard Katz, John Lyons, Nellie McKay, Aldon Nielsen, Theresa Sears, Carole Shaffer-Koros, Lamont Thomas, and Hanna Wallinger. I am also deeply grateful to Tish Crawford, Jon Davies, Ira Dworkin, Eric Sundquist, MJ Devaney, and the readers for the University of Georgia Press for their suggestions for improving the book as a whole, and to Nancy Grayson for her unfailing assistance and support.

Western writers until the middle of the twentieth century [...]
wrote with an exclusively Western audience in mind, even when
they wrote of characters, places, or situations that referred to,
made use of, overseas territories held by Europeans. But just
because [they did so] without any thought of possible responses
by the [...] natives resident there is no reason for us to do the
same. We now know that these non-European peoples did not
accept with indifference the authority projected over them, or the
general silence on which their presence in variously attenuated
forms is predicated. We must therefore read the great canonical
texts, and perhaps the entire archive of modern and pre-modern
European and American culture, with an effort to draw out,
extend, give emphasis and voice to what is silent or marginally
present or ideologically represented [...] in such works.

EDWARD SAID

1 An Overview

The Black Atlantic as a Bridge between Postcolonial
and African American Literary Studies

Widely credited with founding colonial discourse theory in *Orientalism* (1978)
and thus paving the way for postcolonial studies,[1] Edward Said went on, in
1993, to publish *Culture and Imperialism*, which seeks in part to reveal the reci-
procity between colonialism and the English novel. As indicated by the passage
quoted above, in the latter book he draws attention to postcolonial "responses"
to colonial discourse, issuing a call for what he terms "contrapuntal reading,"
a method requiring us to extend "our reading of texts to include what was
forcibly excluded" (66–67). In *Playing in the Dark: Whiteness and the Literary
Imagination* (1992), Toni Morrison analyzes what she calls the "Africanist" or
shadowy black presence in canonical white American literature, contending
that it has had profound and readily identifiable effects on this writing:

I have been thinking about the validity or vulnerability of a certain set of assumptions conventionally accepted among literary historians and critics and circulated as "knowledge." This knowledge holds that traditional, canonical American literature is free of, uninformed and unshaped by the four-hundred-year-old presence of, first, Africans and then African-Americans in the United States. It assumes that this presence—which shaped the body politic, the Constitution, and the entire history of the culture—has had no significant place or consequence in the origin and development of that culture's literature. [. . .] I am convinced that the contemplation of this black presence is central to any understanding of our national literature and should not be relegated to the margins of the literary imagination. Furthermore, American literature distinguishes itself as a coherent entity because of and in reference to this unsettled and unsettling population. ("Black Matter[s]" 310)[2]

As she remarks in "Unspeakable Things Unspoken: The Afro-American Presence in American Literature" (1989), an important precursor to *Playing in the Dark*, "The problem now is putting the question. Is the nineteenth century flight from blackness, for example, successful in mainstream American literature? Beautiful? Artistically problematic? Is the text sabotaged by its own proclamations of 'universality'? Are there ghosts in the machine? Active but unsummoned presences that can distort the workings of the machine and can also *make* it work? These kinds of questions have been consistently put by critics of Colonial Literature vis-à-vis Africa and India and other third world countries. American literature would benefit from similar critiques" (211–12).

Given the formidable similarities between postcolonial and African American literary criticism, exemplified by but by no means limited to Said's and Morrison's projects, it is both surprising and regrettable that only a handful of postcolonial theorists have sufficiently accounted for black American literature and that African Americanists have in general been resistant to postcolonial theoretical concepts. By no means am I suggesting that the two fields can and should be conflated. The experiences and cultural productions of people of African descent in the United States differ markedly and profoundly from those of persons from colonized or formerly colonized lands. Yet throughout history theoretical concepts imported from one discipline or culture into another have resulted in important advances in critical praxis. My purpose, then, is not to blur the distinctions between postcolonial and African American literary studies but rather to identify points of correspondence and build bridges between them. I believe that the establishment of conduits through which ideas and critical approaches can pass will serve to enrich both fields.

In 1985, Henry Louis Gates Jr. guest-edited a special issue of *Critical Inquiry* titled *"Race," Writing, and Difference* comprising fourteen essays by an impressive group of theorists and scholars, including Said, Homi Bhabha, Gayatri Spivak, Barbara Johnson, Jacques Derrida, and Gates himself. (The following year two more articles and seven critical responses to the earlier issue appeared in the same journal and shortly thereafter all of the essays and responses were published in book form by the University of Chicago Press.) The majority of the articles in the 1985 issue addressed subjects that would today be regarded as postcolonial while four others would be categorized as relating to African American scholarship. This special issue represents a key moment of confluence for a variety of theoretical and critical approaches to literature and culture, especially postcolonial and African American studies. In the ensuing years, both fields have grown considerably in terms of prominence and impact within and beyond the academy. Since its coalescence in the late 1980s and early 1990s, postcolonialism has been incredibly fecund, exerting an influence on areas as diverse as Native American, biblical, and Shakespearean studies. Yet despite the precedent of Gates's *Critical Inquiry* issue and the striking points of intersection between the two fields, African American studies has not been significantly influenced by postcolonialism and postcolonial theorists and critics have tended not to explore the long history of African American engagement with issues such as colonialism, displacement, and syncretism, and only occasionally have they chosen black American literature and culture as subjects for contemplation and analysis.

Because exceptions to the insularity or what might be called the territorialization of postcolonial and African American literary studies have been relatively infrequent, they are particularly noteworthy. In the introduction to *The Location of Culture* (1994), a meditation on contemporary attempts to "locate the question of culture in the realm of the *beyond*," Homi Bhabha reads the "freak social and cultural displacements" in the "'unhomely' fictions" of the African American and South African Nobel laureates Morrison and Nadine Gordimer (1, 12).[3] Echoing the Said epigraph and the extended Morrison passage quoted earlier, Bhabha declares that the "act of writing the world, of taking the measure of its dwelling, is magically caught in Morrison's description of her house of fiction—art as 'the fully realized presence of a haunting' of history. Read as an image that describes the relation of art to social reality, my translation of Morrison's phrase becomes a statement on the political responsibility of the critic. For the critic must attempt to fully realize, and take responsibility for, the unspoken, unrepresented pasts that haunt the historical present" (12).

Later in *Location,* a book that emphasizes the porous nature of the borders that separate people(s), Bhabha provides a concise description of postcoloniality that breaks down barriers that some postcolonial theorists have erected: "Postcolonial perspectives emerge from the colonial testimony of Third World countries and the discourses of 'minorities' within the geographical divisions of East and West, North and South" (171). Despite its apparent simplicity, this description builds on Bhabha's highly nuanced conception of the term in "DissemiNation," an essay that engages the work of Benedict Anderson, Walter Benjamin, Jacques Derrida, Michel Foucault, Sigmund Freud, Julia Kristeva, Edward Said, and others: "The postcolonial space is now 'supplementary' to the metropolitan centre; it stands in a subaltern, adjunct relation that doesn't aggrandize the *presence* of the west but redraws its frontiers in the menacing, agonistic boundary of cultural difference that never quite adds up, always less than one nation and double" (318). Although some recent articles and essay collections, including those devoted to postcolonialism and the United States, have embraced Bhabha's inclusive conception of postcoloniality, others have expressed reservations about or openly rejected it.[4]

In "Postcolonialism and Afrocentricity: Discourse and Dat Course" (1994), Ann duCille asserts that "while the designation 'postcolonial' may be new, the thematizing of relations of power between colonizer and colonized is not," as can be seen, she continues, in the shared concerns of, on the one hand, late-nineteenth- and early-twentieth-century African American intellectuals, such as W. E. B. Du Bois and Pauline Hopkins, and, on the other, postcolonial figures like Said (31).[5] Referring to the situation in which contemporary black scholars find themselves, duCille trenchantly observes, "What we seek is a precolonial connection; what we theorize is a postcolonial condition; what we're stuck with is a perennial colonial contradiction" (29). Unfortunately, she actually says very little about African American literary studies, choosing instead to contrast "Discourse" (postcolonialism's emphasis on global theory and its considerable cachet among scholars) with "Dat Course" (Afrocentrism's focus on local politics and its near-pariah status within the academy). Nevertheless, at the conclusion of her essay she raises a key issue when she ponders "what these three discourses—African American studies, postcoloniality, and Afrocentricity—might learn from one another, and in particular they might teach one another about the first world academy that both claims and disclaims them" (41).[6]

Without question Paul Gilroy's ambitious black Atlantic project, outlined in "Cultural Studies and Ethnic Absolutism" (1992) and elaborated in *The Black Atlantic: Modernity and Double Consciousness* (1993), *Small Acts: Thoughts on the Politics of Black Cultures* (1993), and "Route Work: The Black Atlantic and the Politics of Exile" (1996), stands as the most profound attempt to correlate postcolonialism and African American studies. Gilroy's penetrating readings of black American texts indicate the advantages of using postcolonial theoretical concepts, discourse analysis, and an expanded frame of reference to analyze African American literature. Inspired by Gilroy's emphasis on movement (especially via water), the main title of this book is intended to highlight the movement of ideas and influences through space and over time, a process comparable to the joining of two or more streams to form a powerful current. Embracing the flow of people and patterns of thought, *Confluences* aims to make a modest contribution to the globalization of literary study (at least in English) through its consideration of migration, circulation, transit, and related concepts.

In the pages that follow, my goals are, first, to provide concise introductions to three prominent and related theories of how marginalized peoples respond to dominant and dominating discourses for scholars, students, and other interested readers who may not be well acquainted with one or more of them and, second, to convince those people working in postcolonial or African American studies of the importance of breaking down the boundaries separating the two fields. For the former audience, I illustrate and implement the theoretical and critical concepts discussed in this chapter in my readings of individual texts in the second, third, and fourth chapters. For those readers already engaged with one or more of the three theoretical models, I point out their confluences and briefly raise theoretical and critical questions in this first chapter, and then pursue these confluences and explore these questions in more detailed fashion in subsequent chapters.

Postcolonialism

People have been involved in what has been variously known as anticolonial, Third World, and/or Commonwealth studies for many years. The demarcation of a codified domain of literary study now known as "postcolonialism," however, is recent. In *Orientalism,* Edward Said builds on Michel Foucault's contention that discursive formations are systems of power that restrict the way people see and talk about things. Examining the West's depiction of the Orient, especially the Near East, from the early 1800s to the present as its own reverse image, Said asserts that the purpose and results of Orientalist discourse are hegemonic: "My contention is that Orientalism is fundamentally a political doctrine willed over the Orient because the Orient was weaker than the West, which elided the Orient's difference with its weakness" (204). Because of its delineation of colonialist discourse, against which postcolonial texts have been seen as reacting, *Orientalism* has come to occupy the position of an urtext for postcolonial studies. Most observers regard *The Empire Writes Back: Theory and Practice in Post-colonial Literatures* (1989) as a groundbreaking publication in terms of codifying this new or newly renamed field. The title derives from a 1982 essay by Salman Rushdie and refers to how writers at the margins have responded to their colonized status and their exclusion from the literary canon. Not major theorists, along the lines of Said, Bhabha, and Gayatri Spivak, but rather synthesizers, popularizers, and disseminators of theory drawn from a variety of figures, regions, and perspectives, the authors of this book, Bill Ashcroft, Gareth Griffiths, and Helen Tiffin, are responsible to a degree for the widespread use of the term "postcolonialism" today.

As the first major attempt to delimit postcolonial studies, *The Empire Writes Back* sparked considerable critical debate in academic journals during the 1990s, being the subject of or occasion for numerous reviews, articles, and review essays, some of which have had long-term ramifications for the field. The 1991 essay "What Is Post(-)colonialism?" for example, welcomes the appearance of *The Empire Writes Back,* but the authors, Vijay Mishra and Bob Hodge, express certain reservations, particularly about its conflation of white settler countries (such as Australia) with formerly invaded countries (e.g., Nigeria) under the postcolonial rubric. The year 1993 saw the appearance of the first postcolonial anthology, Patrick Williams and Laura Chrisman's *Colonial Discourse and Post-colonial Theory: A Reader,* which criticizes *The Empire Writes Back*'s version of postcolonialism and features substantial selections from books and lengthy scholarly essays. This was followed a year later by Ashcroft, Griffiths, and Tiffin's more comprehensive *Post-colonial Studies Reader,* comprised of relatively brief excerpts from books and articles. In 1995, *PMLA,* one of the most influential and widely distributed academic journals in the fields of language and literature, devoted a special issue to postcolonialism. Since then a truly impressive number of books, anthologies, and essay collections relating to postcolonial theory and its impact on a wide variety of literatures, cultures, periods, and figures has been published. In 1998, Ashcroft, Griffiths, and Tiffin published their third book for Routledge (one of the leading presses in the field of postcolonial studies), a glossary of terms titled *Key Concepts in Post-colonial Studies,* and in 2002 they brought out a second edition of *The Empire Writes Back,* which is identical to the first except for a new chapter and the addition of one paragraph to the conclusion.[7]

The Empire Writes Back discusses three elemental concepts of postcolonial theory: the center-periphery opposition, the displacement experienced by colonized persons, and the hybrid character of postcolonial writing.[8] The metropolitan center serves as the clearinghouse for not only colonial and imperial policy but also the English language and the literary canon. Politically, colonized people at the periphery of empire submit to, openly rebel against, or covertly subvert colonial and imperial strictures. Linguistically, writers in settler cultures in particular but also authors in invaded societies who choose to write in English transform the language into an "english" of their own, which reflects the peculiarities of their environment. In the literary realm, because of their distance from the center and their use of a unique english, writers at the margins are excluded from the canon to which their texts counter-discursively respond.

Ashcroft, Griffiths, and Tiffin regard displacement as an integral component of the postcolonial condition, engendering "the special post-colonial crisis of identity [. . . , i.e.,] the concern with the development or recovery of an effective identifying relationship between self and place" (8). White settlers import and continue to speak the English language; however, they experience a spatial displacement from metropolitan culture. People in invaded societies do not suffer from geographic dislocation but have an alien language and culture forced on them, which results in linguistic displacement and cultural denigration. *The Empire Writes Back* acknowledges the limitations of the settler and invaded society models, citing their inability to describe the West Indian situation adequately: "Like the populations of the settler colonies all West Indians have been displaced. Yet this displacement includes for those of African descent the violence of enslavement, and for others (Indian and Chinese) the only slightly less violent disruption of slavery's 'legal' successor, the nineteenth-century system of indentured labour. As in India and African countries the dominant imperial language and culture were privileged over the peoples' traditions" (25). West Indians of African and Asian descent, like black Americans (about whom *The Empire Writes Back* is curiously reticent), thus experience a treble (i.e., spatial, linguistic, and cultural) displacement.

One of the most striking ideas informing postcolonial literature, hybridity (often used interchangeably with the terms "syncretism" and "creolization") counterbalances the negative connotations of displacement and its attendant identity crisis. In the introduction to the section of *The Post-colonial Studies Reader* devoted to hybridity, Ashcroft, Griffiths, and Tiffin, summing up the work of Bhabha and others, assert that "Most post-colonial writing has concerned itself with the hybridised nature of post-colonial culture as a strength rather than a weakness. Such writing focuses on the fact that the transaction of the post-colonial world is not a one-way process in which oppression obliterates the oppressed or the coloniser silences the colonised in absolute terms. In practice it rather stresses the mutuality of the process. It lays emphasis on the survival even under the most potent oppression of the distinctive aspects of the culture of the oppressed, and shows how these become an integral part of the new formations which arise from the clash of cultures characteristic of imperialism" (183). A direct result of the experience of displacement, hybridity reflects the possession of a "double vision" unavailable to those who have not been exposed to both metropolitan and peripheral culture, which, *The Empire Writes Back* notes approvingly, "ensures that in all post-colonial cultures monolithic perceptions are less likely" (36).

Despite significant similarities between the histories of and recent theories about African American and postcolonial literature, the Australian academics Ashcroft, Griffiths, and Tiffin largely exclude black American writing from the seemingly all-inclusive realm of postcolonialism. Rather than limiting itself to postindependence writing, *The Empire Writes Back* defines its subject area as "all the culture affected by the imperial process from the moment of colonization to the present day" (2). As a result, American literature as a whole qualifies as postcolonial: "Perhaps because of [the United States'] current position of power, and the neo-colonizing role it has played, its post-colonial nature has not been generally recognized. But its relationship with the metropolitan centre as it evolved over the last two centuries has been paradigmatic for post-colonial literatures everywhere. What each of these literatures has in common [. . .] is that they emerged in their present form out of the experience of colonization and asserted themselves by foregrounding the tension with the imperial power, and by emphasizing their differences from the assumptions of the imperial centre. It is this which makes them distinctly post-colonial" (2). *The Empire Writes Back*'s American examples, however, come exclusively from mainstream white writing: Charles Brockden Brown's late eighteenth-century gothic and sentimental novels reveal that he wrestled with questions about the adaptability of inherited forms to a postcolonial environment (15); a quotation from Mark Twain's *Adventures of Huckleberry Finn* illustrates how the vernacular is used to convert the English language into a distinctive "english" in settler cultures (56); Henry James and T. S. Eliot exemplify the tendency of "those from the periphery to immerse themselves in the imported culture, denying their origins in an attempt to become 'more English than the English'" (4).

Meanwhile, *Empire,* which rather arbitrarily limits itself to "those peoples formerly colonized by Britain" (1) and thus concentrates on English language texts, denies the legitimacy of what it calls the "Black writing" model, particularly as manifested in the francophone Negritude movement. Even though Ashcroft, Griffiths, and Tiffin unite such disparate literatures as those of Singapore, Ghana, and (white) America under the umbrella of postcolonialism, they contend that the "Black writing" model founders because of the major difference between the experiences of African Americans and those of other peoples of African descent: "Even where the idea of Black writing has worked well, in comparing and contrasting Black American writing with that from Africa or the West Indies, it overlooks the very great cultural differences between literatures which are produced by a Black minority in a rich and powerful white country and those produced by the Black majority population of an independent nation. This is especially so since the latter nations are often still experiencing the residual effects of foreign domination in the political and economic spheres" (19–20). Ashcroft et al. do not devote any of the eighty-six selections in *The Post-colonial Studies Reader* to African American literature.[9] Moreover, in an entry on "African American and post-colonial studies" in *Key Concepts,* they claim that African American studies "has had a widespread and often quite separate development from post-colonial studies, to which it is related only in a complex and ambiguous way" (6). And yet to illustrate how writers in invaded societies have responded to linguistic alienation, in *The Empire Writes Back* they cite Chinua Achebe quoting James Baldwin to explain how marginalized authors transform the English language so it will "'bear the burden' of their experience" (10).

In "Re-thinking the Post-colonial: Post-colonialism in the Twenty-first Century," the new chapter appearing in the second edition of *The Empire Writes Back,* the authors raise but refrain from answering the key question "Can we really say that slavery and its effects (e.g., the black diaspora) are not a legitimate element of the colonial and should not be part of what we study to try and understand how colonialism worked?" (200). Turning once more to the subject of African American studies, Ashcroft, Griffiths, and Tiffin make the rather puzzling statement, "Like the question of slavery itself, this field emphasizes the flexible boundaries of the post-colonial, for while the phenomenon of African American society is not specifically a consequence of colonization, it is a consequence of colonialism" (202). Apparently for the authors of *The Empire Writes Back* colonization only happens in two forms, people from the metropolitan center either settle un- or underpopulated lands or they invade and dominate already existing cultures; therefore, because Europeans shipped African slaves to plantations in the new world, including the English settler colonies in North America, Ashcroft et al. believe that African American society "is a consequence of colonialism" rather than colonization. Yet people of African descent, whose presence in the English colonies in North America dates at least as far back as 1619, were certainly colonized and, in the process, spatially, linguistically, and culturally dislocated. Although acknowledging a "lively and argumentative" relationship between African American and postcolonial studies, especially in the work of "bell hooks, Henry Louis Gates, and Cornell [sic] West," the authors of *The Empire Writes Back* contend that the former field is "much larger" than the latter (202), by which they presumably mean that African American studies concerns much more than the colonialism and neocolonialism of black Americans. However, even if African American studies encompasses histories and issues not directly connected to postcolonial studies, it does not follow that the fields should be seen as totally isolated from each other, especially given the many areas where they do intersect.

The Empire Writes Back rightly criticizes Negritude for being essentialist and adopting the binarism of Western philosophy. However, it also presents a flawed history of the movement that reduces cross-cultural interactions between black American and African political and literary movements: "In recent years the philosophy of Negritude has been most influential in its derivative form in the Afro-American Black consciousness movement. Senghor's influence in America can be traced to prominent Black intellectuals of the 1920s such as Langston Hughes and Richard Wright; the latter significantly, spent most of the later part of his life in exile in Paris" (21). However, Leopold Senghor and Aimé Césaire did not found Negritude until the 1930s, and the former not only openly acknowledged his movement's debt to African American writing, particularly that of Hughes, but also linked it to the turn-of-the-century anglophone African Personality movement.[10] Moreover, Wright, who was born in 1908, did not begin publishing until the 1930s. Although Ashcroft, Griffiths, and Tiffin point out the continuing pursuit of a black aesthetic in African American criticism, they note approvingly the influence of structuralism and discourse analysis in the early 1980s on critics such as Houston Baker and Henry Louis Gates, whose literary critical approach they regard as a significant advancement over Negritude and the Black Arts movement.

Despite Ashcroft et al.'s attempt to exclude black American writing from their compendium of marginalized literatures, the similarities between certain aspects of their account of postcolonial discourse, on the one hand, and Gates's

Signifyin(g), a major theory about black American literature by one of the best-known and most prolific African American literary critics, on the other, are striking. Just as postcolonial theory has transformed the extent to and ways in which the writings of colonized and formerly colonized people have been discussed and analyzed, Gates's *Figures in Black: Words, Signs and the "Racial" Self* (1987) and *The Signifying Monkey: A Theory of Afro-American Literary Criticism* (1988) have had a profound impact on the study of African American literature. In their efforts to transform their fields, Gates and many postcolonial theorists have made use of poststructuralism. Moreover, they also have proposed similar, politically tinged rhetorical strategies as their fields' signature gestures.

Reflecting the influence of Said, Rushdie, Spivak, and others, Helen Tiffin argues in "Post-colonial Literatures and Counter-discourse" (1987) that post-coloniality neither simply responds to metropolitan culture and/or the literary canon (because a writer could be imitating colonial discourse without questioning its legitimacy) nor merely adopts an anticolonial political stance, which would raise the possibility of a white Briton writing postcolonial literature; rather, it subverts the dominant discourse while calling its own biases into question: "It is possible to formulate at least two (not necessarily mutually exclusive) models for future post-colonial studies. In the first, the post-coloniality of a text would be argued to reside in its discursive features, in the second, in its determining relations with the material situation. The danger of the first lies in post-coloniality's becoming a set of unsituated reading practices; the danger of the second lies in the reintroduction of a covert form of essentialism. In an attempt to avoid these potential pitfalls I want to try to combine the two as overarching models [. . .] by stressing counter-discursive strategies which offer a more general post-colonial reading practice or practices" (96–97).

Tiffin considers counter-discourse superior to other models that are based on nationality, race, or culture, such as Negritude, because of its ability to account for not only a wide variety of literatures that write back to the metropolitan center but also situations in which postcolonials themselves assume the role of colonizers: "If the impulse behind much of post-colonial literature is seen to be broadly counter-discursive, and it is recognized that the resulting strategies may take many forms in different cultures, I think we have a more satisfactory model than national, racial, or cultural groupings based on marginalisation can offer, and one which perhaps avoids some of the pitfalls of earlier collective models or paradigms. Moreover, such a model can account for the ambiguous position of say, white Australians, who, though still colonised by Europe and European ideas, are themselves the continuing colonisers of the original inhabitants. In this model, all post-invasion Aboriginal writing and orature might be regarded as counter-discursive to a dominant 'Australian' discourse and beyond that again to its European progenitor" (96). Tiffin identifies two types of postcolonial counter-discourse. One responds to colonialism and colonialist literature in a general way. The second rewrites a specific, canonical colonialist text. For Tiffin all postcolonial texts are counter-discursive, yet some, such as Jean Rhys's re-vision of Charlotte Brontë's *Jane Eyre* in *Wide Sargasso Sea* and J. M. Coetzee's reworking of Daniel Defoe's *Robinson Crusoe* in *Foe*, are more explicitly so than others. Building on this argument, the authors of *The Empire Writes Back* state in their conclusion, "Thus the rereading and rewriting of the European historical and fictional record is a vital and inescapable task at the heart of the post-colonial enterprise. These subversive manoeuvres, rather than the construction of *essentially* national or regional alternatives, are the characteristic features of the post-colonial text. Post-colonial literatures/cultures are constituted in counter-discursive rather than homologous practices" (221). It should be noted that Tiffin's assertion that postcolonial literatures can themselves be the object of counter-discourse appears to provide a model for thinking about black American literature's relationship to mainstream white literature; however, the authors of *The Empire Writes Back* make no attempt to extend this model to the American context.

Signifyin(g)

Gates's efforts to delineate the African American literary tradition resemble attempts to define postcolonial literature. He rejects the repudiative theories of African American literature proposed by Houston Baker and Robert Stepto as well as Addison Gayle's and Maulana Karenga's Black Aesthetic in favor of "Signifyin(g)," a revisionary, double-voiced response to the "discourse of the black," Gates's term for texts by both whites and people of African descent that portray black characters. His theory builds on Zora Neale Hurston's, Ralph Ellison's, Thomas Kochman's, Geneva Smitherman's, and especially Roger Abrahams's and Claudia Mitchell-Kernan's discussions of "signifying" as a folkloric concept. In an effort to map out a tradition that is distinctively black but avoids the essentialism that characterizes Negritude, the Black Arts movement, and Afrocentrism, Gates argues that black American writing is not simply a repudiation of assertions of black inferiority that either imitates white literature or refutes its assumptions, nor is it a reflection of a distinctive black essence; instead, it is a counter-discursive strategy associated with the

African American trickster figure of the Signifying Monkey, which ultimately derives from the Yoruba trickster and messenger of the gods, Esu-Elegbara.

Conceived as companion volumes, Gates's *Figures in Black* relates African American literature to mainstream white literary theory, reviews the history of black literary criticism, and proposes a theory of Signifyin(g) rooted in the black vernacular tradition, while *The Signifying Monkey* elaborates, illustrates, and situates this theory in a specifically black (primarily African American but also, he asserts, African and diasporic) context.[11] In *Figures* Gates laments and endeavors to remedy African Americans' aversion to theory, an aversion that, as he points out, is nevertheless readily understandable given the manner in which theory has for centuries victimized people of African descent: "Black writers and critics, since [Antonius G.] Amo, have been forced to react against an impressive received tradition of Western critical theory which not only posited the firm relation among writing, 'civilization,' and political authority, but which also was called upon by various Western men of letters to justify various forms of enslavement and servitude of black people. It is no surprise that black people have been theory-resistant" (27). Rather than responding with a theory of their own, according to Gates, African American literary artists and critics up until at least the Harlem Renaissance strived to counter accusations of black inferiority by demonstrating their literacy and rebutting the charges leveled against them. This involved adhering to mainstream white formal and stylistic conventions, publishing biographies of blacks responsible for great achievements, and producing propagandistic texts that had few if any aesthetic aspirations. The emphasis on content and disregard of form and technique continued in the 1930s, 1940s, and 1950s when the influence of Marxist ideas resulted in what Gates punningly calls the "race and superstructure" school of black literary criticism, reaching its "zenith of influence and mystification" with the Black Arts movement in the 1960s (31).

Gates focuses on two works of African American literary criticism from the 1970s that in different ways fall short of providing a rigorous and comprehensive theory of black American literature.[12] The first is Houston Baker's *Long Black Song: Essays in Black American Literature and Culture* (1972), which asserts that white theories of culture were largely responsible for creating a distinct black American culture that arose to repudiate them. Baker also sees repudiation as characteristic of African American folklore and as a key feature distinguishing black and white American literature. Gates discerns two problems with the book's emphasis on repudiation. First, like African American literature and criticism generally, it focuses on the content of a literary work rather than its structure, technique, and rhetoric. Second, by making black American writing dependent on the white theorizing about culture to which it responds, rather than proposing an autonomous (black) source for African American literature, *Long Black Song* is doomed to go to battle against—and have its argument shaped by—those same assertions of black inferiority. As Gates expresses it in an apt analogy to the sweet science, "Baker finds himself shadow-boxing with the ghostly judgments of Jefferson on Phillis Wheatley and Ignatius Sancho; his blows are often telling, but his opponent's feint is deadly" (*Figures* 38). Gates takes issue even more strongly with Addison Gayle's *The Way of the New World* (1975), which elaborates the Black Aesthetic. Once again content dominates over form in this strictly ideological criticism, which regards language and literature as expressions of a black essence. Gates laments Gayle's purely political criticism of writers such as James Baldwin and his literal approach to literature, which cannot do justice to a multivalent text like Ralph Ellison's *Invisible Man*. According to Gates, the major problem with Gayle's theory is its refusal to recognize that literature is a linguistic system and not an expression of external reality: "'Blackness' is not a material object, an absolute, or an event, but a trope; it does not have an 'essence' as such but is defined by a network of relations that form a particular aesthetic unity" (*Figures* 40).[13]

Like the authors of *The Empire Writes Back* vis-à-vis postcolonial writing, Gates regards rigidly essentialized descriptions of African American literature as dead ends and he proposes a more theoretically rigorous alternative that combines aspects of each approach. After calling for "attention to black figurative language, to the nature of black narrative forms, to the history and theory of Afro-American literary criticism, to the fundamental relation of form and content, and to the arbitrary relationship between the sign and its referent" as well as to the "nature of intertextuality, that is, the nonthematic manner by which texts [. . .] respond to other texts" (*Figures* 41)—calling for attention, in short, to key concerns of traditional mainstream white literary criticism and poststructuralist theory that have rarely been broached by African American critics—he introduces his theory of Signifyin(g), which is intended to address these deficiencies. Unlike Baker's repudiation theory in which African American literature opposes but is nonetheless dependent on white literature, Gates asserts that Signifyin(g) "is indigenously black and derives from the Signifying Monkey Tales," which themselves derive from the African trickster Esu-Elegbara (48). Moreover, instead of being obsessively thematic like Baker's, Gayle's, and black American critical theories generally, "Signifyin(g) is a uniquely black rhetorical concept, entirely textual or linguistic, by which a second statement or figure repeats, or tropes, or reverses the first. Its use as a figure for intertextuality allows us to understand literary revision without resource to thematic, biographical, or Oedipal slayings at the crossroads; rather, critical signification is tropic and rhetorical. Indeed, the very concept of Signifyin(g) can only exist in the realm of the intertextual relation" (49).

Instead of concentrating on the content of African American literary texts that repudiate the assertions of white authors, Signifyin(g) focuses on the rhetorical strategies black American authors use to revise the discourse of the black.[14] A major strength of Gates's theory is its ability to account for literary movements and genres that develop in response to earlier ones. Phillis Wheatley critically signifies on Milton's and Pope's poetry and Kant's and Hume's aesthetic theories, the slave narrators revise not only such sentimental figures as the noble Negro of texts like Aphra Behn's *Oronooko* and the "Dying Negro" of the English Romantic poets but also the sentimental and the picaresque novel, and the authors associated with the Harlem Renaissance rewrite turn-of-the-century anti-Negro propaganda. The process does not work in only one direction, however, for Gates regards the plantation novel as a counter-discursive response to the slave narrative. Nor do black texts only signify on white ones and vice-versa. Gates describes Zora Neale Hurston's *Their Eyes Were Watching God* as a "double-voiced" novel that blends African American oral tradition and the free indirect discourse used by European authors such as Gustave Flaubert and Virginia Woolf, and likewise reads Ishmael Reed's *Mumbo Jumbo* as a complex revision of white and black writers, particularly Wright and Ellison. Acknowledging that "all texts Signify upon other texts" and suggesting that this intertextual, revisionary concept may be useful in studying other literatures, Gates nevertheless regards his notion of Signifyin(g), which graphically represents the linguistic difference between white and black pronunciations of the word "signifying," as distinctively black because he believes that "black writers, both explicitly and implicitly, turn to the vernacular in various formal ways to inform their creation of written fictions. To do so, it seems to me, is to ground one's literary practice outside the Western tradition. Whereas black writers most certainly revise texts in the Western tradition, they often seek to do so 'authentically,' with a black difference, a compelling sense of difference based on the black vernacular" (*Signifying* xxiv, xxii).

In *The Signifying Monkey,* Gates makes a useful distinction between motivated and unmotivated Signifyin(g), associating the former with parody and the latter with pastiche and quoting from *The Oxford Classical Dictionary* to distinguish "pastiche, which caricatures the manner of an original without adherence to its actual words" from "parody proper, in which an original, usually well known, is distorted, with the minimum of verbal or literal change, to convey a new sense, often incongruous with the form" (107). He explains that "[b]y motivation I do not mean to suggest the lack of intention, for parody and pastiche imply intention, ranging from severe critique to acknowledgment and placement within a literary tradition. Pastiche can imply either homage to an antecedent text or futility in the face of a seemingly indomitable mode of representation" (xxvii). Both types of literary signification can appear in a single, "double-voiced" text: "Literary echoes, or pastiche, as found in Ellison's *Invisible Man,* of signal tropes found in Emerson, Eliot, Joyce, Crane, or Melville (among others) constitute one mode of Signifyin(g). But so does Ellison's implicit rhetorical critique of the conventions of realism found in Richard Wright's *Native Son, The Man Who Lived Underground,* and *Black Boy*" (xxvii). To "Signify," then, is to repeat with "a black difference" (xxii–xxiii).[15] To do so in the context of a negative critique is to engage in motivated Signifyin(g), as "[w]hen Sterling A. Brown riffs on Robert Penn Warren's line from 'Pondy Woods' (1945)—'Nigger, your breed ain't metaphysical'—with 'Cracker, your breed ain't exegetical'" (122). To do so without the critique, either "as a loving act of bonding," as Gates argues Alice Walker does in *The Color Purple* vis-à-vis Zora Neale Hurston's *Their Eyes Were Watching God,* or "without sufficient revision," as he asserts Paul Laurence Dunbar does in some of his dialect poems in relation to James Whitcomb Riley, is to practice unmotivated Signifyin(g) (xxvii, 113, 120).

Despite the similarities between postcolonial counter-discourse and Signifyin(g), many postcolonial theorists have chosen not to correlate African American and postcolonial literature. Gates also chooses not to pursue such connections. Although he pinpoints an African origin for Signifyin(g) in Esu-Elegbara and magnanimously offers "Signifying" (without the "g" in parenthesis) to "critics of other literatures [who may] find this theory useful as they attempt to account for the configuration of the texts in their traditions" (*Signifying* xxv), he has decided to restrict his focus to African American oral and written literature and does not explicitly relate his theory to the literatures of (other) colonized peoples. However, as I hope to show, this can and should be done.

The Black Atlantic

Like postcolonial theorists and Gates, Paul Gilroy proposes a counter-discourse that is neither completely rhetorical nor rigidly essentialist in his pathbreaking book *The Black Atlantic.* Engaging with philosophical, sociological, historical, political, as well as literary issues, Gilroy explains that he borrowed the term "black Atlantic" from African art history and histories of mercantilism because he "wanted to supplement the diaspora idea with a concept that emphasized the in-between and the intercultural" ("Dialogue" 208). Although he rejects the essentialism that characterizes Negritude and Afrocentrism in favor of a plural (but nevertheless historically grounded) diasporic approach, his theory of the black Atlantic is itself a black writing model, albeit a selective one. Gilroy's subtitle refers to W. E. B. Du Bois's famous concept of African American "twoness." However, his theoretical model is not fully Pan-African. Associated with Du Bois who played a role at all six of the Pan-African meetings that took place between 1900 and 1945, the term refers to the recognition of a shared heritage and common political interests among people of African descent throughout the world. The black Atlantic, defined as "a deterritorialised multiplex and anti-national basis for the affinity or 'identity of passions' between diverse black populations" ("Route Work" 18), is predicated on the experience and/or memory of new world slavery, which links African Americans, black Britons, and West Indians of African descent but does not include other colonized peoples, Africans (with the exception of Sierra Leoneans and Liberians, many of whom are descendents of freed slaves), apparently, among them.

The black Atlantic model is valuable for four major reasons. First, Gilroy's brave attempt to rewrite the history of modernity to include slavery and its attendant racist ideology raises important questions that theorists and historians of the modern era have long needed to address. Second, the black Atlantic accounts for and underscores the many cross-cultural interactions among black American, black British, black West Indian and to a lesser extent African philosophy, music, literature, and political discourse that a sizable portion of postcolonial theorists have chosen not to emphasize. Third, Gilroy convincingly argues that transatlantic (particularly European) travel profoundly influenced the political stances of key African American figures. Finally, he effectively employs postcolonial theoretical concepts in his often brilliant readings of the texts of these black Americans.

Residing "in but not necessarily of the modern, Western world" ("It Ain't" 120) and thus possessing what Gilroy calls a "striking doubleness," black Atlantic peoples share more than a collective history of victimization; they have an ambivalent perspective on modernism and Western notions of progress that differs significantly from that of ruling white populations. Seeing slavery and its attendant horrors as connected to rather than divorced from the Enlightenment ideas associated with modernism, black Atlantic peoples constructed what Gilroy calls a "counterculture of modernity": "[The black Atlantic] was shaped by the need to supply a counter-narrative of modernity that could offset the wilful innocence of those European theories that ignored the complicity of terror and rationality and in so doing denied that modern slavery could have anything to do with the sometimes brutal practice of modernisation or the conceits of enlightenment" (*Black Atlantic* 37; "Route Work" 25). Echoing postcolonial theorists, Gilroy regards the black Atlantic experience of displacement and its "unashamedly hybrid character" as potential sources of strength "capable of conferring insight" rather than unmitigated detriments "precipitating anxiety" ("Route Work" 22). However, Gilroy regards movement through space as more significant than place and displacement, a shift that is nicely expressed through his emphasis on "routes" rather than "roots." For this reason, maritime travel and trade figure prominently in his black Atlantic model: "It should be emphasized that ships were the living means by which the points within th[e] Atlantic world were joined. They were mobile elements that stood for the shifting spaces in between the fixed places that they connected. Accordingly they need to be thought of as cultural and political units rather than abstract embodiments of the triangular trade. They were something more—a means to conduct political dissent and possibly a distinct mode of cultural production" (*Black Atlantic* 16–17).

Gilroy not only uses postcolonial theoretical terminology to delimit the black Atlantic world and characterize its counter-discourse to modernism but also applies it to African American literature, to which he consistently turns (rather than the literary productions of black Britons and West Indians of African descent) to illustrate his points: "In black America's histories of cultural and political debate and organisation, I found another, second perspective with which to orient my own position. Here too the lure of ethnic particularism and nationalism has provided an ever-present danger. But that narrowness of vision which is content with the merely national has also been challenged from within the black community by thinkers who were prepared to renounce the easy claims of African American exceptionalism in favour of a globalised, conditional politics in which anti-imperialism and anti-racism might be seen to interact if not to fuse" (*Black Atlantic* 4). For over two centuries, black Americans have been acutely aware of their peculiar situation, frequently conceiving themselves as the vanguard of the black race, the people most qualified to lead Africa and other members of the diaspora to freedom and prosperity. This is the belief

Gilroy identifies as African American exceptionalism, a viewpoint that his emphasis on African American travel and the cross-cultural interactions among black Atlantic peoples works to problematize.[16] He remarks in "Cultural Studies and Ethnic Absolutism" that "much of the precious political, cultural, and intellectual legacy claimed by Afro-American intellectuals is in fact only partly their 'ethnic' property. There are other claims to it which can be based on the structure of the Atlantic diaspora. A concern with the Atlantic as a cultural and political system has been forced on black historiography and intellectual history by the economic and historical matrix in which plantation slavery [. . .] was one special moment. The fractal patterns of cultural and political exchange and transformation that we try to specify through manifestly inadequate theoretical terms like creolization and syncretism indicate how both ethnicities and political cultures have been made anew in ways that are significant not simply for Caribbean peoples but for Europe, for Africa (especially for Liberia and Sierra Leone), and of course, for Afro-America" (192). In illustrating his theory in *The Black Atlantic,* Gilroy chooses to concentrate on texts by black American men who traveled across the Atlantic to Europe and sometimes Africa. He pinpoints Du Bois's *The Souls of Black Folk* (1903) as "the first place where a diasporic global perspective on the politics of racism and its overcoming interrupted the smooth flow of African American exceptionalism" (*Black Atlantic* 120) and asserts that this foreign experience significantly influenced other key African American figures, altering "their perceptions of America and racial domination" (*Black Atlantic* 17) and often converting them from an exceptionalist position to either a Pan-African or an internationalist outlook.

My intention in this chapter has not been to argue that African American literature should be regarded as postcolonial (although if white American literature is, as has been asserted, it would follow that black American literature, like Aboriginal Australian writing, must be as well) but rather to contend that certain concepts of postcolonial literary theory can usefully be applied to African American literary studies, as Gilroy's *The Black Atlantic* vividly illustrates, and vice versa. Despite the major differences in scope and objectives among them, postcolonial theory, Signifyin(g), and the black Atlantic offer valuable and far-reaching critical insights. Each uses the concept of a historically and politically grounded counter-discourse to describe the process by which one or more marginalized peoples rewrite the dominant discourse imposed on them. Moreover, each of these three influential, revisionary theories devotes attention to the ambivalent, "double" or hybrid position marginalized persons occupy within specific societies. Although this experience of two or more cultures can produce anxieties about identity in the subject, it also confers on him or her a unique perspective that can be advantageous in some contexts. Postcolonialism's stress on place and displacement helps to make comprehensible the attractions and repulsions that African Americans, who like black West Indians are spatially, linguistically, and culturally displaced from their ancestral home, have felt toward Africans and other people of the diaspora. Signifyin(g)'s ability to account for genres and countergenres greatly assists in understanding the relationship between black American literary productions and mainstream, white literature, particularly the ways in which specific genres have long been used to caricature or otherwise stereotype black characters and the means by which African American writers have responded to this. The black Atlantic model not only explores some of the common ground between postcolonial and African American literary studies, but its stress on movement through space also promotes the discovery of cross-cultural influences among peoples of African descent.

Each of the three chapters that follow begins by examining a literary text that illustrates the value of the theoretical model under consideration, strives to extend the model in its analysis of a second text, and concludes with a reading of yet another text that raises one or more questions about the theory. The initial section of chapter 2 examines Salman Rushdie's short story "Chekov and Zulu," both as a counter-discourse to Rudyard Kipling's portrayal of the Great Game in *Kim* and as an exploration of the end(s) of postcolonialism. In the second section, I argue that recognizing that Jean Rhys's *Wide Sargasso Sea* functions as a highly effective counter-discourse to not only Charlotte Brontë's *Jane Eyre* but also Shakespeare's *Othello* aids in the analysis of the racial theme in the novel. In the final section, I discuss the sometimes uncomfortable relationship between the recent Nobel Prize winner V. S. Naipaul and postcolonial studies. In several works, particularly *A Bend in the River,* Naipaul writes back to Joseph Conrad; however, rather than counter-discursively questioning or rebutting *Heart of Darkness,* Naipaul honors the novella and strives to confirm its validity.

In comparison to the texts by major but very different postcolonial writers that I examine in the second chapter, those by African Americans I have selected for discussion in the third and fourth chapters are more eclectic in terms of genre, the prominence of the author, and subject matter. Chapter 3 explores the connections between postcolonial counter-discourse and Signifyin(g). Praising Gates's theory for its insights into the relationship between texts in specific genres and its valuable distinction between motivated and unmotivated signification, I also explore the possibility of moving beyond its focus on African American texts and contexts. First I illustrate the usefulness of the theory in connection with a genre such as mystery writing by discussing how Walter Mosley in *Devil in a Blue Dress* signifies on white hard-boiled fiction and creates a Signifyin(g) detective in the character of Easy Rawlins. Next I analyze Pauline Hopkins's "A Dash for Liberty," a short story that signifies on the white historical record concerning the 1841 rebellion aboard the slave ship *Creole* in a more profound manner than the earlier treatments of the incident by black and white writers as well as on these earlier versions themselves. In addition, I underscore the story's overall trajectory, which encompasses the West Indies and points towards Africa. Finally, I use Toni Morrison's theory of American Africanism to reveal the racial implications of Nathaniel Hawthorne's seemingly raceless tale, "The Birth-mark." If race is already present in classic white American literary texts, as Morrison argues in *Playing in the Dark*, then this raises a question about Gates's definition of Signifyin(g) as repetition with a black difference, for African American texts that thematize birthmarks, including Morrison's own *Sula*, are not so much adding a racial dimension to Hawthorne's story as they are counter-discursively expanding on and making explicit its racial implications.

In chapter 4 I examine African American texts concerning journeys to Europe or Africa for which the black Atlantic model is particularly apposite. The first section establishes the validity of Gilroy's assertion about the profound influence foreign travel has had on the political stances of black Americans through an examination of Harry Dean's *The Pedro Gorino*, an autobiographical text, named after the author's ship, that emphasizes routes through its depiction of an African American sailor traversing the black Atlantic world. Seeking to extend Gilroy's ideas to the life and text of an African American woman, the second section addresses how Harriet Jacobs's ten-month sojourn in England and her depiction of it in chapter 37 of *Incidents of the Life of a Slave Girl* significantly affects the rest of the narrative. In the final section, I call into question the mediating position Gilroy confers on England in the black Atlantic model through an analysis of Alice Walker's *Possessing the Secret of Joy*, a woman-centered novel about an African heroine who, after being politically transformed while residing in United States, returns to her homeland to defy the taboo surrounding female circumcision/genital mutilation.

Acknowledging the numerous and significant differences between the experiences of blacks in the United States and people in colonized and formerly colonized nations, I believe that African Americanists and postcolonial theorists and critics would do well to consider the histories and cultural productions of black Americans vis-à-vis those of postcolonial persons more comprehensively than they may have done heretofore. It is my hope that the chapters that follow contribute to such a project.

[Postcolonialism] confers on colonialism the prestige of history proper; colonialism is the determining marker of history. Other cultures share only a chronological, prepositional relation to a Eurocentred epoch that is over (post-), or not yet begun (pre-). In other words, the world's multitudinous cultures are marked not positively by what distinguishes them but by a subordinate, retrospective relation to linear, European time.

ANNE MCCLINTOCK

2 Postcolonial Counter-discourse

Salman Rushdie, Jean Rhys, V. S. Naipaul

Echoing Anne McClintock, who expresses reservations about the widespread use of the term "postcolonialism" in her essay "The Angel of Progress: Pitfalls of the Term 'Post-colonialism'" (1992), some critics have objected to the concept of postcolonial counter-discourse. Arun Mukherjee, for example, states that it relegates people at the margins to "one modality, one discursive position. We are forever forced to interrogate European discourses, of only one particular kind, the ones that degrade and deny our humanity. I would like to respond that our cultural productions are created in response to our own needs" (qtd. in McLeod 28). Building on Mukherjee's point, John McLeod has raised another major concern about the concept: "[A] re-writing will always remain tethered in some degree to its antecedent. This problematises the extent to which postcolonial re-writings of literary 'classics' ever can be really independent of colonial culture. The re-writing will always invest value in the source text as a point of reference, no matter how much it is challenged as a consequence. For this reason, some critics believe re-writings can never fully challenge the authority of the classic text" (169). Objections of this sort are particularly relevant in a case such as that of Joseph Conrad's *Heart of Darkness,* which has profoundly influenced the way that Westerners have thought about and depicted Africa for over a century.[1]

Nevertheless, counter-discourse remains a useful concept whose application can be expanded to both nonpostcolonial texts and analyses of racial issues within postcolonial texts; it has difficulty, however, accounting for texts that respond to canonical authors without subverting them. Literary texts about Asia, the West Indies, and Africa by three prominent postcolonial writers, each of whom was born in a British colony and eventually settled in the so-called mother country, exemplify the concept's advantages and limitations. Responding to Kipling's treatment of the Great Game in *Kim,* Rushdie's "Chekov and Zulu" illustrates postcoloniality as many critics have defined it. Responding not merely to *Jane Eyre* but also *Othello,* Rhys's *Wide Sargasso Sea* demonstrates that a postcolonial rewriting can be more than merely supplementary to a canonical text and that the concept of counter-discourse can be useful in investigating the racial dynamics within a text. Because Naipaul's *A Bend in the River* pays homage to rather than undermines *Heart of Darkness,* it forces us to return to the question of what exactly is meant by the terms "postcolonial" and "counter-discourse".

Updating the Great Game and Exploring the End(s) of Postcolonialism in "Chekov and Zulu"

A lengthy article relating Rudyard Kipling's writings, especially the depiction of the Great Game in *Kim* (1901) and other works, to the situation the United States found itself in vis-à-vis Afghanistan appeared in the *New York Times* on 26 January 2002 (Rothstein). Nine days later, on 4 February, Salman Rushdie published an Op-Ed piece in the same paper criticizing anti-American sentiments in the Muslim world and Europe, commending the United States for swiftly ousting the Taliban, but presciently warning America not to turn a deaf ear to constructive criticism or to abandon efforts to build consensus with the international community ("America and Anti-Americans"). It might seem merely coincidental that the writer regarded as the chief apologist for Western imperialism and the author of what many believe to be the quintessential postcolonial novel, *Midnight's Children,* were both in the news as the world attempted to come to grips with the events of 11 September 2001. Kipling and Rushdie, however, have much in common: each was born on the subcontinent, spent long periods in England, and became a leading literary figure of his day. In a critical essay titled "Kipling" (1990), Rushdie reveals himself to be well versed in the Briton's works, which he both highly praises and roundly condemns. He attributes the "[a]nger and delight" these writings evoke in him to, on the one hand, the racial bigotry of "Kipling Sahib" and, on the other, "Ruddy Baba's" intimate familiarity with India (74, 75). Although "[t]here will always be plenty in Kipling that I will find difficult to forgive," remarks Rushdie, "[n]o other Western writer has ever known India as Kipling knew it, and it is this knowledge of place, and procedure, and detail that gives his stories their undeniable authority" (80, 75).

Born into a Muslim family and raised in Bombay, Rushdie is perhaps the best-known postcolonial figure, living with a price on his head for writing *The Satanic Verses,* coining the phrase that Ashcroft, Griffiths, and Tiffin would use as the title for their codification of postcolonial studies, and ranking as one of the top ten public intellectuals in the world, according to Richard Posner's recent reckoning. Rushdie's short story "Chekov and Zulu" and the book in which it was published, *East, West* (1994), epitomize postcoloniality, as many critics have defined it. The title of the collection, with its strategic comma placement, writes back to the first two lines of the initial (and the final) stanza of Kipling's "The Ballad of East and West," "*Oh, East is East, and West is West, and never the twain shall meet, / Till Earth and Sky stand presently at God's great Judgment Seat.*" Rushdie does not call the book *East and West,* which would simply echo Kipling and might minimize the differences between these parts of the world; rather, he presents them as if they were items in a series, unique yet syntactically equivalent. *East, West* comprises nine stories equally divided among three sections: "East," "West," and "East, West." Set in India and Great Britain in the 1980s and 1990s, "Chekov and Zulu" appears in the final section and illustrates the concept of postcolonial counter-discourse in its response to colonialism generally and Kipling's treatment of the Great Game in *Kim* in particular; moreover, it explores the end(s) of postcoloniality, especially in connection with a country such as India.

The story's use of pop culture (especially the 1960s American television program *Star Trek,* from which the title characters' names derive) and postmodern narrative techniques, as well as its willingness to tackle questions of morality, exemplify what has come to be regarded as a postcolonial style of writing.[2] Illustrating the contention of many critics that postcolonialism contains the history of colonialism within it, the story not only thematizes India's postindependence present and recent past but also refers to India's colonial past and writes back to Kipling's pivotal novel about the subcontinent. In "Chekov and Zulu," the Great Game has come to England where the eponymous former schoolmates, one a high-ranking Hindu diplomat and the other a Sikh security agent, seek information about the "enemies" of the Indian government. Yet even though his fiction and critical writings have made Rushdie indispensable to postcolonial studies, "Chekov and Zulu" suggests that he himself has reservations about the accuracy and usefulness of the concept of postcoloniality, especially in connection with the nation of India. Anchored by the assassinations of Mrs. Gandhi in 1984 and her son (and Chekov and Zulu's fellow Doon School alumnus) Rajiv in 1991, Rushdie's story exposes the limitations of the very notion of postcoloniality, a maneuver that is itself a hallmark of postcolonial writing, according to specialists in the field.

Rushdie divides "Chekov and Zulu" into three numbered sections. The first takes place on 6 November 1984, roughly a week after the assassination of Indira Gandhi and during a period when many Sikhs are being killed. Chekov, at thirty-three already the number two man at the Indian embassy in London, visits Zulu's wife, explaining to her that because her husband has not checked in since 4 November many people in the government believe that he is affiliated with the radical Sikhs who gunned down the prime minister. The first half of the second section is set three months earlier. Reunited in London after many years apart, Chekov and Zulu, who continue to use their school nicknames from the original *Star Trek* series, take in the sights of the erstwhile seat of empire, the former angrily referring to the English as "burglars," while the latter calmly proclaims that "[t]he colonial period is a closed book" (155, 157). The second half of section 2 begins on the day of the assassination, 31 October, with the two men discussing Zulu's mission to infiltrate Khalistan separatists based in England, recounts Zulu's suspicions on the day he disappears that his undercover operation is a test of his loyalty, and concludes with an account of a dinner hosted by Chekov at which he refers to Zulu going AWOL. The first half of section 3 takes place in February 1985. Finally breaking his silence, Zulu sends an urgent message through his wife to Chekov, who leaves immediately to pick up his friend. When they meet, Zulu turns over a list of names to Chekov, tenders his resignation, and abruptly walks away. The second half of section 3 serves as a coda to the story, informing the reader that the two men never see each other again. Zulu starts a highly successful private security business in Bombay; meanwhile, moments before dying along with Rajiv Gandhi on 21 May 1991 during an attempt to restore the Congress Party to power, Chekov has a vision of himself holding hands with Zulu on the bridge of the starship *Enterprise* a split second before it is destroyed by the Klingons.

Chekov and Zulu's intelligence work and *Kim*'s depiction of the Great Game serve as the most obvious link between the story and Kipling's novel. However, historians and critics who have written about *Kim* do not agree on exactly what Kipling meant by the "Great Game," a phrase that, according to Peter Hopkirk, was first used by Arthur Conolly, a British officer sent to explore central Asia in 1829 (Kling 302). Zohreh Sullivan annotates it as the "cold war between the British Empire and Russia for control over southern and western Asia" (110). Blair Kling offers a similar definition but shifts the disputed territory to "the Middle East and Central Asia" (302).[3] Meanwhile, Edward Said provides a concise gloss—"British intelligence in India" (*Culture* 137)—which derives more from the novel itself than history and once more alters the location. Ian Baucom agrees with Said on an Indian setting for the Great Game but presents yet another explanation of its derivation: "The mapping of the subcontinent, officially known as the Survey of India, and colloquially referred to as the 'Great Game,' was an immense, protracted, and varied task. The survey began in 1767 […] and continued without interruption until India's independence in 1947" (351).[4] For some readers of the novel, then, the Great Game concerns an external threat to British India while for others it is all about India itself.

Rushdie's essay on Kipling provides some insight into this split. He states that he is most fascinated by those early stories in which Kipling's realistic depiction of certain native characters undermines his imperialist fantasy that India will always need outside rulers. However, he believes that by the time Kipling wrote *Kim* his "control had grown," rendering "Kim's torn loyalties" less "interesting" to Rushdie than "the ambiguous, shifting relationships between the Indians and the English" in some of the tales written a dozen years earlier (74). In their attempts to place the novel in its historical context, critics such as Kling and Ann Parry have explained how Kipling exercises the "control" in *Kim* that Rushdie talks about. They argue that Kipling shifts attention away from the real threat to British authority in the subcontinent, Indian resistance as seen in physical form in the 1857 rebellion and in political form in the incipient Indian National Congress, to an external threat—Russia's designs to pluck the jewel from Britain's imperial crown. Clinging to a colonialist fantasy, the novel suggests that the head of the British Secret Service, Colonel Creighton, has to oversee a vast intelligence network involving people of different ethnicities and nationalities, including the Pathan horse trader Mahbub Ali, the Bengali

Babu Haree Chunder Mookerjee, and the Irish orphan Kimball O'Hara himself, because of the Great Game and not because of the growing number of educated Indians seeking rights and opportunities comparable to those available to Anglo Indians.

More intriguing and significant than the espionage are the external versus internal and fantasy versus reality conflicts that lie at the heart of "Chekov and Zulu," just as they do in *Kim*. Before 31 October 1984, Chekov and Zulu are, as the latter declares, "[b]lood brothers" (157), intelligence officers stationed in Britain committed to combating "terrorist" threats to the Indian state. However, when Hindus respond to the assassination of Mrs. Gandhi by killing large numbers of Sikhs and no action is taken to punish these murders, everything changes for Zulu. In their final conversation, Zulu asks Chekov, "Who needs extremists when there are killings in Delhi? Hundreds, maybe thousands, Sikh men scalped and burned alive in front of their families. Boy-children, too," to which he adds, "No Congress workers have been indicted [...]. In spite of all the evidence of complicity. Therefore, I resign. You should quit, too" (168, 168–69). For Zulu it is no longer those agitating for independence who pose the greatest threat but rather people within the ruling Congress Party itself, some of whom fomented and then turned a blind eye to the widespread slaughter. The external-internal divide can also be seen in Chekov's statements about the origins of the revolutionary ideas motivating those who have sought to overthrow the colonial and postcolonial governments in India, as well as in the names of the main characters. At the dinner party, he declares, "England has always been a breeding ground for our revolutionists," citing Nehru and Gandhi. "Now that England's status has declined," Chekov states further, "I suppose it is logical that the quality of revolutionists she breeds has likewise fallen," and then he angrily denounces the "Kashmiris" and "Khalistan types" (164). Yet when time stops during the instant that Dhanu shakes Rajiv Gandhi's hand, he notes, "These Tamil revolutionists are not England-returned [...]. So, finally, we have learned to produce the goods at home, and no longer need to import" (170). What Chekov has failed to consider, both immediately following the 1984 assassination and in the ensuing six and a half years, is why the Indian government is "produc[ing such] goods." *Star Trek*, too, comes from the outside. Zulu's wife complains about the nicknames, objecting that her husband's name should be spelled with an "S" (in keeping with the television series in which the character was Asian) rather than a "Z." (153). During the party, Chekov explains that at school "we never saw one episode of the TV series. [...] The whole thing was just a legend wafting its way from the US and UK" (165). A female guest agrees with him that only Zulu's and his own name stuck because they somehow go together, and to illustrate her point she proceeds to misquote the lyrics of the song "Love and Marriage" made popular by Frank Sinatra. In typical postcolonial fashion, the story suggests that when external ideas and influences are imported to India they are subject to both mistranslation and reinterpretation.

On the day he goes undercover, Zulu suggests that Chekov lives in a fantasy world rather than the real world. In contrast to himself, a "soldier" who operates in "the world of life and death," Zulu claims the diminutive diplomat resembles the hobbits in Tolkien's Middle-earth who "work and squabble and make merry and [...] have no fucking clue about the forces that threaten them, and those that save their tiny skins" (162). Chekov, however, remains loyal to the Congress Party (and its new leader Rajiv Gandhi), does his best to keep up appearances, and continues to live in his *Star Trek*-inspired fantasy world: "The policy was business as usual. The dreadful event must not be seen to have derailed the ship of State: whose new captain, Chekov mused, was a former pilot himself. As if a Sulu, a Chekov had been suddenly promoted to the skipper's seat" (163). When they are briefly reunited three months later and Chekov asks Zulu why he went through with his dangerous mission if he no longer believed in the government, Zulu takes a clear moral position: "I am security wallah [...]. Terrorists of all sorts are my foes. But not apparently, in certain circumstances, yours" (169). At the moment of his death, Chekov appears to acknowledge the truth in Zulu's assertion that he has refused to face reality: "'The tragedy is not how one dies,' he thought. 'It is how one has lived'" (170). The very end of the story, moreover, functions as a fantasy within a fantasy. Chekov imagines himself on the bridge of the *Enterprise* with not only Captain Kirk, Mr. Spock, and Dr. McCoy but also Zulu, whose hand he takes "firmly, victoriously, as the speeding balls of deadly light approached" (171). Yet Zulu is no longer his friend and dying in a bomb blast while participating in a campaign that was doomed to fail hardly qualifies as a triumph.

To dismiss Chekov's ongoing and Zulu's former faith in a Congress Party–run state of India as simply a fantasy, however, is to minimize the complexity of both the country and the short story. In an essay written in the wake of the 1984 assassination, Rushdie discusses two paradoxes at the heart of what he calls the "India-idea" and, like Zulu, takes a moral stand against Congress Party corruption and excesses. The first paradox is that the fledgling central government of India "holds sway" over states that have "cultures and independent existences going back centuries" ("Assassination" 41). The second is that the "ethic" of independent India "has always been secular" even though religion plays such a central role in its citizens' lives (42–43). He blames the Nehru-Gandhi family, who "make the Kennedys look like amateurs" (43), for its dynastic aspirations and the slain prime minister, in particular, for "going out to get the Hindu vote" (43).[5] Deploring the choice of the untried Rajiv to succeed his mother, Rushdie calls on the new government "[t]o show that India is not in the grip of any new *imperium*. And to restore our faith in the India-idea," which he contends must "base itself firmly on the concept of multiplicity, of plurality and tolerance, of devolution and decentralization wherever possible. There can be no one way—religious, cultural, or linguistic—of being an Indian; let difference reign" (44). The alternative to Chekov's fantasy world, then, is not Realpolitik but the proper mixture of idealism and realism.[6] Rushdie suggests that instead of being a fantasy, like Gene Roddenberry's idealistic sci-fi series or Tolkien's novels, the India-idea functions as a standard of perfection to be striven for and one by which India must measure itself. The challenge involves being realistic without becoming cynical, keeping the objective in sight without being corrupted by power or seduced by rhetoric.

In 1899, the year that Kipling was to begin working on *Kim* in earnest, he published "The White Man's Burden," a copy of which he sent to his friend Theodore Roosevelt, on the occasion of the American victory in the Spanish-American War. Once a British colony itself, the United States had now acquired a Caribbean and Pacific empire. Beyond voicing a racist belief in white superiority over "savage" races, the poem vividly chronicles the resentment such "new-caught, sullen peoples" (7) feel toward those who rule over them. Ironically, as anti-British as Chekov's sentiments are, his contempt for those in India who fail to accept the justice and inevitability of Congress Party rule is aptly expressed in the fifth stanza of Kipling's poem:

> *Take up the White Man's burden—*
> *And reap his old reward:*
> *The blame of those ye better,*
> *The hate of those ye guard—*
> *The cry of hosts ye humour*
> *(Ah, slowly!) toward the light:—*
> *'Why brought ye us from bondage,*
> *Our loved Egyptian night?' (33–40)*

As powerful as "Chekov and Zulu" is when read within its Indian context and as a counter-discourse to *Kim*, the story also has relevance beyond the country's borders and its reworking of Kipling, raising questions about the postcolonial condition generally. If, as the story seems to assert, India under the Congress Party, particularly during the 1970s and 1980s, became a virtual empire, a "new *imperium*" recklessly ruling over peoples of widely divergent ethnic origins and religious affiliations, then does the term "postcolonial" have any meaning when applied to the nation? If indigenous people take over from outside rulers and simply replace one form of domination with another, then has independence truly been achieved? And if new leaders keep preaching multiplicity, secularism, and democracy but their actions produce antithetical results, then have these ideals become mere fantasies? Quite possibly, in the changing world wrought by the events of 11 September 2001 and their aftermath, Rushdie's ideas about the end(s) of postcolonialism in his counter-discursive "Chekov and Zulu" have even more significance today than they did when the story was originally published.

Betraying the Other, Controlling Female Desire, and Legally Destroying Women in *Wide Sargasso Sea*

In a setting far from the metropolitan center, a newly married man is informed by another man that his wife has betrayed him. Rather than defending his spouse, the man believes the accusations without substantive proof and sets about to revenge himself on the woman, convincing himself that his cause is just. In contrast to the wife, who passively submits to her fate, her female servant denies the husband's charges and refuses to allow him to get away with destroying his wife without a fight. Seemingly this summary could only describe Shakespeare's *Othello,* in which the title character, the military and de facto political leader in war-threatened Cyprus, accepts Iago's testimony that Desdemona has been unfaithful and suffocates her in her bed, only to learn from the outraged Emilia that her mistress Desdemona was true and that "honest" Iago has deceived him. Yet this précis applies equally well to *Wide Sargasso Sea* (1966) by the white Dominican-born Jean Rhys. This novel has been consistently read as a rewriting of the plotlines of *Jane Eyre*. However, it depicts the Rochester figure[7] taking Daniel Cosway's slanderous statements about Antoinette as the truth, driving his wife to madness, and, prior to transporting her to a smothering imprisonment in England, being aggressively confronted about what he is doing by Antoinette's childhood nursemaid and her family's former slave, Christophine.

These and other parallels between the novel and the tragedy serve as the foundation for my argument that, in addition to functioning as a rewriting of *Jane Eyre*, *Wide Sargasso Sea* serves as a postcolonial and feminist re-vision of *Othello*. *The Tempest* has long been the Shakespearean text most frequently invoked and analyzed by postcolonial critics,[8] yet *Othello* concerns such matters as empire, colonization, slavery, race relations, miscegenation, and the male desire to control the female, and these are precisely the subjects addressed by Rhys in her novel. The comparison between the tragedy and the novel can be elaborated to include not only Daniel Cosway and Iago, as outlined in the previous paragraph, but also Antoinette's cousin Sandi and Cassio[9]; however, in the reading that follows, I want to concentrate on the links among Antoinette, Rochester, Othello, and Desdemona—specifically those between Antoinette and Othello as colonized Others and victims of betrayal, Antoinette and Desdemona as women destroyed by their husbands, and Rochester and Othello as men of power who take what they consider to be righteous vengeance on their spouses. Additionally, I examine the connections and contrasts between Christophine and Emilia in order to address the novel's racial dynamics.

Anticipating Gayatri Spivak's plea for the production of "a narrative in literary history, of the 'worlding' of what is now called 'the third world'" (262) and Edward Said's call in *Culture and Imperialism* for contemporary readers to supply the silenced people in colonial texts with voices, Rhys makes Bertha Mason, the madwoman in the attic permitted only animal-like utterances and uncanny laughter in *Jane Eyre,* the protagonist and predominant speaker in *Wide Sargasso Sea.*[10] As daring, significant, and well executed as Rhys's famous rewriting of Brontë's canonical novel is, her subtler reworking of one of Shakespeare's greatest dramas is at least as audacious, skillfully managed, and remarkable. In *Othello,* the general plays the dual role of victim and victimizer, falling into Iago's trap to bring him down and pitilessly extinguishing the life of his innocent wife. However, because the play, reflecting the patriarchal ethos of its era, is unquestionably Othello's tragedy, Shakespeare puts greater emphasis on the protagonist's reversal of fortune than on the crime he commits, constructing his plot so that Desdemona's death serves to increase Othello's misery (precisely as Iago planned that it would). Thus, even though it is Othello who cruelly murders Desdemona, she ultimately resolves into one of Iago's victims, joining a list that includes Roderigo, Emilia, Cassio, and of course Othello himself. Rhys redresses this inequity at the core of the tragedy by creating in her novel a pair of figures, each of whom reflects one aspect of Othello's character.

Like the general, Antoinette is a colonized Other destroyed by a person from the metropolitan center whom she trusted. Acquiescing to Rochester's appeal that they attempt to make their arranged marriage work, Antoinette not only sacrifices her fortune and what little independence she has to her new husband but allows herself to fall in love with him, thereby finding a purpose for living, only to have him spurn her affections, deliberately undermine her sanity, remove her from her native environment, and lock her away for the rest of her life. Meanwhile, despite the differences in their origins, ages, accomplishments, and fates, Othello and Rochester, as husbands and men of status and power, act in remarkably similar ways. Each is altered by the emotions and appetites that his wife stirs in him; each obsessively seeks to control his wife's passion, which he himself has elicited and that he jealously and erroneously comes to believe is not directed solely toward him; and each regards himself as morally or legally justified in punishing his wife for her supposed betrayal. In rewriting *Othello* Rhys positions the white creole Antoinette at the center of *Wide Sargasso Sea*, depicting her as doubly victimized by her status as a non-European and as a married woman.

   A vast majority of the action in each text unfolds in a colonial location: the first act of Shakespeare's play takes place in Venice, the imperial center, but thereafter the action shifts permanently to Cyprus; *in Wide Sargasso Sea,* the brief, final section is set in England, but otherwise all the events occur in the West Indies. Moreover, in each text a character from the mother country gains the trust of a colonized subject and uses this trust to destroy the Other's sense of him- or herself. Having appeared to serve Othello loyally for several years, often fighting side by side with him, Iago has won the general's complete confidence. Thus, he can use male camaraderie and a soldier's sense of honor, as well as his superior knowledge of Venetian customs, in his plot to devastate Othello. In a similar manner, Rochester gains Antoinette's trust and thereby her money, only later to use these and his status as her husband and an Englishman to erode her sense of herself so much that she loses her ability to distinguish what is real from what isn't.

Although Iago makes trouble for Othello in act 1 by rousing Brabantio and alerting him that his daughter and the general have eloped, it is not until the setting has shifted to Cyprus, where martial law has replaced civil law and where the rules of war rather than the rules of polite society are in effect, that he embarks on his scheme to convince Othello that people are not what they appear to be, specifically that Desdemona is not a faithful wife and Cassio is not a loyal friend. More significantly, playing on the self-doubts that these accusations awaken, Iago aims to persuade Othello that he himself is not the happily married, highly successful man people believe him to be. Iago correctly surmises that if he can show the general that things are not as they seem, Othello will respond as a warrior whose honor has been insulted and perhaps even revert to his erstwhile non-Christian beliefs. And he knows that nothing will better serve to destroy Othello's sense of himself as a loyal servant of imperial Venice advantageously married to a member of one of its leading families than for him to kill his wife in the mistaken belief that she has cuckolded him. In one of the few critical essays to examine the tragedy from a postcolonial perspective, Philippa Kelly explains that the words Othello speaks just before killing himself indicate Iago's success in obliterating the general's self-image by revealing "his compulsion, at the play's end, to deal with ambivalence by externalizing his otherness into images of 'the base Indian,' the 'turbaned Turk.' By telling the story of 'the Venetian' who 'took by th' throat the circumcised dog, / And smote him—thus' (5.2.358–59), he radically splits himself and kills off his other. Disposing of the other leaves intact the Venetian self, yet […] the irony is that through this naive inscription, Othello destroys the text, his self, altogether" (4). Othello's suicide thus serves as the final and most harrowing instance of Iago's success in manipulating people into doing his dirty work for him.

From the beginning of her postcolonial novel, Rhys connects her protagonist to Shakespeare's tragic hero—a former slave of African origin hired by imperial Venice to run its army—by stressing Antoinette's in-between status and the vulnerability that accompanies it. People perceive Antoinette as neither black nor completely white, neither French nor truly English, neither native nor colonizer. Burned out of her childhood home, sent to a convent to be groomed for marriage, and told she should accept a man from a distant land whom she has just met as her husband, Antoinette has always lacked power over the circumstances that shape her destiny. In a rare act of defiance on her part, she initially refuses to marry Rochester. However, by portraying himself as a kindred spirit, someone similarly at the mercy of forces he cannot control, by suggesting that in working together they can make their marriage work ("I'll trust you if you'll trust me. Is that a bargain?"), and by promising her "peace, happiness, safety" (47), Rochester secures Antoinette's tacit approval for their union to take place as planned. Yet in becoming Rochester's wife, Antoinette not only surrenders her wealth but also abandons the emotional defense mechanism she developed as a child in response to being rejected by her mother and her playmate Tia. For years she has directed her love toward familiar places and things but not people (with the possible exception of Christophine, who is nearly as alienated from the black and white communities as Antoinette). Now, however, Antoinette falls passionately in love with her new husband. After asking Rochester "Why did you make me want to live?" (54) and wondering what she would do if he "took this happiness away when I wasn't looking … ," she whispers, "If I could die. Now, when I am happy. Would you do that? You wouldn't have to kill me. Say die and I will die" (55).

This passage, the novel's most explicit reference to *Othello,* reveals the method by which Rhys goes about recasting Shakespeare's tragedy. In act 1 Othello greatly underestimates the depth of his feelings for Desdemona, asserting before the Duke and the senators that "the young affects / In me [are] defunct" (1.3.266–67); however, when he is reunited with his wife on Cyprus, he can barely contain his emotion, telling her

> *If it were now to die,*
> *'Twere now to be most happy, for I fear*
> *My soul hath her content so absolute*
> *That not another comfort like to this*
> *Succeeds to unknown fate. (2.1.187–91)*

Observing this uncharacteristic display of passion, Iago knows for certain how to engineer the general's downfall. In *Othello,* one man uses another man's deep feelings for a woman, emotions he has never experienced before, to cause him to make a series of mistakes that leads to his destruction. Othello's declaration of love for Desdemona suggests that she has power over him.[11] However, patriarchal Venice does not allow a woman like Desdemona to wield any real power. Act 1, scene 3 basically shows male control over Desdemona being transferred from her father, Brabantio, to her husband, Othello. Like Desdemona, Antoinette has her fate decided for her by men; yet, in contrast to Desdemona's elopement with Othello, which represents an act of rebellion against her father, Antoinette's marriage amounts to a business transaction in which her stepfather's money is bartered for Rochester's reputable English name, with her stepbrother acting as the middleman who clinches the deal. The key to Rhys's re-vision, not only in the "Say die" passage but throughout the novel, is that while Othello is a man, he is also, like Antoinette, a colonized Other and therefore does not wield the total power over Desdemona that Rochester, as both a man and a European, wields over Antoinette. Reflecting his complete dominance over his wife, Rochester, as Antoinette unwittingly but accurately predicts, has the ability to destroy her without physically killing her (i.e., through words alone). By taking his love away from her, causing her to hate the only place she truly loves, and using his own form of voodoo to turn Antoinette into her deranged mother, Rochester in effect says "die" to his wife.

Just as Iago poisons Othello's mind with images of Desdemona's supposed infidelity, Rochester treats Antoinette as though she were mentally unsound and uses one of her mother's names, Bertha, to address her. As a result of these deliberate attempts to alter the personality of these colonized Others, Othello and Antoinette are transformed into something people from the metropolitan center regard as monstrous or bestial and eventually the protagonists take their own lives. Othello changes spiritually, emotionally, and even physically. He abandons his Christianity in act 3, scene 3, calling on the forces of darkness to assist him in achieving his revenge on Desdemona and Cassio. In act 4 this once imperturbable man openly weeps. Moreover, his metamorphosis manifests itself physically in the final two acts, in which he, respectively, suffers an epileptic fit and, according to Desdemona, rolls his eyes demonically. Similarly, Rochester's calculated steps to undermine his wife's psyche cause Antoinette to change drastically. After he turns against her on Dominica in part 2, she reverts to a childish dependence on Christophine, begins to consume large quantities of rum, appears noticeably different to her husband, and at one point bites Rochester. In the novel's final section, Antoinette not only savagely plunges her teeth into the arm of her stepbrother but is so strikingly altered after an extended period of confinement that she fails to recognize her own image in a mirror.[12] Moreover, in a final link between Antoinette and Othello, Rhys's main character apparently commits suicide, presumably emulating Brontë's Bertha Mason in jumping to her death after setting fire to the house that for so long has been her prison.

As a colonized Other deceived by someone from the metropolitan center, Antoinette resembles Othello; however, as a wife falsely accused of betraying, and then unjustly destroyed by, the man she married, her fate reenacts Desdemona's. Marriage causes each woman to become completely reliant on, and thus puts each at the mercy of, her husband. Just as Desdemona loses her father's approbation and concomitant social standing by wedding Othello, Antoinette gives up all claim to her money and property when she becomes Rochester's wife. Falsely accused of betrayal, the women are initially subjected to acts of violence—Othello striking Desdemona in act 4, scene 1 and Rochester roughly forcing himself sexually on Antoinette—and later destroyed by their husbands. Not only do Emilia and Cassio attest to the falsity of the charges against Desdemona, but the latter is so innocent that she cannot even bring herself to speak the word "whore" that Othello has hurled at her. Similarly, Rochester himself indicates that he is the one who initiates Antoinette, a seventeen-year-old girl fresh out of a convent school, into the mysteries of sexuality: "I watched her die many times. In my own way, not in hers. In sunlight, in shadow, by moonlight, by candlelight. In the long afternoons when the house was empty. Only the sun was there to keep us company. We shut him out. And why not? Very soon she was as eager for what's called loving as I was—more lost and drowned afterwards" (55). Moreover, Antoinette's recollection of her final days in the West Indies in part 3 of the novel suggests that the sexual dimension of her relationship with Sandi began after Rochester rejected her and embarked on his plan to destroy her: "Sandi often came to see me when that man was away and when I went out driving I would meet him. I could go out driving then. The servants knew, but none of them told. Now there was no time left so we kissed each other in that stupid room. Spread fans decorated the walls. We had kissed before but not like that. That was the life and death kiss and you know a long time afterwards what it is, the life and death kiss. The white ship whistled three times, once gaily, once calling, once to say good-bye" (110).

This fascinating passage, one of several in the book that alludes to Peter's denial of Christ, signals a chain of betrayal in the novel—a chain initiated by Rochester and not Antoinette. It is also pervaded by a sense of foreboding, indicating that at the time Antoinette intuitively senses the miserable fate that lies ahead of her in England. In act 4, scene 3 of *Othello*, Desdemona evinces similar intimations of her impending demise. Yet neither woman offers staunch resistance to her husband's unjust behavior. Despite her suspicions that Othello might kill her, Desdemona does not flee but rather goes to sleep in their bed, and, when he tells her that that is precisely what he intends to do, she does not cry for help or aggressively defend herself but rather begs him for mercy. Antoinette, too, offers very little resistance at first to Rochester's plot against her, rejecting Christophine's advice that she leave her husband. Later she strongly rebels, but only after Rochester has driven her mad and long confined her in a storage room like an exotic bauble brought back from the colonies in which he has lost interest.

Whereas in Antoinette Rhys combines Desdemona's status as a woman in patriarchal society destroyed by the man she marries with one aspect of Othello's character—that of a colonized Other betrayed by someone from the metropolitan center—in Rochester she creates a figure who embodies the other part of Othello's character, namely that of a husband so consumed by jealousy that he seeks to gain control of his wife's passionate nature by any means necessary. Like the general, the newly married Rochester experiences emotions he has never felt before, becomes obsessed with his wife's supposedly illicit desires, and avenges himself on her pitilessly while convincing himself that he is acting justly.

Just as Othello is overwhelmed by the passions that Desdemona stirs in him, Rochester describes himself as "thirsty for" Antoinette, connecting her to the alien landscape whose secret he continually expresses a desire to learn. It is not love he feels for her, as he explicitly states (55), but rather an uncontrollable and unquenchable lust that unnerves him. Rochester strives to gain the upper hand over his desire for Antoinette by projecting his raging libido on her and then taking drastic steps to control *her* desires. This act of projection is apparent when Rochester, rejecting Christophine's plea that he attempt to recapture what he once had with Antoinette, characterizes his wife as the one who cannot restrain her sexual impulses: "She thirsts for *anyone*—not for me" (99). Yet, like Othello who continues to declare his undying love for Desdemona even after he has killed her, Rochester acknowledges that his desire for Antoinette remains as strong as ever despite the calculated steps he has taken to destroy her: "Above all I hated her. For she belonged to the magic and the loveliness [of the place]. She had left me thirsty and all my life would be thirst and longing for what I had lost before I found it" (103).

In his only soliloquy, Othello laments that husbands cannot control every aspect of their wives' lives: "O curse of marriage, / That we can call these delicate creatures ours / And not their appetites!" (3.3.284–86). As a man and a colonizer, Rochester, too, has a compulsion to gain the upper hand—physically, mentally, emotionally, financially, even linguistically. For instance, he devises a plan to become the person in charge of the servants and the household finances at Granbois, telling himself soon after arriving there that he must bide his time before taking over, "Not now [...]. Not yet" (53). This mania for control also explains why the chaotic feelings Antoinette unleashes disturb him so profoundly. A basic insecurity at the heart of Othello's and Rochester's character accounts for their need to be in control. Despite a storied career that has brought him to the pinnacle of his profession, Othello is a black man in white society who is taking potentially catastrophic emotional, social, and political risks by marrying Desdemona. Likewise, although Rochester comes to the West Indies as a colonizer, he is nevertheless an inexperienced and dislocated youth still reeling from the staggering blow dealt to his self-image by the mercenary actions of his father and brother. Thus, where more secure men would be able to dismiss or dispassionately evaluate and if need be calmly investigate the accusations made by Iago and Daniel Cosway, Othello and Rochester quickly become convinced that the charges are true because they confirm fears these newlywed husbands have themselves harbored.

Totally self-absorbed, neither man defends his wife to her accuser nor can he bring himself to communicate his suspicions in an open and honest manner to the woman he has married. On the contrary, each man decides that the only way to control his wife is to destroy her. Othello hyperbolically tells Iago that Desdemona's supposed infidelity makes it impossible for him to continue to be a soldier, "Othello's occupation's gone" (3.3.373), but then he proceeds to regard his wife and his lieutenant as enemies who have insulted his honor and must be hunted down. Revealing that murder is the sole means by which he believes he can gain power over his wife's desires, Othello says to the sleeping Desdemona "I will kill thee, / And love thee after" (5.2.17–18). Similarly, Daniel Cosway's claims that Antoinette not only engaged in a sexual relationship with her mixed-race cousin Sandi before Rochester met her but also knowingly participated in the plot of the Masons and his father and older brother to trick him into marriage wound Rochester's pride and whet his appetite for revenge: "As I walked I remembered my father's face and his thin lips, my brother's round conceited eyes. They knew. And Richard the fool, he knew too. And the girl with her blank smiling face. They all knew" (62). Moreover, despite lacking Othello's training and experience as a warrior, Rochester also uses martial imagery to describe those things he associates with Antoinette, from the "enemy trees" (62) that surround him after he follows the path leading away from Granbois; to the island of Dominica, which he tells Antoinette "is my enemy and on your side" (78); to "[t]hat green menace" (90), a phrase he applies to the natural world generally. Convinced that only in this way can he ensure that he alone will possess her, Rochester endeavors to drive Antoinette insane: "She's mad but *mine, mine*" (99).

Othello and Rochester seek not only to control their wives but to punish them for their putative betrayals, regarding themselves as justified in doing so. At the beginning of the final scene of the play, Othello states "It is the cause, it is the cause my soul," implying that he does not want to kill Desdemona but that he must go through with it for the sake of a higher moral principle, a sentiment that is echoed when he later identifies himself with "Justice" and describes his premeditated act of killing his wife as a "sacrifice" rather than a "murder" (5.2.17, 69). However, when he elaborates his "cause"—"Yet she must die else she'll betray more men" (5.2.6)—his motive sounds both confused and self-deceiving. Although Othello suggests here that he has come not to punish Desdemona for her crimes against him but rather to defend the male world from the contagion of female infidelity, the hollowness of this statement and of his appeals to some higher law becomes apparent a short time later when the tears Desdemona appears to shed for Cassio, whom Othello claims is dead, enrage him, and he asphyxiates her.

Othello decides to kill Desdemona before he enters their bedroom and shortly thereafter pitilessly snuffs out her life in a fit of anger. Soon after convincing himself that Antoinette has betrayed him, Rochester likewise devises a plan both to punish and control her and then heartlessly carries it out, invoking his legal authority as a husband and an Englishman to do so. Victimized by both primogeniture and his father and brother's unscrupulous behavior, Rochester frequently refers to the unjust way in which he has been treated. Yet rather than openly decrying English and patriarchal law, Rochester chooses to blame Antoinette for his situation and then uses his status as a man and a Briton to make her pay for it. Rochester invokes the concept of justice but refuses to see that he is unjustly destroying his wife. In a conversation with Antoinette about his deliberate act of betrayal with Amelie, he dispassionately invokes the word "justice" while alluding to slavery, suggesting that its legacy taints her because her father owned slaves, and then he proceeds to address her with the name "Bertha" (88). Although in his confrontation with Christophine he admits to himself that his betrayal of Antoinette was deliberate—"Yes, that didn't just happen. I meant it" (93)—and later even briefly considers the possibility that everything he has assumed to be true is false (100), in both instances he quickly reverts to his earlier conviction that these non-European women are in error and he alone has both the truth and the law on his side. His position of authority enables him to dismiss the charges Christophine levels against him, accuse her of being "to blame for all that has happened here" (95), and use the letter from Mr. Fraser, the Spanish Town magistrate, to threaten her with the police. It also allows him to follow through relentlessly with his plot to destroy Antoinette, a course of action whose pitilessness is underscored at the conclusion of part 2 by his decision to sell Granbois for whatever he can get and by his callous response to the young boy who loves Rochester and cries as the couple leaves Dominica: "[I thought] that I'd sell the place for what it would fetch. I had meant to give it to her. Now—what's the use? That stupid boy followed us, the basket balanced on his head. He used the back of his hand to wipe away his tears. Who would have thought that any boy would cry like that. For nothing. Nothing ..." (104).[13]

Rochester's repeated appeals to justice to defend his patently unjust actions epitomize an additional component of Rhys's re-vision of *Othello*, a play pervaded by legalistic imagery and structured around a series of trial scenes. For if *Othello* is about justice, *Wide Sargasso Sea* concerns colonial and patriarchal injustice. In the tragedy, Othello is accused of witchcraft in act 1, Cassio of drunkenness and disorderly conduct in act 2, Desdemona of infidelity in acts 3, 4, and 5, Othello of treason in act 5, and Iago of villainy in act 5.[14] At the very end of *Othello*, as Lodovico prepares to return to Venice and report what has happened, the implication is that the lawlessness of the colonial outpost has significantly contributed to the perversion of the legal system and loss of life that has occurred. Yet despite being undermined throughout most of *Othello*, justice ultimately remains an ideal to strive for and one that can, however belatedly, be attained, as indicated by the fact that eventually the real culprit is captured, tried, and punished. No such faith in justice can be found in the postcolonial novel. In part 1 the legacy of slavery and its outrages hangs over Coulibri and ultimately leads to its ruin. In part 2 Antoinette and Christophine comment on the inequity of the fate of the once-beautiful and cultured Annette, who loses her sanity and endures a life of abuse at the hands of those paid to care for her. Rochester likewise becomes obsessed with the injustice of his life in the book's middle section, believing he has been betrayed by not only his father and brother but also the entire Mason family, including Antoinette. Never having witnessed or experienced justice, Antoinette fails to expect, much less demand, it, telling Rochester pointedly, "There is no justice" (88), and thereby, ironically, leaving it up to the former slave Christophine to articulate the unfairness of Rochester's treatment of his wife. Moreover, as Gayatri Spivak has rightly noted (268–69), it is Richard Mason's reference to the justice system and not an inexplicable impulse for violence that triggers Antoinette's attack on him in part 3. Oblivious to the significance of the incident, Grace Poole tells her prisoner, who cannot remember what happened, "I was in the room but I didn't hear all he said except 'I cannot interfere legally between yourself and your husband.' It was when he said 'legally' that you flew at him and when he twisted the knife out of your hand you bit him" (109). Finally, even though there is indeed an appropriateness to Antoinette's fiery destruction of Thornfield Hall, a symbol of Rochester's English and patriarchal power, the fact that she is largely unaware of what she is doing and why greatly compromises the justice of this action.

In the foregoing I have sought to establish connections between Antoinette and Othello, Antoinette and Desdemona, and Rochester and Othello. In this section I discuss Christophine's relationship to Emilia and its connection to the depiction of race in the novel. Both Emilia and Christophine denounce violence against women, refute the charges leveled against their mistresses, show no fear when standing up to their mistresses' husbands, defy the men who have betrayed their mistresses, and are silenced for their temerity (though Iago accomplishes this through murder, whereas Rochester does so by means of the colonial legal system). Many critics have read the novel primarily as a rewriting of Brontë's text, regarding Antoinette and not Christophine as *the* colonized other. As a result, the trebly displaced black population in the West Indies occupies a position inferior to that of the white settlers not only within the hierarchy of the colonial system but also within the interpretative framework critics have used to analyze Rhys's novel.

Subordinate to both her husband and her mistress, Emilia nevertheless defies Iago in defense of Desdemona and pays the ultimate price for it. Once Emilia stops acknowledging her husband's authority over her—"'Tis proper I obey him, but not now. / Perchance, Iago, I will ne'er go home" (5.2.205–6)—he can only silence her by killing her. Denied moral authority as a result of his schemes that have led to the death of an innocent, high-class woman, Iago also loses the legal authority patriarchal society confers on him as husband. A defiant wife—as Desdemona was accused of being—can justifiably be killed by her husband; however, because Emilia's disobedience serves the cause of truth and defends the honor of her unjustly murdered mistress, it has a legitimacy of its own that poses a real threat to Iago. Yet because the play presents Othello as Iago's primary victim and thus de-emphasizes the cruelty of the general's murder of Desdemona, Emilia, being a servant, a woman, and a wife, simply becomes the latest and least important of Iago's victims.

Subordinate to Antoinette and Rochester by caste and class, Christophine defies the latter in defense of the former. However, unlike Iago who kills Emilia to silence and punish her, Rochester does not use violence against Christophine. Recently liberated from slavery and, unlike Emilia, not subject to the dominating presence of a husband, Christophine is nevertheless prey to the law enforcement system. Just as patriarchy enables Rochester to destroy his wife legally, colonialism provides him with the means of silencing and banishing Christophine. Had Rochester killed Christophine, as Iago does Emilia, *Wide Sargasso Sea* would be radically different because such a murder would highlight the physical—and racial—violence of the colonial system. It would also shift the focus of the book away from Antoinette's victimization to that of a member of the nonwhite population and greatly reduce the impact of the protagonist's imprisonment and rebellion in England.

Spivak and Benita Parry discuss the counter-discursiveness of *Wide Sargasso Sea;* however, they offer two very different readings of Christophine's role in the novel. For the former, although she "is the first interpreter and named speaking subject in the text" and it is she "alone whom Rhys allows to offer a hard analysis of Rochester's actions, to challenge him in a face-to-face encounter, Christophine is nonetheless tangential to this narrative. She cannot be contained by a novel which rewrites a canonical English text within the European novelistic tradition in the interests of a white creole rather than a native" (271, 272). Parry dissents, seeing the character as "disrupting" rather than "marking the limits" of the novel's discourse: "Christophine's defiance is not enacted in a small and circumscribed space appropriated within the lines of the dominant code, but is a stance from which she delivers a frontal assault against antagonists, and as such constitutes a counter-discourse" (248, 249). The question is not whether Christophine offers a critique of the colonial system (Spivak and Parry agree that she does), but rather whose colonized status and counter-discourse is at issue here. Unlike Parry, who focuses on Christophine's words, Spivak looks at the overall effect of Rhys's novel, in which Christophine plays a limited role. Impressively as she performs in her extended encounter with Rochester, Christophine does not speak up for herself and her people as victims of colonialism. Instead, her concern is Rochester's exploitation of his wife, namely, his plea that Antoinette marry him, his seizure of her assets, his rejection of her love, and his destruction of her psyche. At bottom, the debate between Christophine and Rochester concerns Antoinette's money. Yet for all her savvy about the wiles of white people, Christophine does not make the connection between this money and the labor of black slaves.[15]

At the end of *Othello,* order has been restored. Cassio rules in Cyprus, the bulk of the Venetian army and its entourage prepare to return home, and the injustice perpetrated by Iago has been recognized and is in the process of being rectified. Critics have argued, unsuccessfully I believe, that the destruction of Thornfield Hall in the third section of *Wide Sargasso Sea* represents an unequivocal victory for the colonized female Antoinette over the patriarchal colonizer Rochester; however, there can be no question that in the final section the absence of Christophine (whose departure from the novel Spivak believes lacks narrative justification, but that Parry defends by asserting that her obeah powers would have no effect in England) underscores the unabated colonial domination of the nonwhite population in the West Indies. Rather than focusing on the transportation, enslavement, and continued subordination of people of African descent after 1833, *Wide Sargasso Sea* depicts the trials of the white settlers Annette and Antoinette, portraying them as victims of both the vindictiveness of the recently emancipated slaves and the mercenary designs of the English colonizers.

Through Antoinette's echo of Othello's expression of his readiness to die for the person he loves, Jean Rhys establishes a connection between these characters, a connection that is reinforced by their shared fate as colonized Others victimized by people from the metropolitan center. This is the basis of Rhys's postcolonial re-vision of *Othello*. Yet she also rewrites the tragedy from a feminist perspective by associating Antoinette with Desdemona and Rochester with Othello. Like Shakespeare's "ill-starred wench," Antoinette is destroyed by a jealous, sexually insecure husband who not only fails to investigate fully the charges leveled against his wife but believes himself completely justified in vengefully punishing her for her supposed disloyalty. Rather than diminishing the profound impact *Wide Sargasso Sea* has had and will continue to have on critical considerations of *Jane Eyre*, acknowledging that Rhys's book powerfully responds to a second canonical text may serve not only to enhance the novel's status as a postcolonial and feminist tour de force but also to inspire critics to reevaluate Shakespeare's *Othello*.

Despite McLeod's reservations about postcolonial counter-discourse, he believes that Rhys takes great pains to preserve the integrity of her text, asserting that it "both *engages with* and *refuses Jane Eyre* as an authoritative source" (162). She accomplishes this, according to McLeod, through the use of competing points of view and the names she confers—or refuses to confer—on the two main characters. Rhys's rewriting of not simply Brontë's novel but also *Othello*, I would argue, serves to establish more fully the autonomy of *Wide Sargasso Sea*. Reading the novel primarily in relation to a single canonical text, that is, *Jane Eyre*, as postcolonial critics up to now have done, has made it difficult for them to account adequately for the racial theme and evaluate effectively Christophine's role in Rhys's text. Recognizing that Rhys responds to Shakespeare as well as Brontë, however, makes it possible to grapple with the issues of race in *Wide Sargasso Sea* more effectively. It also serves to reinforce the validity of Spivak's contention that within Rhys's counter-discursive story of the betrayal and destruction of the white settler Antoinette the black servant Christophine has a significant but ultimately marginalized part to play.

Reflecting Conrad's Darkness: Naipaul's *A Bend in the River*

Whereas "Chekov and Zulu" vividly illustrates the concept of postcolonial counter-discourse and *Wide Sargasso Sea* demonstrates that postcolonial texts can gain autonomy by responding powerfully to more than one classic text, V. S. Naipaul's *A Bend in the River* (1979), with its Conradian assessments of Zaire and Africa generally, raises questions about not only counter-discourse but the concept of postcoloniality. Numerous critics, including most notably Naipaul himself in "Conrad's Darkness" (1974), have connected the Trinidadian-born author of Hindu descent to the writer of *Heart of Darkness*. Responding to Naipaul's statement in this essay that he "found that Conrad— sixty years before, in a time of great peace—had been everywhere before me," Fawzia Mustafa correctly points out that the author's "map is Conrad's writing rather than colonial history, and his quest canonical rather than historical" (3). What has not often been recognized, however, are the links between Conrad's novella and narratives about Africa by outsiders that have followed it, especially *A Bend in the River*. In *Heart of Darkness* (1899), Africa functions as a metaphor for a condition of unlimited power and lack of external restraint that tests the basic beliefs of an outsider. It thus offers one of the earliest in-depth treatments of the European fear of "going native" as a result of exposure to the tropics.[16] In *A Bend in the River*, the narrator, an Indian Muslim born on the continent's east coast, plays a role similar to that of Kurtz, succumbing to Africa's violence, corruption, and lack of restraint. Naipaul quite consciously writes Salim's story so that it serves to update and validate his forerunner's portrayal of the Congo.[17]

Just as Conrad writes *Heart of Darkness* so that places (such as Brussels and Leopoldville) and people (e.g., King Leopold II) are decipherable without being named, making it possible to read the text both as time- and place-specific and as a more or less timeless portrayal of Africa, Naipaul sets his novel in the town "at the bend in the river" (Kisangani, formerly Stanleyville and the location of Kurtz's Inner Station) during the first decade of the reign of the "Big Man" (i.e., Mobutu Sese Seko, leader of Zaire). In *A Bend in the River*, Naipaul portrays independent Africa as flawed and failed colonialism grafted on African primitivism, an assessment he elaborated earlier in his nonfictional account of Zaire, "A New King for the Congo: Mobutu and the Nihilism of Africa" (1975). Having lost Africa because of either a lack of conviction in the colonial mission or its sheer falsity, outsiders no longer have a place in Africa. There are no more heroic or tragic whites, like Kurtz, to fall morally, just insignificant, obsolete outsiders who have become part of the problem. However, despite acknowledging the bankruptcy of the colonial approach to the continent, Naipaul leaves Conrad's and other colonial writers' assessment of Africa basically intact, adjusting it to postindependence conditions: Africa and Africans remain the seat and source of corruption, the continent is still riddled with contradictions, and, with the Europeans' departure, Africa reverts to its former state of absolute blankness, lacking history, a past, and a future. Thus, while Naipaul's choice of Salim rather than a white character as his protagonist and his decision to give some Africans significant speaking roles represent a divergence from Conrad's narrative, *A Bend in the River* follows the basic pattern established by *Heart of Darkness:* prolonged exposure to a corrupt African environment results in the moral decline of a non-African. A man with divided loyalties, born and raised in Africa but of Indian descent, Salim is both an insider and an outsider, a person whose fate is inextricably linked with the continent's but who has a foreign perspective on the events he narrates. His position between two worlds, as he himself sees it, makes him "a man apart," so much so that even near the end of his story when he is imprisoned and hears the screams of Africans who are his fellow prisoners, he "never felt closer to them, or more far away" (269).

Salim has a qualified respect for European civilization because it produced the history books in which he learned about his people's past. Without the introduction of a Western perspective he doubts whether this past would be remembered or even exist; however, history books and a Western sense of time also enable Salim to look in a detached way at familiar things, including the Indian enclave in East Africa, which has uncomfortable consequences for him: "It was from this habit of looking that the idea came to me that as a community we had fallen behind. And that was the beginning of my insecurity" (15–16). Even more isolated from the European historical perspective than Salim's Indian community, Africans had no past of their own until the Europeans came. When the colonialists left, history left with them and Africa began to revert to what it was before they arrived: bush and primitive people. Thus, it has no future as well.[18] Salim often reflects on the words used by Nazruddin, the Indian from whom he purchases his shop and whose daughter Salim has long been expected to marry, to describe the property in a ruined colonial-era suburb outside of the town—a description that Naipaul apparently intends to apply to all of the New Africa: "This isn't property. This is just bush. This has always been bush" (23). Echoing Selwyn Cudjoe's observation that the bush serves as Naipaul's "central metaphor for colonial backwardness and futility" (156), Rob Nixon asserts, "Drawing a mental moat around the metropole, he has declared everything inside, Civilization; everything outside, Bush" (42), adding that "'Bush' is simply Naipaul's buzzword for barbarism; it has nothing to do with vegetation. Deserts can be Bush" (183).

Despite his admiration for Europeans, Salim recognizes the flaws in their civilization. Not content with simple greed, Europeans lied to themselves about their motivations in building and maintaining their empires. Salim feels that, in addition to history, falsity is the legacy Europe bequeathed to Africa, and he succinctly identifies the hypocrisy toward Africa that resulted from the contradictory impulses inherent in European civilization: "The Europeans wanted gold and slaves, like everybody else; but at the same time they wanted statues put up to themselves as people who had done good things for the slaves. Being intelligent and energetic people, and at the peak of their powers, they could express both sides of their civilization; and they got both the slaves and the statues" (17). Without question this passage counter-discursively lays bare the contradictions inherent in European modernism, a major focus of Gilroy's *The Black Atlantic*. However, in contrast to those writers who question or rebut the canonical texts they rewrite, Naipaul does not subvert *Heart of Darkness* here; rather, he pays homage to Conrad, who himself saw and exposed the mendacity of the European civilizing mission.

When the Europeans departed at independence, Africans not only took over political power but they also inherited the use of duplicity from their former rulers; moreover, without the constraints of colonial rule, widespread violence erupted throughout the continent. As the New Africa takes shape, Salim "fear[s] the lies—black men assuming the lies of white men" (16). The creation and operation of the postcolonial state, particularly the Big Man's efforts to erect modern cities in the jungle and transform children from the bush into university-trained intellectuals, epitomize the falseness that characterizes independent Africa. Salim's description of the New Domain—a complex built in the ruined suburb dismissed by Nazruddin, which begins to deteriorate soon after it is completed—emphasizes this sense of falsehood: "The Domain, with its shoddy grandeur, was a hoax. Neither the President who called it into being nor the foreigners who had made a fortune building it had faith in what they were creating" (103). Similarly, the Big Man has created a bogus image for himself in the photographs of him hung in every shop in the country. Zabeth, a *marchande* from a village in the interior who comes to the shop to purchase her goods, informs Salim that the elaborately carved stick the Big Man carries, supposedly a symbol of his immense power, is a sham: "[T]hat isn't a fetish he's got there. It's nothing" (224). In addition to being riddled with falseness, the country teems with violence. Arriving after the civil war following independence has ended, Salim lives through the "Second Rebellion," which dominates the first section of the book, and leaves in the midst of another battle. The killing of people from one tribe by members of another, on which Salim comments early in the novel, is presented as emblematic of the entire continent: "Africa was big. The bush muffled the sound of murder, and the muddy rivers and lakes washed the blood away" (53).

Rather than Salim, Naipaul uses one of the New Africans to present his final assessment of the flawed civilization and reemergent primitivism of independent Africa, namely Zabeth's son Ferdinand, who excels in the country's educational system, eventually becomes a member of the government, and releases Salim from prison at the end of the novel. Unlike Salim, however, Ferdinand has no place to which he can flee. Decrying the state of the nation and renouncing his education and accomplishments, Ferdinand, the Big Man's New African, has become a nihilist. He explains that his schooling has robbed him of the one thing that was truly his (and for Naipaul the only thing truly African), the simple life of the bush: "Everything that was given to me was given to me to destroy me. I began to think I wanted to be a child again, to forget books and everything connected with books. The bush runs itself. But there is no place to go to. I've been on tour in the villages. It's a nightmare. All these airfields the man has built, the foreign companies have built—nowhere is safe now" (272).

In this world without a past and future, full of lies and violence—where everyone, African, European, and Indian, is left dangling, and from which there is no escape—the position of an outsider becomes especially perilous. The white headmaster of the local *lycée* and an amateur anthropologist, Father Huismans, is killed while traveling through a remote region collecting artifacts. The death takes on great significance because Huismans, like Salim, is "a man apart"; moreover, through this Catholic priest, Naipaul echoes *Heart of Darkness* by making reference to the Roman Empire. Huismans provides Salim with a translation and identifies the source of a Latin motto, "*Miscerique probat populos et foedera jungi*" ("He approves of the mingling of the peoples and their bonds of union"), carved on a ruined monument near the docks (63). The motto is a line from the *Aeneid* that has been deliberately modified. When Aeneas comes to Africa and the affair with Dido jeopardizes his mission to found Rome, the gods intervene, declaring their disapproval of relations between Africans and Europeans. In Naipaul's novel, however, the owners of a steamship company have changed the line into an assertion that relations between Europeans and Africans are approved. This revelation shocks Salim: "I was staggered. Twisting two-thousand-year-old words to celebrate sixty years of the steamer service from the capital! Rome was Rome. What was this place? To carve the words on a monument beside this African river was surely to invite the destruction of the town. Wasn't there some little anxiety, as in the original line from the poem?" (63). Salim certainly believes in the veracity of Virgil's line, and Naipaul constructs *A Bend in the River* so as to confirm it. The murder by Africans of Father Huismans, the key who unlocks this mystery for Salim and a great believer in the future of the continent, is surely meant to indicate that the "gods" do not approve of the mingling of Europeans and Africans "at the bend in the river." Salim himself attributes Huismans's death to the incompatibility between the headmaster's civilization and the African environment: "The idea Father Huismans had of his civilization had made him live his particular kind of dedicated life. It had sent him looking, inquiring; it had made him find richness where the rest of us saw bush or had stopped seeing anything at all. But his civilization was also like his vanity. It had made him read too much in the mingling of peoples by our river, and he had paid for it" (82).[19]

Although Salim's insecurity, insignificance, and powerlessness differentiate him from Kurtz, like his predecessor Salim brings traditions and principles with him when he comes to the bend in the river, and he is aware of his decay as he chronicles his drift into licentiousness, self-deception, violence, criminality, and betrayal. Soon after his arrival in the town, Salim receives word that African independence on the coast has destroyed his family's position and forced most of the Indian community to emigrate; as a result, he has been permanently severed from the restraints on his behavior he knew as a child. Salim has no place to return to, no life to fall back upon, as he once thought he would. He remarks that his new way of living "was the opposite of the life of our family on the coast. That life was full of rules. Too many rules, it was a prepacked kind of life. Here I had stripped myself of all rules. During the rebellion—such a long time ago—I had also discovered that I had stripped myself of the support the rules gave" (191). At first Salim delights in the "sexual casualness" of this part of Africa, but it later grows to perturb him. He comes to agree with Mahesh, an Indian living with his wife in the town, who views this casualness as "part of the chaos and corruption of the place" (39). Salim does inherit one thing from his family, the responsibility for a family servant, who acquires the name Metty soon after his arrival because of his mixed racial background. An eyewitness to the violence directed against the Indian community on the coast, Metty serves as a reminder that, with the destruction of Salim's past life, his fortunes are now tied to those of the town at the bend in the river.

Like many of the Africans and expatriates around him, Salim is gradually seduced by the lies of the Big Man. Amidst an economic boom that follows the chaos of the Second Rebellion, Salim begins to lose his detached perspective on the newly independent country, regarding the bush as more than just blank space and believing in the future: "We felt that there was treasure around us waiting to be picked up. It was the bush that gave us this feeling. During the empty, idle time, we had been indifferent to the bush; during the days of rebellion it had depressed us. Now it excited us—the unused earth, with the promise of the unused. We forgot that others had been here before us, and had felt like us" (95). He succumbs to the lure of the New Domain more than any other aspect of the Big Man's attempt to build modern Africa in the bush. There Salim meets a wide variety of interesting people unavailable to him in the town. As he becomes dependent on the excitement that the Domain offers him, Salim begins to feel "tenderness" for the Big Man and forgets the "vainglory" of the Latin motto Father Huismans translated for him. Through the people of the Domain, Salim feels "bound more closely with the fact of the President's power" and therefore more dependent on him (184). Thus, in contrast to visiting foreigners who laugh at the Big Man's promotion of the "African madonna," Salim has invested too heavily in the president's impossible dream to scoff at any part of it. He eventually recognizes the falsity of the Big Man's endeavors but not before it costs him financially, emotionally, and morally.

The main reason Salim becomes so enmeshed in the life of the New Domain is his affair with a married white woman, Yvette, which he recognizes as corrupting and which ends in shocking physical violence. From the time he sees her at a party in a European blouse, Salim becomes obsessed with her. However, he derives little pleasure from their frequent sexual encounters; rather, he experiences only a void, an unfulfilled need, and he believes his manhood has been reduced by his compulsion to give Yvette pleasure. As a result of their relationship, Salim grows increasingly concerned about how he has changed. After closing his shop for three hours to meet Yvette at his flat on a busy day, and thus missing a great deal of business, Salim explicitly links his decline to the process of going native: "I had my first alarm about myself, the beginning of the decay of the man I had known myself to be. I had visions of beggary and decrepitude: the man not of Africa lost in Africa, no longer with the strength or purpose to hold his own" (179). Realizing that adultery has become a way of life for him, Salim thinks how "sly and dishonourable and weak-willed" such behavior would seem if he were still on the coast (191). That past, however, is gone, and Salim attributes the affair with Yvette to the unreal African environment: "In no other place would it be just like this, and perhaps in no other place would our relationship be possible" (202).

Having been corrupted by the licentiousness and falseness of his African surroundings, Salim in time succumbs to the continent's pervasive violence and lawlessness. When his affair with Yvette becomes routine and she behaves mechanically with him during one of their now less-frequent encounters, Salim responds with startling brutality: "She was hit so hard and so often about the face, even through raised, protecting arms, that she staggered back and allowed herself to fall to the floor. I used my foot on her then, doing that for the sake of the beauty of her shoes, her ankles, the skirt I had watched her raise, the hump of her hip" (219). Naipaul implies that, just as Salim and Yvette's relationship could only take place in Africa, it is the lack of restraint, corruption, and violence of the continent that drives the once-principled Salim to such savagery. When he later returns from a trip abroad to find that his shop has been taken away from him by the government and placed in the hands of an incompetent, comic-book-reading alcoholic, Salim must find a means of raising capital quickly so that he can flee the country and start over somewhere else. To do so he resorts to smuggling both gold and, in a link to Kurtz, ivory. In order to exchange the local banknotes for hard currency, he seeks out the foreigners in the Domain. At the mercy of those with whom he illegally changes money, Salim loses any illusions he might have had about this place and its inhabitants he once found so fascinating.

The final stage of Salim's decline occurs when he abandons Metty, who represents the last vestige of Salim's past life that exists in the New Africa.[20] Demoted from owner to shop manager, Salim tries but can do little to stop the new man in charge from mistreating Metty. As a result, Metty believes Salim has failed him, and Salim concurs: "So the old contract between Metty and myself, which was the contract between his family and mine, came to an end" (264). When Salim refuses to give him money so that he can escape somewhere, Metty stops bringing Salim his morning coffee and reveals Salim's hiding place for smuggled goods to the police. After Ferdinand releases Salim from prison and amidst rumors of an imminent bloodbath, Metty begs Salim to take him with him when he flees. However, Salim no longer acknowledges a link between them and asserts that he can only fend for himself.

Naipaul crafts Salim's story so as to echo and update *Heart of Darkness*. Now that the whites have gone, Salim represents the last person possessing any kind of moral compunction in the country and by extension on the whole continent. When Salim returns to the town after a journey abroad, he duplicates the route taken by Marlow to reach Kurtz, traveling from London to Kisangani via Brussels and Kinshasa. More importantly, his departing by steamboat, down the same river Kurtz and Marlow sailed up, and from Kisangani, the location of Kurtz's Inner Station, is meant by Naipaul to close a chapter in history. Salim narrowly escapes from a collapsing Africa that is returning to the state Kurtz found it in almost ninety years earlier. Naipaul suggests that Africa's encounter with civilization, with time and history, was doomed to fail from the beginning because that imported civilization was flawed and African primitivism was too strong to overcome. Although Naipaul de-emphasizes the importance of whites, shifting attention away from them to the African-born outsider Salim, he preserves the Conradian motif of going native, which entails the corruption of all things African. For Naipaul, England, the United States, and Canada may no longer be Africa's polar opposites, may no longer provide guaranteed safe havens, having themselves entered into flux and decline. Nevertheless, in these places Nazruddin has managed to survive, hold on to some of his past, and look ahead to some kind of a future, and presumably Salim will manage to do so as well. In contrast, with the end of colonialism, Africa has become Kurtz's realm once more, a place with no past, no future, no rationality, no moral framework.

Because Naipaul strives not to subvert but to affirm and offer obeisance to the colonialist text he rewrites, *A Bend in the River* does not fit the model of postcolonial counter-discursiveness. The author does not simply accuse colonialists of hypocrisy, mendacity, and the exportation of flawed and failed civilization. He also shifts the focus of the novel to the metropolitan center at times, revealing the long-term effects of colonialism on the former seat of empire, through the lengthy description by Indar (Salim's childhood friend who comes to teach at the university in the New Domain) of his years in England and Salim's account of his six-week stay in London, highly significant sections of the book that have rarely received critical scrutiny. However, these aspects of the novel have largely been overlooked because Naipaul so deliberately patterns his narrative on *Heart of Darkness,* the subject of intense critical and pedagogical controversy for more than a generation. For some readers, including Naipaul, *Heart of Darkness* presents one of the most profound indictments of European colonialism. For others, like Chinua Achebe, Conrad was a "bloody racist," whose distorted depiction of Africa and Africans resulted in "an offensive and totally deplorable book" (328, 330). Not surprisingly, Naipaul's texts generally and *A Bend in the River* in particular have similarly polarized readers.[21] The novel and its author thus raise thorny issues for postcolonial critics. On the one hand, to deny postcolonial status to the

narrative because of its neocolonial politics may satisfy one faction of postcolonial writers, critics, and readers but not without compromising some of the
basic tenets of postcolonialism as outlined by others. On the other hand, to
classify the book as postcolonial may alienate precisely those people who are
most likely to embrace the postcolonial enterprise. In "The License of Exile," the
second chapter of his book on Naipaul that bears the main title *London Calling*,
Nixon skeptically examines the writer's and his critics' frequent assertions of his
"exile" status and his "homelessness." Noting that Naipaul has lived in England
since 1950 and that his political views (especially his nostalgia for Victorian
times) resemble those of Margaret Thatcher, Nixon argues that he should be
regarded as a "metropolitan" writer. This designation, especially when combined with the fact that Nixon subtitles his book *V. S. Naipaul, Postcolonial
Mandarin*, serves as further evidence of the sometimes imprecise nature of the
term "postcolonial."

Whereas the concept of postcolonial counter-discourse
has difficulty accounting for a text such as Naipaul's, the African Americanist
Henry Louis Gates's ideas about literary revisionism do not. Looked at through
the lens of Signifyin(g), which will be the focus of the next chapter, "Chekov
and Zulu" and *Wide Sargasso Sea* exemplify motivated signification while *A
Bend in the River* constitutes an example of unmotivated signification. This link
between the concept of counter-discursiveness and Signifyin(g) suggests that
postcolonial and African American literary theory can work effectively in concert, a thesis that will be confirmed and expanded on in chapters 3 and 4.

Repetition and revision are fundamental to black artistic forms, from painting and sculpture to music and language use. I decided to analyze the nature and function of Signifyin(g) precisely because it *is* repetition and revision, or repetition with a signal difference. Whatever is black about black American literature is to be found in this identifiable black Signifyin(g) difference. That, most succinctly if ambiguously, describes the premise of this book. Lest this theory of criticism, however, be thought of as only black, let me admit that the implicit premise of this study is that all texts Signify upon other texts, in motivated and unmotivated ways. Perhaps critics of other literatures will find this theory useful as they attempt to account for the configuration of the texts in their traditions.

HENRY LOUIS GATES

3 Signifyin(g)

Walter Mosley, Pauline Hopkins, Toni Morrison

Henry Louis Gates's Signifyin(g) has been one of the most influential of the many theories about the African American literary tradition advanced in the last thirty years in part because of its brilliance and in part because of its propounder's stature as one of the leading African American academics and literary and cultural critics. The assertions about how authors rewrite and respond to earlier texts that Gates advances in *Figures in Black* and *The Signifying Monkey* have proven extremely useful in reading African American literature, and, as I mentioned at the end of the previous chapter, they offer insights to critics of postcolonial literary texts. Some observers, however, have expressed concerns about his attempt in the latter book to provide a coherent, totalizing theory of the black American literary tradition. Sandra Adell, for example, contends that Gates's statement in the passage above from *Signifying* that "all texts Signify upon other texts" "undermines his own efforts to establish a principle of black cultural identity based on a 'black signifyin(g) difference'" (133). Reacting to

Gates's statement that his "idea of tradition, in part, turns upon [... the notion] of texts [being] read by an author and then Signified upon in some formal way, as an implicit commentary on grounding and on satisfactory modes of representation" (*Signifying* 145), Adell sees a contradiction in the entire project:

These, then, are the grounds and the limits of the black literary tradition: to participate in the tradition one must read other authors in the tradition and then signify on their works in some formal way, which would not be signifyin(g) at all. For as Gates so cogently argues in chapter 2 of *The Signifying Monkey*, an important aspect of signifyin(g) is its dreaded, yet playful "condition of ambiguity." To signify is to engage in a spontaneous verbal game of one-up-manship that cannot be harnessed by writing. Consequently, to signify in "some formal way" is to deprive the game of that condition of ambiguity and the element of surprise intended to provoke a signifyin(g) response. Indeed, within Gates's critical paradigm, the disruptive play and subversiveness of the Signifying Monkey [...] has been tamed. (133–34)

More to the point for the purposes of this study, Gates's attempt to establish Signifyin(g) as *the* defining gesture of the African American literary tradition explains why he has chosen not to connect counter-discursive texts by black Americans with those by marginalized people outside of the United States— despite the Yoruba origins he claims for Signifyin(g). However, his assertion that blackness is merely a trope raises questions about his attempt to delineate a specifically black tradition of Signifyin(g). If there is no racial essence, as Gates argues in his critique of Addison Gayle, and in his later assertion that "a claim of blackness" functions as the Negritude movement's "transcendent signified" (*Figures* 39–40, 53), then the "identifiable black Signifyin(g) difference" that makes African American literature distinctive had to have been created by the material conditions in which a particular group of people (arbitrarily) designated as black found themselves. In other words, specific historical events and political conditions produced the black literary tradition Gates writes about. Beneath the sometimes esoteric terminology of poststructuralism, and despite his protestations to the contrary, a major purpose of Gates's project seems to be to outline a *history* of black American literature from the eighteenth century to the present.[1] Thus, at least in connection with the relationship it posits between African American texts and white writing, Gates's Signifyin(g), like postcolonial counter-discourse, frequently involves a historically based and politically motivated response to a dominant discourse that calls the terms of that discourse, as well as its own, into question.

Although he endeavors to disassociate Signifyin(g) from the repudiative (i.e., content-based) theories of African American literature that preceded it, "the black difference" Gates writes about often has as much to do with content as with form. His discussion in *Signifying* of T. Thomas Fortune's "The Black Man's Burden," for example, emphasizes the poem's formal revision of Kipling's "The White Man's Burden" and downplays content even though his argument makes clear that the thematic revision is as important as the formal one:

> Rhetorical naming by indirection is central to our notions of figuration, troping, and of the parody of forms, or pastiche, in evidence when one writer repeats another's structure by one of several means, including a fairly exact repetition of a given narrative or rhetorical structure filled incongruously with a ludicrous or incongruent context. T. Thomas Fortune's "The Black Man's Burden" is an excellent example of this form of parody, Signifyin(g) as it does upon Kipling's "White Man's Burden":
>
> *What is the Black Man's Burden,*
> *Ye hypocrites and vile,*
> *Ye whited sepulchres*
> *From th' Amazon to the Nile?*
> *What is the Black Man's Burden,*
> *Ye Gentile parasites,*
> *Who crush and rob your brother*
> *Of his manhood and his rights? (103)[2]*

To focus on the formal aspects of Fortune's poem, as Gates implies should be done, would be to rob it of its counter-discursive significance, for this parody, an example of motivated signifying, would have little meaning without its pointed critique of imperialism and references to the exploitation of dark-skinned peoples. The issue here is not so much the infusion of black content as the insertion of incongruous (i.e., liberatory) content or context into a white form, for race clearly plays a role in Kipling's poem. Adopting an anti-imperial perspective that anticipates that of postcolonial writers and critics, Fortune signifies on "The White Man's Burden" by portraying blacks as the ones who must shoulder the load and whites as hypocritical oppressors. And, as evidenced by Gates's assertion in the context of a discussion of Alice Walker's *The Color Purple* in the final chapter of *Signifying* that the novel "disrupts the patterns of revision (white form, black content) that we have discussed [previously]" (255), he acknowledges that he does indeed see content as relevant to his theory.

Neither Gates nor his critics have been consistent in their spelling of the word "signifying." Referring to Jacques Derrida's neologism *différance*, Gates explains in chapter 2 of *Signifying*, "I have encountered great difficulty in arriving at a suitably similar gesture. I have decided to signify the difference between these two signifiers by writing the black signifier in the upper case ('Signification') and the white signifier in lower case ('signification'). Similarly, I have selected to write the black term with a bracketed final *g* ('Signifyin(g)') and the white term as 'signifying.' The bracketed *g* enables me to connote the fact that this word is, more often than not, spoken by black people without the final *g* as 'signifyin'" (46). Because I have some reservations about "the black difference" that anchors Gates's *literary* theory of Signifyin(g) (as opposed to the idea of verbal sparring and one-upmanship for which the bracketed *g* seems entirely appropriate to me), in *Confluences* I use the lowercase and eschew the parentheses, except when quoting Gates, referring to his theory by name, or adverting to oral wordplay, whether it be within or outside of literary texts.

Signifyin(g) proves especially valuable in analyzing how texts within specific genres respond to other texts, and, as Gates himself suggests (but chooses not to explore) and I asserted at the end of the previous chapter, the theory can be usefully applied to texts outside the African American literary tradition. In *Devil in a Blue Dress,* the character of Easy Rawlins, a detective adept at manipulating linguistic and rhetorical codes, exemplifies Signifyin(g) as Gates defines it; moreover, in revising the hard-boiled writing of Raymond Chandler and others, Mosley engages in literary signification in order to explore African American themes. In "A Dash for Liberty," Hopkins signifies on white and black texts about the 1841 *Creole* rebellion to promote unity among black Americans at the turn of the twentieth century. However, she also anticipates Paul Gilroy's emphases on routes and intercultural connections among black Atlantic peoples, incorporating a dimension into her story that falls outside the scope of Gates's theory through the explicit connection she makes between the slaves aboard the *Creole* and colonized black West Indians, as well as through her implicit link between these black Americans and Africans. Gates's definition of Signifyin(g) as "repetition with a black difference," however, encounters difficulty when considered in the light of Toni Morrison's concept of American Africanism. Applying her ideas about literary whiteness to Nathaniel Hawthorne's "The Birth-mark" and comparing the story to black American texts involving birthmarks, I ask in the final section of this chapter whether African American writers who use the figure of the birthmark in their texts are adding a racial dimension absent from

Hawthorne's tale, as Signifyin(g) suggests, or counter-discursively responding to its inherent racial implications.

An Un-Easy Relationship: Walter Mosley's Signifyin(g) Detective and the Black Community

Only a handful of people would recognize the names of Venus Johnson and Sadipe Okukenu, two of the earliest black detectives to appear in African American fiction. More but by no means a large number of readers are familiar with the detective teams of John Archer and Perry Dart and Coffin Ed and Grave Digger Jones. In contrast, by the early 1990s the popularity of Walter Mosley's private eye Ezekiel (Easy) Rawlins extended all the way to the White House (Muller 300–301). Focusing mainly on *Devil in a Blue Dress* (1990), the originary novel in the series in which Easy decides to become a detective, I draw on Gates to indicate how and suggest why Mosley emulates and diverges from earlier detective fiction. Although *Devil* follows the hard-boiled formula quite closely, it innovatively casts Easy as a Signifyin(g) detective, adept at juggling linguistic and social codes to deceive and outwit both white and black characters. Mosley goes further, however, signifying on the conventions of the genre in order to reflect on black freedom and the relationship between the individual and the community in African American society.

For the black writer of any era, detection presents at least two challenges. First, as a popular form with clearly recognizable conventions, crime fiction would seem a restrictive vehicle for an African American author aspiring to do more than simply entertain readers by satisfying their expectations. Second, because the genre requires the detective to solve the crime or crimes and thereby restore the established order, the mystery is notoriously conservative. As a result, the question for black crime writers becomes how to preserve the integrity of their detectives. No matter how brilliant or brave they are, black sleuths in the pay of white clients or the white power structure risk coming off as lackeys. In short, African American mystery writers must strike a difficult balance between genre conformity and genre subversion.[3] From Pauline Hopkins and John Edward Bruce in the first decade of the twentieth century, who sought to educate their black readers about America and the world, to contemporary writers such as Mosley (who turned to mystery writing after he failed to find a publisher for his nonmystery stories about heroic yet flawed African American males), detective fiction has provided the means for black writers to convey a specific message to a target audience.

Hopkins's 1900 locked-room story, "Talma Gordon," is believed to be the first work of mystery writing published by an African American. A year later, in *Hagar's Daughter: A Story of Southern Caste Prejudice,* the earliest known African American novel to feature a black detective, Hopkins finesses some of the problems that the mystery formula poses for a black writer by waiting until the last third of her melodramatic and polemical narrative (set during and twenty years after the Civil War) to turn to the detective genre. Although the young African American maid Venus Johnson unravels the racially and politically convoluted case that the head of the federal government's detective agency has been unable to crack, her solution of the mystery by no means resolves all of the crimes depicted in the novel, especially those related to racial intolerance and the legacy of slavery. In *The Black Sleuth* (1907–9), Bruce also subordinates his detective plot to his political agenda of providing his readers with a positive image of Africa and Africans through Sadipe Okukenu, his Yoruba crime solver, and exposing American racial intolerance by depicting at considerable length Sadipe's fiery baptism into segregation, white racism, and mob violence in the South during his journey to and sojourn at a black college that resembles Booker T. Washington's Tuskegee Institute. Hopkins and Bruce initiate African American mystery writing by signifying on white writing to critique late-nineteenth- and early-twentieth-century racial politics; they also anticipate key elements of hard-boiled fiction and illustrate the flexibility of the detective form.

In *The Conjure-Man Dies: A Mystery of Dark Harlem* (1932), Rudolph Fisher created not only the first detective novel by a black American writer to be published in book form, but also the first to take place in a distinctly black environment. In this narrative (and in the 1935 story "John Archer's Nose"), Fisher teams the erudite Harlem physician Archer with no-nonsense New York police detective Perry Dart. *Conjure-Man Dies* features two other crime solvers, the city worker turned private investigator Bubber Brown and the African title character, N'Gana Frimbo, who provides clues to the identity of his own murderer. Commencing serially in October 1935, the month the Italo-Ethiopian War started, *The Ethiopian Murder Mystery: A Story of Love and International Intrigue* is one of a pair of novellas George Schuyler wrote concerning a conflict that elicited an intense reaction from black America and one of several Harlem detective stories he published between 1933 and 1939 in the *Pittsburgh Courier,* the country's most widely read black newspaper. The combined talents of the inductive black New York police lieutenant Big Jim Williston and the ratiocinative black newspaperman Roger Bates are required to figure out that the Ethiopian secret service killed Prince Haile Destu in order to prevent him from turning over the plans of a death ray to a seductive white spy working for the Italians. Like Fisher and Schuyler, Chester Himes began writing crime fiction in the 1930s. It was not until 1957, however, that he produced *For the Love of Imabelle* (also known as *A Rage in Harlem*), the first of his nine-volume "Harlem domestic series," featuring the police detectives Coffin Ed Johnson and Grave Digger Jones. The novels chronicle the violence, upheaval, corruption, and growing disillusionment that gripped Harlem during the 1950s and 1960s, culminating in the posthumously published *Plan B* (1984), in which the collaboration between Coffin Ed and Grave Digger comes to an abrupt end.[4]

By setting his books in the corrupt, violent, and ethnically diverse milieu of postwar Los Angeles, Mosley places Easy on the familiar turf of the hard-boiled detective.[5] Like his white counterparts created by writers such as Chandler, Easy is tough, street smart, fiercely independent, and yet vulnerable to the attractions and deceptions of women. Easy, however, like Dart and Archer and Coffin Ed and Grave Digger, operates in a distinctly black environment. He lives (at least initially) in Watts, has access to black nightspots and organizations the police and white operatives cannot infiltrate, belongs to an extensive network of black Houstonians who have migrated to Los Angeles, and comes to regard his role as a sleuth as a matter of doing "[p]rivate investigations" for "[p]eople I know and people they know" (*Devil* 214) rather than a strict fee-for-services-rendered form of employment. In the nine books featuring Easy published thus far—*Devil in a Blue Dress* (1990), *A Red Death* (1991), *White Butterfly* (1992), *Black Betty* (1994), *A Little Yellow Dog* (1996), *Gone Fishin'* (1997), *Bad Boy Brawly Brown* (2002), *Six Easy Pieces* (2003), and *Little Scarlet* (2004)—Mosley has taken Easy from 1939 to 1965, stopping in 1948, 1951, 1956, 1961, 1963, and 1964 along the way. In each installment, Easy tells his own story in his idiosyncratic voice from a vantage point at a considerable temporal distance—internal evidence suggests the late 1980s—from the events he describes. This enables Easy to reflect on how things (and he himself) have changed in the intervening years and thereby either overtly or subtly comment on the progress or lack thereof that has been made by African Americans over the course of that fifty-year period. Apart from his use of a Signifyin(g) African American detective who operates in a black environment, Mosley remains remarkably faithful to hard-boiled crime writing; however, in detailing how Easy's decision to become a private investigator complicates his relationship with his friends and the black community generally, he innovatively uses the detective genre to illustrate the conflict between personal and racial freedom.

Comparing Easy to a prime example of the hard-boiled detective, such as Chandler's Philip Marlowe, reveals how closely Mosley adheres to the conventions of the tradition.[6] Like Marlowe, Easy tells the story of his adventures as a private investigator in the violent, amoral world of mid-twentieth-century Los Angeles. However, Mosley uses an African American detective-narrator who lives and operates in the black section of the City of Angels to anchor his novels. Although tough-guy private eyes frequently disguise their actual intentions to achieve their goals, Easy deceives people and wears masks to an even greater extent than Marlowe and his cohorts. The hard-boiled hero operates in a world where appearance and reality seldom mesh. By definition a seeker of truth, the detective is not always truthful in pursuing this end. A hard-boiled sleuth such as Marlowe will normally identify himself and his profession; however, the seediness of his office and his lower-middle-class standard of living can cause people to underestimate him, and he occasionally finds it expedient and prudent to disguise his true intentions when gathering information or pursuing a criminal. Nevertheless, the hard-boiled lifestyle and moral code perfectly suits a man like Marlowe. For Easy, in contrast, deception is a necessity rather than an option and the role of a detective is much more of a consciously chosen pose. I do not mean to minimize the role deception plays in Chandler's novels or Marlowe's participation in it. As Liahna Babener correctly observes of Marlowe, "Nominally on the side of truth, the detective becomes in effect an agent of deceit. He gives consent to the lies because in the end they are both pervasive and invincible" (143). This is especially true of *The Big Sleep* (1939), which could easily be titled *The Big Lie* because of Marlowe's decision, in an attempt to protect his fragile employer General Sternwood, not to reveal Rusty Regan's murder. However, rather than a consistent Signifier like Easy, Marlowe is only "something of a pretender," as Babener also remarks. Not only in his relations with whites, like Bruce's Sadipe, but especially in his dealings with blacks, Easy is a trickster who employs Signifyin(g) methods common in African American folk tradition.

In Mosley's 1948 Los Angeles, a black man does not acquire a detective's license and hang a shingle advertising his services as a private eye.[7] With no models on which to pattern himself, Easy must invent a detective persona that will work in his milieu. When DeWitt Albright, a veritable Moby Dick of murderous whiteness, surfaces in Joppy's bar asking Easy to do some investigative work for him, Easy knows he is in deep, uncharted waters; nevertheless, the one hundred dollars Albright offers is too tempting for the recently unemployed Easy to refuse. Unlike Marlowe, to survive and succeed Easy must invent a method for dealing with not only Albright and the corrupt white power brokers who employ killers like him but also the violent oppressed black community in which he lives. The method Easy chooses is based on the well-established African American strategy of Signifyin(g). As Easy explains at the end of *Devil in a Blue Dress*'s second chapter, he can speak in two languages: "I always tried to speak proper English in my life, the kind of English they taught in school, but I found over the years that I could only truly express myself in the natural, 'uneducated' dialect of my upbringing" (10). This ability links him to the great trickster, the Signifying Monkey, a figure that "seems to dwell at th[e] space between two linguistic domains"—the European American and the African American (Gates, *Figures* 245). In the many versions of the story of the Signifying Monkey, the mischievous Monkey persuades his friend the Lion that their friend the Elephant has insulted him. When the Lion seeks satisfaction from the innocent Elephant, he is soundly thrashed. The Lion returns to punish the Monkey but cannot reach him in the trees. Thus, through words alone the Monkey succeeds in diminishing the status of the king of beasts. Some of the specific varieties of Signifyin(g) delineated by Gates and the critics on whom he draws include ribbing, complaining, and lying; implying without specifically stating; ridiculing a person or situation; exposing and overturning pretense; and pitting neighbors against one another simply by telling tales (*Figures* 238–40). Most of these types of Signifyin(g) can be found in some form in Easy's interactions with either whites or blacks in *Devil*.

Mosley may in fact be slyly alluding to the Signifying Monkey tales in the remarkable seventeenth chapter of *Devil* when Easy, in desperate straits, finds a way to get behind the facade of white power and respectability in search of answers and a means of changing the rules of a game that is rigged against him. Convinced that once Albright has what he wants he will kill him, Easy violates both the social and linguistic codes that segregate whites and blacks when he goes to a company significantly named Lion Investments in search of Maxim Baxter, whose card Albright has given him. Things come into clearer focus for Easy when a bronze plaque informs him that Todd Carter, Daphne Monet's former boyfriend and the person who has hired Albright to search for her, is the president of the firm. The rules of propriety dictate that a poor black man like Easy has no business entering the offices of Lion, much less demanding to see its senior officers. These rules also dictate that menials should never discuss the personal lives of the kingpins. Easy, however, has no intention of observing propriety, and by exposing the hypocrisy of such niceties when people have been killed and more lives are on the line, he is able to cut through the layers of subordinates insulating the president and gain direct access to Carter.

Dressed in his best suit and courteously addressing the secretary in "proper English," Easy is nevertheless rebuffed. When he produces the card, he is told Baxter is too busy to see him and he must state his business then and there, to which he replies, "Mr. Albright hired me to find Mr. Carter's girlfriend after she ditched him" (111). This calculated shift into slang and breach of decorum produces the desired effect, enabling Easy to speak with Baxter, but now he will be satisfied with nothing less than an interview with Carter. Like the secretary, Baxter tells Easy his request is impossible and chides him for openly discussing Carter's business. However, Easy refuses to acknowledge the validity of such social codes and totally eschews standard English in favor of the vernacular: "I said I don't wanna hear it, Mr. Baxter. It's just too much goin' on fo' me t'be worried 'bout what you think ain't right" (112). Yet it is not until Easy bluffs that Carter's reputation is in jeopardy that Baxter relents and leads Easy to his boss's posh office: "'All I'm 'a tell ya is that he might be runnin' Lion from a jail cell if he don't speak to me and real quick too.' I didn't exactly know what I meant but it shook up Baxter enough for him to pick up his phone [to call Carter]" (113). Easy's ensuing conversation with the president of Lion is crucial because he learns that Albright's real objective is the thirty thousand dollars Daphne stole from Carter and forges an alliance with an influential businessman who late in the novel will legitimize the story he tells to the police. In his masterpiece of Signifyin(g) at Lion, Easy manipulates linguistic and social codes and invents a story to gain access to and momentarily achieve equality with one of the most powerful men in Los Angeles, thereby greatly increasing his chances of surviving and sorting out the mystery.

However, Easy's Signifyin(g) does not occur exclusively or even primarily in his dealings with white people. What makes him a successful detective in Watts is his ability to exploit his southern roots and manners to gain information from people, often without their realizing his true objective. We see what quickly becomes Easy's modus operandi as a detective in the fourth, fifth, and sixth chapters of *Devil* when he goes to John's illegal club looking for Daphne or information about her and later winds up making love to Coretta James, the girlfriend of his passed-out friend, Dupree Bouchard. Through casually talking with Hattie, who controls access to the club, Easy learns of the grisly death of Howard Green. Moments later, after buying a beer for an old foe, the bouncer

Junior Fornay, Easy finds out who Green was working for. Unable to get anything about Daphne out of Junior, Easy nonchalantly asks people, including Dupree, Coretta, and his buddy Odell Jones, "if they had seen a white girl Delia or Dahlia or something" (37).[8] A few hours afterward, in Coretta's arms, he learns that the two women are friends and that Todd Carter used to be Daphne's boyfriend. In an extended passage in chapter 18 describing his unsuccessful search through the shadiest places in Watts for the man he assumes is Daphne's current lover, Easy explicitly acknowledges his role-playing:

> During the next day I went to the bars that Frank Green sold hijack to and to the alley crap games that he frequented. I never brought up Frank's name though. Frank was skitterish, like all gangsters, and if he felt that people were talking about him he got nervous; if Frank was nervous he might have killed me before I had time to make my pitch.
>
> It was those two days more than any other time that made me a detective.
>
> I felt a secret glee when I went into a bar and ordered a beer with money someone else had paid me. I'd ask the bartender his name and talk about anything, but, really, behind my friendly talk, I was working to find something. Nobody knew what I was up to and that made me sort of invisible; people thought they saw me but what they really saw was an illusion of me, something that wasn't real. (128)

Easy's ability to Signify is his greatest asset as a detective. In an environment where appearance rarely reflects reality, Easy creates masks for himself more consistently and consciously than his hard-boiled predecessors like Marlowe in order to deceive others and find the truth. In contrast to Bruce's Sadipe Okukenu, whose Ellisonian invisibility is imposed by and limited to the white world in which he operates, Easy deliberately makes himself invisible in the black world as well as the white. Like Hopkins's Venus Johnson, who dresses as a boy to uncover the place where her father, one of the villains of *Hagar's Daughter*, is hiding her kidnapped grandmother, Easy disguises himself to fool people. However, where Venus's disguise is physical, Easy's is linguistic and rhetorical.[9]

Rather than merely imitating hard-boiled fiction, Mosley signifies on it, problematizing and particularizing the form by emphasizing how Easy's decision to pursue the independent life of a detective makes his relationship with his fellow blacks more difficult. Although the active, autonomous life of a private investigator provides Easy with a degree of freedom he has never experienced before, the role-playing it entails greatly complicates his relationship with friends, acquaintances, and the black community generally. As Chandler indicates in his admonition that "A really good detective never gets married. He would lose his detachment, and this detachment is part of his charm" ("Twelve Notes" 59), sleuths, particularly the hard-boiled variety like Marlowe, are by definition loners.[10] The question for Easy becomes can he and must he live disengaged from the black community in segregated, post-war America in order to be a detective? Although *Devil* refuses to provide a conclusive answer, it presents two major foils to Easy that help to clarify his position—one who apparently will never change and one whose compulsion to deceive others ensnares her. Easy's ambivalent relationship with his deadly old friend Raymond Alexander (aka Mouse) and his encounters with *Devil*'s femme fatale, Daphne Monet, underscore the tensions caused and the dangers posed by his new profession. In contrast to the static Mouse, who represents the past from which Easy tries to but can never quite escape, Easy has gone through many changes, having served in World War II, moved to Los Angeles, bought a house, and become a detective. Like Easy, Daphne, the devil in a blue dress, disguises herself; however, instead of being liberated by the role she plays as a white woman for white and black men, she is imprisoned by it. Although Easy survives and even prospers by the end of *Devil*, subsequent novels will return to the question of whether Easy Rawlins the detective can maintain his friendships and remain engaged with the black community.

As the long passage describing Easy's search for Frank Green quoted above reveals, Easy takes great delight in his detective work despite its enormous risks. The independence, intellectual challenge, and financial gain it offers appeal to him. Even though his friend Joppy does not own the building that houses his small bar and it stinks because it is surrounded by a slaughterhouse, Easy envies his ability to call his own shots: "Joppy had six tables and seven high stools at his bar. A busy night never saw all his chairs full but I was jealous of his success. He had his own business: he owned something" (8). Similarly, Easy is fiercely proud of his modest house, the only thing of importance he has ever owned, and his need to meet his mortgage payment convinces him to take the investigative work Albright offers, despite his misgivings. Even though Easy has no illusions about Albright, almost immediately pegging him as a cold-blooded killer like Mouse, he can't help but admire Albright's independence and defiance of conventions. He also realizes that now that he has invested in a house—and the version of the American dream it represents—the friendships that characterized his youth are no longer sufficient for his needs: "When I was a poor man, and landless, all I worried about was a place for the night and food to eat; you really didn't need much for that. A friend would always stand me a meal, and there were plenty of women who would have let me sleep with them. But when I got the mortgage I found that I needed more than just friendship. Mr. Albright wasn't my friend but he had what I needed" (21). The tension here at this key moment when Easy decides to become a detective is between, on the one hand, Easy's definition of himself and what he requires to be reasonably happy and have pride in himself—a degree of independence, some property of his own, and a modicum of status—and, on the other, Easy's relationship to his former life, his friends, and his community.

As it turns out, Easy can get his position back at Champion Aircraft and thus keep his house without working for Albright. However, when Easy compares his old boss, Benito Giacomo, and the type of life he offers with Albright and the prospect of becoming a detective, he finds he cannot beg for his old job: "I tried to think about what Benny wanted. I tried to think of how I could save face and still kiss his ass. But all I could really think about was that other office and that other white man. DeWitt Albright had his bottle and his gun right out there in plain view. When he asked me what I had to say I told him; I might have been a little nervous, but I told him anyway. Benny didn't care about what I had to say. He needed all his children to kneel down and let him be the boss. He wasn't a businessman, he was a plantation boss; a slaver" (66). After refusing to submit to Giacomo and thereby failing to be rehired, Easy experiences a feeling of elation: "My chest was heaving and I felt as if I wanted to laugh out loud. My bills were paid and it felt good to have stood up for myself. I had a notion of freedom when I walked out to my car" (67). Although he associates the new life he has chosen with independence (in contrast to the slavery his old boss offers), this independence is qualified—"a *notion* of freedom"—hinting at the tensions his career as a detective will entail.

The tenuousness of Easy's freedom becomes eminently clear in two widely separated scenes in *Devil*. Shortly after leaving Champion and exalting in his newfound freedom, Easy is arrested by the police, taken to the 77th Street station, and beaten while being questioned about Coretta's death. A nearly identical deflation occurs at the end of the novel. Having just sold his story to police bigwigs (with the help of Todd Carter), Easy leaves city hall reveling in what he believes is his independence: "I took the stairs. I thought I might even walk home. I had two years' salary buried in the backyard and I was free. No one was after me; not a worry in my life. Some hard things had happened but life was hard back then and you just had to take the bad along with the worse if you wanted to survive" (212). However, before he reaches the bottom of the steps, Miller, one of the two policemen who interrogated him earlier in the novel, confronts Easy and threatens to harass him constantly unless he provides information about the remaining unsolved murder. Recognizing the seriousness of Miller's threat, Easy fingers the real killer, Junior Fornay. Although Junior is not Easy's friend and he appears to have little choice but to hand Junior over if he wants to keep the life he has created for himself in Los Angeles, turning a fellow black in to the police represents a watershed moment for Easy, as his ambivalent and ambiguous statement reveals: "It might be that the last moment of my adult life, spent free, was in that walk down the City Hall stairwell. I still remember the stained-glass windows and the soft light" (213). At least two types of freedom, personal and racial, have come into conflict, and Easy has no option but to choose between them. Looked at from another perspective, Easy here learns his limits. Remarkably, given the odds against him, he has come out ahead, having solved the mystery, turned a profit, and protected Mouse and Daphne. But his success comes at a price. He can't save everyone; the police need a fall guy (and who better than the real murderer and one of Easy's old enemies?). Although it is a very good compromise in many ways for Easy, it is still a compromise and thus limits Easy's sense of who he is and the ideal of true freedom he has set for himself.

The whole issue of friendship becomes and remains tricky for Easy in his career as a detective. Orphaned at age eight, Easy has no family he is connected to (although he will marry, unsuccessfully, and have a child in *White Butterfly,* and in *Black Betty* begin to construct a family of orphans like himself that eventually includes Jesus, the abused two-year-old Mexican boy from *Devil;* Feather, the mixed-race daughter of a murdered stripper from *White Butterfly;* and Frenchie, the irascible canine from *A Little Yellow Dog*). Thus, more so than for most people, friends are important to Easy, but whether he can have and hold onto them while working as a detective becomes a major issue. Other than Joppy, who betrays him, Dupree, who stops being his friend because he suspects Easy of being involved in Coretta's death, and Odell, Easy's only close friends are Primo, a Mexican he met while working as a gardener, and Mouse, his pal from the streets of Houston. Significantly, Primo (like Saul Lynx, the private eye who takes a bullet for Easy in *Black Betty,* and Chaim Wenzler, the communist labor organizer in *A Red Death,* both of whom Easy befriends) is not part of the black community and does not live in Watts; thus, his detective work does not complicate their relationship in the same way it does his relationship with a African American like Dupree, and Easy can be himself with him.[11]

Epitomizing the tension between personal independence and engagement with the black community brought about by Easy's decision to become a detective, his relationship with Mouse stands as far and away the most important and complex friendship in *Devil* and one of the most innovative features of Mosley's mystery series. Looked at as an allegorical figure, Easy can be read as representing those black Americans who hope to improve themselves and participate more fully in the post–World War II United States but at the same time remain wary about their status and the promises the future seems to offer; Mouse, on the other hand, can be seen as black America's segregated and often violent and amoral past. Easy, in fact, leaves Houston, first for the war and then five years later for Los Angeles to escape Mouse and his own personal past, which Mouse in many ways represents. Whenever he is reminded of Mouse, Easy shudders. And yet, when he finds himself over his head with Albright, the police, and Frank Green, it is Easy who makes the call to Houston trying to locate Mouse.

Never having learned to read or write (in contrast to Easy, who is a reader, gets his G.E.D., and in later novels takes community college courses), Mouse has remained the same person during the many years Easy has known him.[12] After rescuing Easy from Frank Green, one of the first statements Mouse makes is "Easy, you changed," referring to Easy's self-assurance and bold, new lifestyle. Even though he has just been handed back his life and has not yet properly expressed his gratitude for this, Easy so fears Mouse and what he stands for that he regrets summoning him: "Raymond, I did call ya, but that was when I was low. I mean I'm glad you saved me, man, but your kinda help ain't nothin' I could use" (152–53). Easy has been trying to create a new life for himself and has embarked on a career that he believes offers him real independence. Mouse's timely arrival and the assistance he renders not only remind Easy of his past life but illustrate the limits of Easy's independence. Mouse tells Easy that he cannot go it alone, that he must rely on his friends, and that he has bought into a false white dream of freedom and self-improvement: "Nigger cain't pull his way out the swamp wit'out no help, Easy. You wanna hole on t' this house and git some money and have you some white girls callin' on the phone? Alright. That's alright. But, Easy, you gotta have somebody at your back, man. That's just a lie them white men give 'bout makin' it on they own. They always got they backs covered" (153). Although it comes from a tainted source, an inflexible man who is an amoral killer, Easy cannot and does not take the argument Mouse advances here lightly.[13] At the climax of *Devil*, in a scene that parallels the rescue of Easy from Frank Green, Mouse appears again at precisely the right time to assist Easy when he is outgunned. In short order, Mouse disarms and ties up Joppy, mortally wounds the fleeing Albright, and kills Joppy execution-style to convince Daphne to hand over the thirty thousand dollars. Once more, Easy's response to Mouse is a conflicted one. Although happy that he and Daphne have survived, Easy is horrified, though not surprised, by Mouse's cold-blooded murder and rapacity.

If the immutable, amoral Mouse, a living reminder of Easy's past, represents one dangerous path for Easy, then the ever-changing Daphne Monet, whom Easy first encounters in the present (story time) of the novel, embodies another. According to Chandler, "The only effective kind of love interest is that which creates a personal hazard for the detective" ("Casual Notes" 70). In Daphne, Mosley creates not only a love interest that puts Easy's life in jeopardy but, signifying on a key motif of both classic and hard-boiled detective fiction, an uncanny double for Easy. Like Easy, Daphne is adept at deception, possessing the ability to change her accent, looks, and personality at will. When they first meet, Easy has difficulty reading Daphne's features. She has "[w]avy hair so light that you might have called it blond from a distance, and eyes that were either green or blue depending on how she held her head" (89). Daphne initially affects a French accent and asserts she is "just a girl" in need of Easy's help; however, after they discover the murdered body of Richard McGee, the accent vanishes and Daphne transforms into an aggressive sexual predator: "She leaned back and smiled at me for a moment and then she kissed me again. This time it was fierce. She lunged so deep into my throat that once our teeth collided and my canine chipped" (95).

Although Daphne's ability to change herself gives her great power over men, including Easy, she lacks the ability to control her role-playing. As becomes clear in Easy's second and most extended encounter with Daphne, she needs others to accept the fantasy version of herself that she creates. If a man comes to know the real person behind the mask, she must leave him. According to Easy, "Daphne was like the chameleon lizard. She changed for her man. If he was a mild white man who was afraid to complain to the waiter she'd pull his head to her bosom and pat him. If he was a poor black man who had soaked up pain and rage for a lifetime she washed his wounds with a rough rag and licked the blood till it staunched" (183). Not only is Daphne's power to deceive limited to men, but she has essentially only one role to play—that of an attractive white woman—for either a white or a black man. Daphne wants to keep Easy in the fantasy world she has created for them in the secluded house Primo owns. After hours of lovemaking, she asks him whether he feels the private world of pleasure and pain she has constructed:

> "Do you feel it?"
>
> "Yeah, I feel it."
>
> She released me. "I don't mean that. I mean this house. I mean us here, like we aren't who they want us to be."
>
> "Who?"
>
> "They don't have names. They're just the ones who won't let us be ourselves. They never want us to feel this good or close like this. That's why I wanted to get away with you."
>
> "*I* came to you."
>
> She put her hand out again. "But I called you, Easy; I'm the one who brought you to me." (182)

Daphne's obsession with escaping the unnamed people who would keep her and Easy from being themselves and her insistence on taking credit for the fantasy they are acting out reveals how little actual control she wields over her roleplaying. Not yet knowing Daphne's past or understanding how much her sense of herself is controlled by others, Easy tells her that they can ignore other people and stay together so long as they love each other. Daphne, however, knows this is impossible.

In the climactic confrontation scene of the novel, Mouse once again forces a character to face up to his or her past. Turning his attention to the money after tying up Joppy and shooting Albright, Mouse addresses Daphne as "Ruby" and tells her that her half brother, Frank Green, is dead. Even though the news that the apparently white Daphne Monet is really part black triggers an earthshaking epiphany for Easy, he still fails to understand the ramifications of this information and his possession of it. Like Carter before him, the knowledge of Daphne's true identity disqualifies Easy as her lover:

> "What's wrong?"
>
> "You know what's wrong. You know who I am; what I am."
>
> "You ain't no different than me. We both just people, Daphne. That's all we are."
>
> "I'm not Daphne. My given name is Ruby Hanks and I was born in Lake Charles, Louisiana. I'm different than you because I'm two people. I'm her *and* I'm me." (203)

Despite Daphne's assertion of the difference between Easy and herself, they are really quite similar. Both were born in Louisiana, both migrated to Los

Angeles, and both play roles to deceive others. What distinguishes them is Easy's ability to manipulate the masks he wears rather than be manipulated by them, as Daphne has been. Nevertheless, her fate remains one into which Easy in his role as a Signifyin(g) detective could fall at any moment.

At the close of *Devil*'s crucial twenty-ninth chapter, Mouse perceptively pinpoints Daphne's tragedy: "She wanna be white. All them years people be tellin' her how she light-skinned and beautiful but all the time she knows she can't have what white people have. So she pretend and then she lose it all. She can love a white man but all he can love is the white girl he think she is" (205). Resisting any kind of change and pursuing his own agenda of winning Easy back to his amoral approach to life, Mouse accuses Easy of being "just like Ruby" and betraying his race: "That's just like you, Easy. You learn stuff and you be thinkin' like white men be thinkin'. You be thinkin' that what's right fo' them is right fo' you. She look like she white and you think like you white. But brother you don't know that you both poor niggers. And a nigger ain't never gonna be happy 'less he accept what he is" (205). Mouse is only half right, however.

Daphne, in trying to deceive other people with her mask of whiteness, has indeed deceived herself, allowing a mask imposed by others to imprison her and render her unable to form meaningful relationships with other people. In his attempt to define himself, Easy, on the other hand, has been able to blaze the precarious, uncharted path of the Signifyin(g) detective, successfully managing the personae he has created for himself to outmaneuver both blacks and whites. Yet the choice that Easy makes to lead the independent life of a private investigator comes at a cost. Although his Signifyin(g) liberates him on a personal level, it complicates his relationship with his friends and the black community as a whole, leaving him sensitive to Mouse's largely self-serving accusation that Easy has deceived himself and betrayed his race.

In the novel's final chapter, Easy remains troubled about the imperfect justice that has been meted out and the role he has played in effecting it. Sitting with his longtime friend Odell, he expresses his concern that because of him one killer, his old friend Mouse, will once again escape retribution while another will be punished:

> "Odell?"
>
> "Yeah, Easy."
>
> "If you know a man is wrong, I mean, if you know he did somethin' bad but you don't turn him in to the law because he's your friend, do you think it's right?"
>
> "All you got is your friends, Easy."

"But then what if you know somebody else who did something wrong but not so bad as the first man, but you turn this other guy in?"

"I guess you figure that that other guy got ahold of some bad luck." (215)

Although the sustained laughter of the two men that follows suggests that Odell succeeds in mollifying Easy's troubled conscience, Mosley will make sure that such moral dilemmas continue to confront Easy. Having lost Joppy and Dupree in solving the mystery in *Devil,* in the next novel, *A Red Death,* Easy sees his friendship with Odell evaporate because of his detective work. This leaves him with the one friend he feels the most ambivalent about, Mouse, a living reminder of Easy's past who through his words and actions denies the validity of Easy's efforts to better himself and lead the independent life of a Signifyin(g) detective.

Through Easy, Mosley signifies on mainstream tough-guy fiction so that he can explore themes such as black male friendships and personal versus communal freedom. As the following section demonstrates, in "A Dash for Liberty" Pauline Hopkins signifies on both white and black texts to engage issues relevant to her turn-of-the-century black readers, including lynching, disenfranchisement, and concubinage. However, because she also connects the efforts of black Americans to free themselves from slavery to the anticolonial struggles of West Indians and Africans, she broaches a subject beyond the boundaries Gates has established for Signifyin(g).

Taking Liberties: Pauline Hopkins's Recasting of the *Creole* Rebellion

The following passage from the preface to the novel *Contending Forces: A Romance Illustrative of Negro Life North and South* (1900) expresses two key tenets of the literary philosophy of Pauline Hopkins, the most prolific African American woman writer and the most influential black literary editor of the first decade of the twentieth century: "Fiction is of great value to any people as a preserver of manners and customs—religious, political and social. It is a record of growth and development from generation to generation. *No one will do this for us; we must ourselves develop the men and women who will faithfully portray the inmost thoughts and feelings of the Negro with all the fire and romance which lie dormant in our history,* and, as yet, unrecognized by the

Anglo-Saxon race" (emphasis in original). Hopkins believed that an intimate relationship should exist between African American fiction and African American history. Not only could novels and short stories be an effective means of making the race's past familiar to newly literate classes of black Americans but African American history, containing countless episodes filled with "fire and romance," offered writers material that could be readily adapted to political and artistic purposes. Hopkins also believed, however, that it was up to African American authors to exploit the didactic, propagandistic, and artistic potential that lay "dormant" in their history. If the race did not produce a group of writers committed to the achievement of this goal, then black Americans risked having their past consigned to oblivion or willfully distorted by their enemies.

Hopkins puts her ideas about African American literature into practice in "A Dash for Liberty," a story that not only commemorates a significant moment in African American history, the 1841 *Creole* rebellion, but also rewrites this historical episode so that it resonates with the turn-of-the-century challenges confronting black Americans. Moreover, "A Dash for Liberty," the first twentieth-century treatment of the *Creole* revolt, can be read as Hopkins's declaration of independence from both the white historical record and earlier writing by African American and white abolitionist authors. Before turning my attention to Hopkins's story, I provide some background information on the *Creole* affair and the nineteenth-century literary texts based on it.

        Madison Washington was a Virginia slave who led a successful revolt on the slave ship *Creole* in 1841 and whose life inspired Frederick Douglass's "The Heroic Slave" (1853), William Wells Brown's "Madison Washington" (1863) and "Slave Revolt at Sea" (1867), and Lydia Maria Child's "Madison Washington" (1865). In 1901 Hopkins published "A Dash for Liberty," a new version of the *Creole* uprising and the life of its leader, whom she renames Madison Monroe.[14] Although a number of critics have discussed Douglass's "The Heroic Slave"—the earliest and longest version of the story—to my knowledge only Richard Yarborough and Celeste-Marie Bernier have commented on the versions of Brown, Child, and Hopkins. In addition to exploiting the patriotic and romantic potential of Washington's story, as her literary antecedents do, Hopkins incorporates into her version a theme particularly relevant to conditions African Americans faced at the beginning of the twentieth century: the need for unified action to combat white oppression of both black men and black women.[15]

In late October of 1841, the United States brig *Creole* left Virginia with a cargo of tobacco and slaves bound for New Orleans. The 135 slaves on board were strictly segregated by sex, the men being kept in the forward hold and the women in the rear of the vessel. The revolt began on the evening of 7 November when the overseer, William Merritt, found Madison Washington, described in the depositions as a large and powerfully built man and the head cook for the slaves, in the main hold aft with the women. Merritt and the first mate, Zephaniah Gifford, tried to grab Washington, but he broke free while another slave, Elijah Morris, fired a pistol at Gifford. Washington then called on the other slaves to join him. A fierce battle raged between the nineteen slaves who participated in the rebellion on one side and the ten members of the crew and four white passengers on the other. By 1:00 A.M. the rebels had control of the ship, one white man was dead and some others wounded, and two slaves were seriously injured, one mortally. Washington wanted to sail for Liberia, but when Merritt, who agreed to navigate the ship, told him there were not enough provisions for such an extended voyage, Washington settled for Nassau in the Bahamas. On the morning of 9 November, the *Creole* reached this British colony where slavery was illegal.

Despite the protestations of John Bacon, the American consul, the slaves who did not participate in the revolt were allowed to go free. Likewise, in defiance of American demands for their extradition, the nineteen insurrectionists were held for a few months and then released.[16] Although abolitionists applauded the British actions, politicians in the South and the North deplored what they regarded as Great Britain's unwarranted interference in a purely American affair. Daniel Webster expressed the Tyler administration's displeasure to London, and the *Creole* episode greatly complicated the negotiations that eventually led to the August 1842 Webster-Ashburton Treaty, which defined the boundary between British and American territory from Maine to Minnesota. Over a decade later, the Anglo-American Claims Commission awarded the United States $110,330 for the slaves lost in the *Creole* affair.

Although the uprising on the *Creole* figures prominently in Douglass's, Brown's, and Child's literary versions of the story, Madison Washington's life prior to the rebellion plays an even more important role in these texts. On this subject, however, there is almost no historical record at all. The three nineteenth-century stories based on Washington's life were all influenced directly or indirectly by a June 1842 *Liberator* article. As speculative as it is informative, "Madison Washington: Another Chapter in His History" remains one of the only sources of biographical information about Washington, along with a few brief references to him in some of Frederick Douglass's speeches in the 1840s, Henry Highland Garnet's "Address to the Slaves of the United States," and the white abolitionist Joshua Coffin's history of slave insurrections.[17]

Repeating earlier descriptions of Washington as a freedom fighter (and thus a patriot worthy of his name), the *Liberator* article offered a "new clue" to the character of the "hero" of the *Creole* revolt that added a romantic dimension to his story: reports from Canadian and northern abolitionists that Washington had been free in Canada but returned to Virginia to liberate his wife. The article hypothesizes that Washington's wife might have been on board the *Creole,* which would explain his presence among the women slaves that triggered the revolt, and calls for British abolitionists to gather more information about Washington, which apparently was never forthcoming.[18] As William Andrews notes, "This effort by the *Liberator* to infer a romantic plot underlying the *Creole* incidents testifies to a strong desire of American abolitionism for *a* story, if not *the* story, about Washington that would realize him as a powerful symbol of black antislavery heroism" (28).

In contrast to the significantly shorter versions that followed it, Douglass's "The Heroic Slave," the only version published before the Civil War, runs over thirty pages.[19] This novella, Douglass's sole foray into fiction, was written primarily for a white northern male audience, as Andrews, Yarborough, and Robert Stepto have noted. Unlike Brown and Child, Douglass divides his story into four sections. The first emphasizes the patriotic (i.e., liberatory) aspect of Washington's history but also introduces the romantic element. In a Virginia forest, a northern white man, Mr. Listwell, determines to become an abolitionist after overhearing Madison Washington's to-be-or-not-to-be-free soliloquy, in which he expresses both his desire to escape and his reluctance to do so because of his love for his wife Susan. In part two, Washington, now a fugitive, arrives by chance at the Listwells' home in Ohio, tells them about his escape and the five years he passed in the Virginia woods, during which he was sustained only by weekly meetings with Susan, and, aided by the abolitionist couple, reaches Canada safely, a free man at last. In the third section, Douglass cuts short the romantic plot to focus on the patriotic story line. Listwell and Washington meet again in Virginia a year later, the latter having returned in an effort to liberate his wife, who was then killed in their escape attempt. Before Washington boards the slaver bound for New Orleans, Listwell slips him files with which to cut himself free. In the final section, two Virginia sailors discuss the *Creole* revolt, which one of them experienced firsthand. Like Listwell, who in part one is converted to abolitionism by Washington's words, this sailor has changed his mind about slavery as a result of witnessing Washington's bravery, leadership, and restraint during the rebellion and its aftermath.

Brown's and Child's stories depicting the *Creole* incident have much more in common with each other than they do with "The Heroic Slave"; however, there are significant differences between them.[20] Literacy rates and socioeconomic conditions at the time were such that Brown, like Douglass, was still writing mainly for a white audience. Nevertheless, the dynamics of the situation for black Americans in general and black writers in particular had changed greatly in the decade since the publication of "The Heroic Slave." Brown actually wrote two versions of the story: one titled "Madison Washington" appeared in *The Black Man, His Antecedents, His Genius, and His Achievements;* the other, "Slave Revolt at Sea," was the fourth chapter of Brown's *The Negro in the American Rebellion.* However, apart from the deletion of the final sentence of "Madison Washington" and the addition of one paragraph to the start and three paragraphs to the end of "Slave Revolt at Sea," the versions are identical. Both books in which Brown's account of Washington appeared were early attempts to write black history. More ambitious than its successor, *The Black Man* stresses continuity by beginning in antiquity and concluding with portraits of notable African Americans. In the preface to *The Negro in the American Rebellion,* Brown states that this text began as an attempt "to serve for future reference an account of the part which the Negro took in suppressing the Slaveholders' rebellion" to which he added "a sketch of the conditions of the race previous to the commencement of the war" that emphasized African American bravery and resistance (v).

Unlike the versions written by Douglass and Brown, African Americans writing mainly for a white audience, "Madison Washington," penned by the white abolitionist, fiction writer, and essayist Lydia Maria Child, appeared in her *Freedmen's Book,* an anthology of biographical sketches, poems, essays, and household tips designed to be used in advanced classes of the freedmen's schools. Although Child's aims were in part didactic,[21] she clearly regarded the volume as historically significant, referring to it in her preface, "To the Freedmen," as the "true record of what colored men have accomplished under great disadvantages."

Richard Yarborough notes that, in contrast to "The Heroic Slave," the subsequent versions not only greatly limit the role assigned to white characters in order to emphasize the nobility and bravery of the protagonist—whom they, unlike Douglass, describe as an unmixed African—but also explicitly depict the violence of Washington's rebelliousness and maximize the romantic possibilities of the story. In the versions of Brown, Child, and Hopkins, Washington—both in his attempt to liberate Susan from the plantation and in leading the slave revolt on the *Creole*—fells his white adversaries, either with his fists or a club. Moreover, following through on the *Liberator* article's suggestion, Susan is on board the *Creole* when the uprising takes place in the three later versions. Child opts for a surprise melodramatic ending, waiting until the last page of the sketch to reveal Susan's presence on the boat. In Brown's and Hopkins's versions, however, the reader learns early on that Susan is aboard, but the husband and wife do not discover that the other is there until the morning after the rebellion. In contrast to Douglass and Brown, as Yarborough points out, Child hints that the possibility that Susan will be sexually abused in part motivates Washington to return to Virginia for her, which becomes a major theme in Hopkins's version.

Several elements make "A Dash for Liberty" unique among the literary renditions of the *Creole* rebellion. One of the most important of these is the fact that the story was written by a black female writer for the readers of the *Colored American Magazine*, "the first significant Afro-American journal to emerge in the twentieth century" (Johnson and Johnson 4).[22] In addition to contributing a remarkable number of essays, articles, biographical sketches, short stories, and serial novels to the periodical, Hopkins played a major editorial role at the magazine. Although she was not identified as the general editor until February 1904, there is strong evidence to suggest that she may have been functioning in that capacity for a considerable period.[23] Hazel Carby describes Hopkins's editorial philosophy as follows: "The *Colored American Magazine* was a direct response to the political climate of the turn of the century—that is, to black disenfranchisement, Jim Crow laws, the widespread murder of black people in the South, and political apathy in the North. Hopkins viewed the journal as a vehicle for social intervention, as an attempt to replace the politics of compromise with political demands for change in social relations. The first editorial asserted that the *Colored American Magazine* 'aspire[d] to develop and intensify the bonds of that racial brotherhood, which alone can enable a people, to assert their racial rights as men, and demand their privileges as citizens'" (xxxii). Hopkins was convinced that fiction could be instrumental in this struggle, as the quotation from *Contending Forces* at the start of this section indicates. In her introduction to *Short Fiction by Black Women, 1900–1920*, Elizabeth Ammons underscores the key role that Hopkins's solicitation, selection, and promotion of poetry, short stories, and novels for publication in *Colored American Magazine* played in the development of black literature at the start of the twentieth century. Hopkins believed that fiction could be used "to enlist the sympathy of all classes of citizens" to the injustices suffered by African Americans through its unique ability to reach "those who never read history or biography" ("Pauline E. Hopkins" 219).

Without question, the most distinctive feature of Hopkins's version of the *Creole* story is her decision to rechristen the main character Madison Monroe. Writers and scholars have pointed out the pivotal role that naming and unnaming have played in black experience. As Michael G. Cooke notes, African American literary texts often concern "the presence or absence of names, their status and their scope" (172).[24] A person's name holds the key to his or her identity. To rob someone of his or her name is to cut that person off from his or her ancestry, family, and history, whereas to give someone a name situates the person within a societal, genealogical, and historical framework. As devastating as it can be for a person to be deprived of a name, being given a false one can be even more destructive. Observers since the 1840s have commented on the appropriateness of Madison Washington's name in view of the actions attributed to him;[25] however, from another perspective, it can be seen as a fictional and potentially meaningless appellation given to a slave (of pure African ancestry, according to some accounts), presumably by his white owner. As the writer of two extended biographical series in the *Colored American Magazine,* "Famous Men of the Negro Race" and "Famous Women of the Negro Race," and a literary artist who consistently incorporated history into her novels and short stories, Hopkins would not have altered the name of an early black figure in a fictional text without careful premeditation, particularly given the historical and political repercussions of such an action.

The search for a strictly historical motivation behind the name change, while far from conclusive by itself, turns up some interesting facts. George Washington and James Monroe (like James Madison) were Presidents from Virginia who served in the Revolutionary War. They also held slaves. Neither Monroe's response as governor of Virginia to Gabriel Prosser's ill-fated 1800 slave insurrection in and around Richmond, nor his actions as president during the debate over and passage of the Missouri Compromise between 1819 and 1821 seem meritorious enough to warrant Hopkins's substitution of his name for Washington's. On the other hand, Monroe did approve emigration to Liberia, and the first settlement, which would later become the country's capital, was named in his honor by the American Colonization Society. This indeed seems relevant given that the leader of the *Creole* rebellion is described as an "unmixed African" in all but Douglass's version of the story, historical accounts of the uprising report that on gaining control of the vessel Washington originally wanted to sail to Liberia, and the whole trajectory of Hopkins's story (as I discuss later) points in the direction of Africa. Lest Monroe be mistaken for an abolitionist, however, it should be noted that he has been characterized as a typical southern liberal who "became an ardent advocate of the colonization of freed slaves in Africa as the best means of resolving the problem" that he, like Jefferson, believed liberated blacks posed to the country (Ammon 189). Nevertheless, the Virginian's association with Liberia, his support—qualified though it was—of an effort by free blacks to form their own community may account for Hopkins's decision to change her main character's name *to* Monroe.

As to the question of why she changed the name *from* Washington, the contemporary struggle within the black community between those allied with Booker T. Washington and his policy of accommodating white constraints placed on African Americans and those opposed to Washington's ideas, particularly W. E. B. Du Bois, may be even more pertinent. A year earlier in her novel *Contending Forces,* Hopkins had thematized this debate through the contrasting philosophies of her characters Arthur Lewis and Will Smith. In "A Dash for Liberty," changing the name of her protagonist—who organizes a brave corps of African Americans that will lead their fellow blacks to freedom—from Washington entailed an implicit criticism of the leading black figure in turn-of-the-century America, someone whose program Hopkins regarded as inimical to the best interests of African Americans. Whether cognizant of this subtle slight or not, the powerful Booker T. Washington would later revenge himself on Hopkins for her more overt questionings of his policies by having an ally, Fred Moore, buy the *Colored American Magazine* in 1904, remove it to New York from its strong base of support in Boston, and eventually fire Hopkins.

An even more compelling explanation for the name change is that Hopkins recognized that the earlier versions of Madison Washington's life were already consciously crafted fictions based only partly on historical fact; by changing the hero's last name she was emphasizing the fictiveness of her version.[26] Both Stepto and Andrews have credited Douglass's "The Heroic Slave" with being the first attempt to break out of the autobiographical-biographical mode of African American writing rooted in oral storytelling and use fiction as a means to convey a political message. By naming her protagonist Madison Monroe rather than Madison Washington, Hopkins signals that she is creating a new fiction inspired by the historical events relating to the *Creole* episode that differs substantively from those that preceded it. Signifying on the Douglass, Brown, and Child versions that were written just before, during, and immediately following the Civil War and aimed at a northern white or newly freed black audience, "A Dash for Liberty" uses the historical facts relating to the *Creole* revolt to address issues that directly concerned her turn-of-the-century black readers.

Complicating matters, the following citation (which Yarborough notes the existence of but does not comment on [187]) is affixed to the top of "A Dash for Liberty" between the story's title and the author's name: "Founded on an article written by Col. T. W. Higginson, for the Atlantic Monthly, June 1861." However, Higginson's article is a sixteen-page account of Denmark Vesey's abortive slave uprising in Charleston, South Carolina, in 1822 that makes no specific mention of Madison Washington or any other leader of a slave rebellion. Given the fact that Hopkins was generally quite scrupulous in acknowledging her sources, particularly when these were African Americans and white abolitionists whose work was often little known, we can discount deliberate obfuscation on her part. Two explanations, then, come to mind: either the headnote is a mistake, or something in Higginson's description of Vesey inspired Hopkins to rewrite Washington's story.

On one hand, there is a piece of evidence that at first glance appears to support the argument for error. *The Black Man* by William Wells Brown, whom Hopkins met and who became a major influence on her life and work, contains not only a sketch of Madison Washington but one of Denmark Vesey. In an uncharacteristic move, according to his biographer William Farrison, Brown specifically cites Higginson's *Atlantic Monthly* article at the end of the pages devoted to Vesey. Thus, it certainly seems possible that Hopkins could have carelessly confused the two sketches, believing that Higginson's article inspired Brown's account of Washington; however, one wonders why she would cite Brown's source rather than Brown himself. On the other hand, it also seems possible that Hopkins, with Brown's description of Washington fresh in her mind, looked up Higginson's article after reading *The Black Man*'s account of Vesey and found something there that inspired her to write her own version of the *Creole* affair. An important link exists between Washington and Vesey that supports this theory: both men were free when they conceived of their plans to liberate those still in bondage. According to the June 1842 article in the *Liberator,* Washington had escaped to Canada but returned to Virginia to free his wife only to be captured, sold, and transported on the *Creole.* Similarly, in an anecdote that according to Higginson "reveal[s] the secret soul of Denmark Vesey," a fellow insurrectionist reports that "Vesey, on first broaching the plan to him, said 'he was satisfied with his own condition, being free, *but, as all his children were slaves, he wished to see what could be done for them'"* (731–32,

Higginson's emphasis). Like Brown's version, Hopkins's story begins with the free Monroe deciding to leave Canada and return to Virginia to liberate his wife, thereby underscoring his commitment to freeing others despite risks to himself. Thus, it seems not only plausible but likely that in "A Dash for Liberty" Hopkins was inspired in part by Higginson's depiction of the effort by Vesey to organize blacks to fight for their freedom. Her headnote, then, can be seen as reinforcing the "fictive" nature of "A Dash for Liberty." By citing Higginson at the start of her story, Hopkins emphasizes the uniqueness of her version of the *Creole* episode, which signifies on not only the white historical record but her literary antecedents (Douglass, Brown, Child, *and* Higginson) and addresses the situation in which black Americans found themselves at the turn of the century.

Hopkins devises a structure at once compact, rife with meaning, and symmetrical. In the earlier versions of the story, Washington's return to the South for his wife serves as the high point of the romantic plot while his liberation of the slave ship functions as the climax of the patriotic plot. Hopkins does not simply weave these narrative threads into her story; she also demonstrates the need for unified action to combat white oppression of blacks in general and the sexual exploitation of black women in particular, a story line that reaches its turning point at nearly the same moment in section 3 as the patriotic plot.

In contrast to her literary antecedents, Hopkins places a great deal of emphasis on the vulnerability of black women to sexual assault by white men in "A Dash for Liberty." Whereas Douglass, Brown, and Child follow the *Liberator* article's lead in stressing the romantic aspect of Washington's return South, Hopkins makes it clear that Monroe fears—rightly as subsequent events show—that his wife will be subject to sexual abuse and that he acts primarily to protect his wife from such abuse. In the first section, Monroe tells his Canadian employer: "Imagine yourself in my place; how would you feel? The relentless heel of oppression in the States will have ground my rights as a husband into the dust, and have driven Susan to despair in that time. A white man may take up arms to defend a bit of property; but a black man has no right to his wife, his liberty, or his life against his master! This makes me low-spirited, Mr. Dickson, and I have determined to return to Virginia for my wife. My feelings are centered in the idea of liberty" (89/243).[27] Here, at the start of the story, Hopkins intertwines the sexual exploitation theme with the patriotic plot. When Monroe and his eighteen companions free themselves and 116 other slaves in the *Creole* revolt in the second half of the story, he unwittingly achieves his original purpose as announced in the first section. Monroe and his men not only free his wife Susan, who unbeknownst to them happens to be on board, but their rebellion puts a stop to the captain's attempted rape.

At this point I must take issue with one aspect of Yarborough's otherwise perceptive comments about "A Dash for Liberty." After noting Hopkins's introduction of the theme of sexual exploitation into her *Creole* story and her innovation of giving a voice and a force to Susan, Yarborough describes Hopkins's depiction of the behavior of her protagonist and his wife as stereotypically romantic: "[By] having Madison fortuitously appear and interrupt the assault on Susan like some white knight rushing to the aid of a damsel, Hopkins ultimately falls back on the conventions of sentimental romance. Hopkins does succeed in reinserting the black female into a field of action dominated, in Douglass's fiction, by the male. However, in claiming for Susan a conventional role generally denied black women, she necessarily endorses the accompanying male paradigm in her depiction of Madison, a paradigm drawn from the same set of gender constructions that provides Douglass with his heroic model" (178). Yet, as Yarborough himself acknowledges, the first act of violence performed by a black person on board the *Creole* is Susan's striking of the captain to stop his attempt to violate her. Moreover, although there can be no disputing that in the climactic moments of section 3 Monroe acts while Susan waits for some kind of deliverance, Yarborough misses what I believe to be a major innovation in Hopkins's retelling of the *Creole* story: her stress on the fact that Monroe does not act independently. To substitute one figure of speech for a more apposite one, rather than bursting in like a solitary white knight seeking to rescue a fair maiden, Monroe successfully leads a black cavalry into battle against the forces of white oppression. Douglass, Brown, and Child all create an inspiring figure who embodies the "white" values of an unswerving commitment to freedom (to match his suggestive name) and an undying love for one's spouse—the patriotic and romantic plots. In contrast, Hopkins stresses communal action—the dash for liberty—even changing the main character's last name (but not altering his circumstances) to de-emphasize the individual person in favor of what he and his companions succeed in accomplishing through a concerted effort.[28]

Furthermore, the inclusion of the attempted rape scene in the third section balances the structure of Hopkins's story and underscores the importance of creating black unity because in a number of ways it parallels the depiction of Monroe's return to his former place of enslavement in the second section with one essential difference. Both in Virginia and on board the *Creole,* Susan is separated from the other slaves because of her refinement and great beauty. As a lady's serving maid on the plantation, she sleeps in the main house away from the slave quarters. Similarly, on the slave ship she receives her own cabin because of the captain's designs on her. In both scenes Monroe takes advantage of distractions to mask his assault: in Virginia, he strikes during a party; on the *Creole* a rainstorm enables the rebels to free themselves without being detected by the whites. In both scenes Monroe fights bravely, armed with a club. However, whereas he fails in Virginia because he acts alone, Monroe succeeds on the *Creole* because he is joined by a dozen and a half other men.

By playing on the multiple meanings of the word "dash," Hopkins's title reinforces her story's four-part structure and emphasizes the need for action to enhance black unity and defend against black women's sexual exploitation. At least five distinct "dash[es] for liberty" occur in the story. A "dash" can mean a sudden movement or a rush, normally on foot, and this clearly describes Monroe's escape from his Virginia plantation to Canada and freedom, which has already been accomplished before section 1 opens the story. Like her literary predecessors who emphasize Washington's romantic motivations, Hopkins through her title also refers to Monroe's return to Virginia to free Susan, which is the subject of the second section. In section 3 when Hopkins uses the title phrase to describe the revolt, she relies on another definition of "dash," that being the verve or spirited action Monroe and his companions will demonstrate in attempting to take over the ship: "The 'Creole' proceeded slowly on her way towards New Orleans. In the men's cabin, Madison Monroe lay chained to the floor and heavily ironed. But from the first moment on board ship he had been busily engaged in selecting men who could be trusted in the *dash for liberty* that he was determined to make" (95/246, emphasis added). The word "dash" also denotes physical violence, the striking or smashing of someone or something. In the third section, Hopkins incorporates an additional "dash for liberty" into her story—a dash by a black woman for the freedom to control her body. On board the *Creole*, Monroe's wife Susan tries to thwart the captain's attempt to rape her first by "dash[ing] his face aside" and then striking him with "a stinging blow across the eyes" (96/246).[29] A further violent "dash" for liberty occurs later in the third section when Monroe uses a capstan bar to kill a white man who has just shot dead a black rebel. In the story's fourth section, one more "dash" is recorded: the *Creole*'s landing or splash against the dock in Nassau where the slaves will find freedom.

Hopkins's illustration of the need for united action to combat various forms of white oppression in "A Dash for Liberty" is what made her story relevant to the conditions facing blacks at the turn of the century. This aspect of the story also resonates with her other writing. In her nonfiction she comments on the violence and political machinations being directed against African Americans in the 1890s and the early 1900s and advocates unified responses to combat these racist actions. For example, in her *Primer of Facts Pertaining to the Early Greatness of the African Race and the Possibility of Restoration by Its Descendents*, published at her own expense in 1905, Hopkins angrily denounces the assertions being made about African Americans by the southern "plantation" writers and boldly rejects Booker T. Washington's accommodationist policies:

> Because of the desire and commands of our enemies, shall agitation stop, and shall we sit in silence while our traducers go unanswered? This question answers itself. We cannot cease from agitation while our wrongs are the sport of those who know how to silence our every complaint and plea for justice. NEVER SURRENDER THE BALLOT.
>
> The iron heel of oppression is everywhere; it has reached every section of the country, and every black citizen has a duty to perform. [...] It has reached a pass where the educated Black will handle any subject in his assemblies but politics. The South and its friends have said: "Not a word of complaint, no talk of lynching, not an offensive word, or it will go hard with you," and the race leaders have bowed to that decree in abject submission. (27–28)

Furthermore, in her fiction, Hopkins repeatedly shows a concern for black women and the fact that their relationships with white men, while often resulting in children, are rarely matrimonial. In *Contending Forces,* for instance, Hopkins deplores not only the lynching of black males by southern mobs but also the sexual abuse and concubinage that many black women were subjected to at the turn of the century. She decries white America's insane and impossible pursuit of supposed racial purity, often used as a justification for acts as contradictory as the lynching of black men and the sexual exploitation of black women by "chivalrous" southern men, the very group responsible for widespread amalgamation in the first place. Frequently in her novels, characters' "blood," their often-hidden or unknown familial and racial ancestry, is revealed and plays a major role in determining their fate.

Along these lines, I would argue that the name of the slave ship, the *Creole,* perhaps even more than Madison Washington's suggestive name (which, as noted, she deliberately changes), may have been the key factor attracting Hopkins to the slave rebellion as the subject for a *Colored American Magazine* short story. Like "dash," the word "creole" has various meanings, one of which is a person of both white and black ancestry. Echoing Brown and Child, Hopkins describes Monroe as an "unmixed African" and his wife as a "beautiful octoroon." Moreover, in contrast to Douglass who stresses a symbolic connection between Madison Washington and the founding fathers in the opening paragraph and elsewhere in "The Heroic Slave," Hopkins, incorporating something unique to Brown's version into her story, emphasizes a direct blood connection between Susan and one of the founding fathers: "It was a tradition that her grandfather served in the Revolutionary War, as well as both Houses of Congress. That was nothing, however, at a time when the blood of the proudest F.F.V.'s was freely mingled with that of African slaves on their plantations. Who wonders that Virginia has produced great men of color from among the exbondsmen, or, that illustrious black men proudly point to Virginia as a birthplace? Posterity rises to the plane that their ancestors bequeath, and the most refined, the wealthiest and the most intellectual whites of that proud state have not hesitated to amalgamate with the Negro" (94/245).[30] Hopkins's concern in the story with the sexual exploitation of black women leads her to signify in this passage on the male bias, the stress on patriotism, and even some of the phrasing of Douglass's first paragraph, which reads in part as follows:

> The State of Virginia is famous in American annals for the multitudinous array of her statesman and heroes. She has been dignified by some the mother of statesmen. History has not been sparing in recording their names, or in blazoning their deeds. Her high position in this respect, has given her an enviable distinction among her sister States. With Virginia for his birth-place, even a man of ordinary parts, on account of the general partiality for her sons, easily rises to eminent stations. Men, not great enough to attract special attention in their native States, have, like a certain distinguished citizen in the State of New York, sighed and repined that they were not born in Virginia. Yet not all the great ones of the Old Dominion have, by the fact of their birth-place, escaped undeserved obscurity. By some strange neglect, *one* of the truest, manliest, and bravest of her children,—one who, in after years, will, I think, command the pen of genius to set his merits forth, holds now no higher place in the records of that grand old Commonwealth than is held by a horse or an ox. (473–74)

Instead of emphasizing how the heroic actions of the black Virginian patriot Washington link him to the white Virginian founding fathers, as Douglass appears to do, Hopkins calls into question the honor of "the most refined, the wealthiest and the most intellectual whites" from Virginia by pointing out the extent to which these men engaged in sexual relations with slave women, thereby fathering mixed-race offspring and founding a stigmatized subclass of people to which both Susan and many of the African American women suffering sexual exploitation at the turn of the century belong.

In "A Dash for Liberty," the woman Susan, a Creole, and the boat, the *Creole*, are images of one another. Thus, by liberating the one, Monroe and his companions liberate the other. It is only by failing to save Susan by himself and being retaken into slavery in Virginia in the second section, that Monroe, at the head of a score of firmly committed men, can truly free her, the other slaves on board the *Creole,* and himself in sections 3 and 4. Just as the rebels put an end to the captain's figurative rape of black America—the transportation of human cargo to the slave market of New Orleans—they also stop the captain's actual rape of Susan. In the process, Monroe fulfills the purpose he announced in the first section to protect his wife's virtue and thereby preserves their mixed-blood marriage, itself one more and perhaps the story's most important "dash," this time referring to a blending, for liberty.[31]

In "A Dash for Liberty," Pauline Hopkins not only evokes the "fire and romance" inherent in the *Creole* revolt but also significantly rewrites this historical episode and signifies on the earlier literary versions of it to produce her own brand of sophisticated and politically engaged fiction. She implicitly argues that black America will only be fully free when its women no longer suffer sexual oppression and concubinage and that a unified response by and for African American men and women is needed to combat the lynchings, sexual exploitation, and disenfranchisement campaigns directed against them.

Signifyin(g) proves indispensable in analyzing Hopkins's literary revisionism in "A Dash for Liberty," yet the broader implications of the story extend beyond the limits that Gates in his emphasis on the African American literary tradition has chosen to impose on his theory. Like Douglass, Hopkins divides her version into four parts; however, she devotes each to a different geographic location— two American settings sandwiched between two foreign ones. Each move takes Monroe to the southeast, roughly in the direction of Africa. Moreover, as the story progresses, Monroe surrounds himself with an increasingly large number of black people committed to freedom. Section 1 presents Monroe free in Canada but alone. The second section depicts Monroe trying to free his wife in Virginia. Section 3 is set in the north Atlantic on board the southbound *Creole,* where a black community is created that acts in concert to free themselves and the other slaves. The final and shortest section describes the slave ship's arrival in Nassau; here the newly free community of men and women are "offered protection and hospitality" (98/247) by a black British colony where slavery is illegal. Thus, through the four-part structure and transatlantic trajectory of her story, Hopkins links the *Creole* rebellion and by extension the African American fight for freedom with the liberation struggles of colonized peoples in the Caribbean and Africa.

Unspeakable Things Unspoken and Spoken: Birthmarks in Hawthorne and African American Literary Texts

Hopkins's "A Dash for Liberty," like Mosley's *Devil in a Blue Dress,* illustrates the usefulness of Signifyin(g) but also connects the battle against the oppression of blacks in the United States to anticolonial resistance abroad. Utilizing the conventions of (white) literary critical discourse to argue that a phantom blackness haunts classic white American literature, Toni Morrison in *Playing in the Dark* demonstrates that African American critical as well as literary texts signify in motivated ways, yet her project raises a question about Gates's theory as well. Whereas Signifyin(g) holds that African American writers repeat or imitate the discourse of white authors with a black difference (white form, black content or context), Morrison contends that an Africanist presence already exists in canonical American literary texts. The application of her ideas about whiteness and the literary imagination to the relationship between Nathaniel Hawthorne's "The Birth-mark" (1842) and African American narratives that feature birthmarks (including Morrison's own *Sula*) suggests that the authors of these texts are not actually adding something that is missing from Hawthorne's tale but rather making overt what is already implicit therein.

Presciently, in *Figures in Black* Gates anticipates and calls for a project similar to Morrison's: "No one, to my knowledge, has yet discussed the relationship among the slave narratives, the Confederate romance, and the American Romantics, which we may think of as three terms of the dialectic—thesis, antithesis, synthesis—wherein the themes of black and white, common to the bipolar moment in which the slave narratives and the plantation novel oscillate, inform the very structuring principles of the great gothic works of Hawthorne, Melville, and Poe" (50–51). Morrison's study, which is only slowly beginning to receive the attention it deserves from Americanists,[32] examines American Africanism, her "term for the denotative and connotative blackness that African peoples have come to signify, as well as the entire range of views, assumptions, readings, and misreadings that accompany Eurocentric learning about these people" (6–7). Like Said in *Culture and Imperialism* vis-à-vis colonialist texts, Morrison in *Playing in the Dark* is not seeking to expose racism but rather to read American literature more comprehensively. Morrison explains that her interest lies not in racism's effect on its victims but rather in attempting to "avert the critical gaze from the racial object to the racial subject" (90). "Through the simple expedient of demonizing and reifying the range of color on a palette," she asserts in a key passage, "American Africanism makes it possible to say and not say, to inscribe and erase, to escape and engage, to act out and act on, to historicize and render timeless. It provides a way of contemplating chaos and civilization, desire and fear, and a mechanism for testing the problems and blessings of freedom" (7). Contending that the concept of freedom so often explored by white American writers was necessarily formulated in part as a response to those people in society who were enslaved and were thus, by definition, unfree, Morrison states, "There is no romance free of what Herman Melville called 'the power of blackness,' especially not in a country in which there was a resident population, already black, upon which the imagination could play; through which historical, moral, metaphysical, and social fears, problems, and dichotomies could be articulated" (37).[33]

Morrison has examined American Africanism in Melville's *Moby Dick* in "Unspeakable Things Unspoken: The Afro-American Presence in American Literature" (1989) and in Poe's *The Narrative of Arthur Gordon Pym,* "The Gold-Bug," and "How to Write a Blackwood Article" in *Playing in the Dark.* However, although she unmistakably alludes to Hawthorne in the passage quoted above and elsewhere in her discussion of the gothic and romance in the chapter titled "Romancing the Shadow," she has never, as far as I am aware, published a reading of the senior and, in his lifetime, most popular and most critically acclaimed member of the triumvirate of American Renaissance fiction writers. Nonetheless, the prefatory essay in *Mosses from an Old Manse* provides a telling example of the tendency of white authors to use the presence of slavery in American society to highlight conceptions of white freedom. Hawthorne labored for months on "The Old Manse," which immediately precedes "The Birth-mark" in this collection originally published in 1846. In his ruminations on the venerable house where Emerson wrote "Nature" and he himself composed the majority of the pieces in *Mosses* between 1842 and 1845, Hawthorne recalls his fishing trips on nearby rivers with his neighbor, the poet Ellery Channing, as liberating experiences: "[T]he chief profit of those wild days, to him and me, lay [...] in the freedom which we thereby won from all custom and conventionalism, and fettering influences of man on man. We were so free to-day, that it was impossible to be slaves again tomorrow. When we crossed the threshold of a house, or trod the thronged pavements of a city, still the leaves of the trees [...] were whispering to us—'Be free! Be free!'" (25). The objection that the references to "fettering influences of man on man" and "slaves" in this passage are entirely conventional only serves to validate Morrison's point: white Americans so frequently contrasted their notions of and aspirations for freedom with that of the enslaved population in the country that they no longer were conscious of doing so. Furthermore, as Morrison remarks, many critics of American literature have failed to explore connections between slavery and the pervasive American literary concern with freedom.[34]

Hawthorne's "The Birth-mark" has been interpreted as a story about aesthetics, the duality of human existence, the preference for an idea over a human life, the dangers of science, male fears of menstruation or female sexuality, the murder of a wife without legal consequences, and nineteenth-century labor conditions and practices. Despite the striking diversity of these readings, they all agree on one key point: the obsessive nature of Aylmer's reaction to the small red mark on Georgiana's otherwise white cheek. In some of his best-known fiction, Hawthorne depicts characters who are separated from other people because particular aspects of their appearance make them unusual. To cite two examples, the Reverend Mr. Hooper in "The Minister's Black Veil" creates an unbridgeable gulf between himself and his congregation by donning a simple piece of black crepe, and in *The Scarlet Letter*, the Puritan elders decree that Hester Prynne must wear a red A on her breast as a reminder to herself and the community of her sin of adultery. Like Mr. Hooper's veil and Hester's embroidered letter, the small, crimson nevus in the shape of a human hand on Georgiana's face elicits a wide variety of reactions and symbolic interpretations from those who see it. Hawthorne's decision to make a birthmark the focus of his story merits particular attention because it is not something artificial a person chooses or is forced to wear; rather, it is a permanent part of Georgiana's physiology.[35] Attributable to "an overgrowth of blood vessels," as one encyclopedia puts it, the birthmark on her face relates directly to Georgiana's blood and all of the significance attached to that word, especially during the antebellum period ("Birthmark").[36]

In "The Birth-mark," Aylmer reifies whiteness, associating it with perfection. Any deviation from the white norm apparently makes a person susceptible to ugliness, sin, evil, deformity, and mortality. Although Aylmer sets the standards for beauty, spirituality, and perfection in the story, the narrator refers to this character's own coloring with the unflattering word "pale" on four occasions, describing him, for example, "as pale as death" when Georgiana observes him in his laboratory (50). As scientist, husband, and arbiter, Aylmer deems Georgiana's appearance not merely deficient but offensive to him, claiming that

Georgiana's birthmark "shocks" him, "as being the visible mark of imperfection" (37), a judgment echoed in the comparison made between it and a "crimson stain upon the snow" (38) and the use of adjectives such as "Bloody," "frightful," "spectral," "terrible," and "fatal" to describe it.

In response to her husband's habit of shuddering whenever he beholds the birthmark, Georgiana grows to loathe it as much as he does, referring to it as "this odious hand" (39) and begging Aylmer to remove the "hateful mark" even if it kills her in order to prevent her from going insane (41). When Aylmer, frantically engrossed in efforts to eradicate the birthmark, informs his wife that only one possible treatment remains to be undertaken but it is fraught with danger, Georgiana hysterically declares, "There is but one danger—that this horrible stigma shall be left upon my cheek! [...] Remove it! remove it!—whatever be the cost—or we shall both go mad!" (52). Instead of revolting against a husband who has become so obsessed with an insignificant aspect of her appearance that he can hardly bear to look directly at her, Georgiana comes to worship Aylmer and detest that part of herself he finds offensive. As the following passage reveals, she has been brainwashed by his rhetoric about the beauty and perfection of whiteness and in the process she internalizes his prejudices: Georgiana "considered the character of Aylmer, and did it a completer justice than at any previous moment. Her heart exulted, while it trembled, at his honorable love, so pure and lofty that it would accept nothing less than perfection, nor miserably make itself contented with an earthlier nature than he had dreamed of. She felt how much more precious was such a sentiment, than that meaner kind which would have borne with the imperfection for her sake, and have been guilty of treason to holy love, by degrading its perfect idea to the level of the actual" (52). However, if Aylmer's "perfect idea" of whiteness is really a delusion, then "the actual" is precisely what he cannot see.

Indeed, from the start of the story, there is ample evidence that Aylmer reacts to the birthmark not in a lofty and principled way but rather in an unscientific and fanatical manner. Significantly, the narrator's initial description of the birthmark does not reify whiteness: "in the centre of Georgiana's left cheek, there was a singular mark, deeply interwoven, as it were, with the texture and substance of her face. In the usual state of her complexion,—a healthy, though delicate bloom,—the mark wore a tint of deeper crimson, which imperfectly defined its shape amid the surrounding rosiness. When she blushed, it gradually became more indistinct, and finally vanished amid the triumphant rush of blood, that bathed the whole cheek with its brilliant glow. But, if any shifting emotion caused her to turn pale, there was the mark again" (37–38). If this passage privileges any color, it is rose or pink, the blending of red and white. Moreover, most people regard Georgiana's mark as either becoming or inconsequential, and those who do criticize it are referred to as "fastidious persons [...] exclusively of her own sex" (38). Yet in comparison to these negative reactions, Aylmer's proves so maniacal that the mark comes to assume the character of a fetish for him; despite his repeated expressions of revulsion at the birthmark, late in the story Aylmer impulsively presses his lips to it as the supposed cure does its work on the sleeping Georgiana (54). In time, he can think of little else and even his dreams are filled with images of the birthmark. Untroubled by the blemish before their marriage, after the ceremony Aylmer chooses to make it an obsession: "[S]electing it as the symbol of his wife's liability to sin, sorrow, decay, and death, Aylmer's sombre imagination was not long in rendering the birthmark a frightful object, causing him more trouble and horror than Georgiana's beauty, whether of soul or sense, had given him delight. At all seasons which would have been their happiest, he invariably, and without intending it—nay, in spite of a purpose to the contrary—reverted to this one disastrous topic. Trifling as it at first appeared, it so connected itself with innumerable trains of thought, and modes of feeling, that it became the central point of all" (39). The narrator's use of the word "selecting" indicates the arbitrary nature of Aylmer's fixation on the birthmark.

For these reasons, it is not surprising that at the conclusion of the story too much whiteness, as in the work of Melville and many other nineteenth- and twentieth-century American writers, results not in perfection but something horrifying and deadly.[37] As the potion Aylmer has prepared for Georgiana begins to work and the birthmark starts to fade, he begins to think he has achieved his greatest success. But then he himself sounds a note of alarm when he remarks, "But she is so pale!" (55). Failing or refusing to recognize that Georgiana is moribund, however, Aylmer proudly tells his now totally white wife that she is "perfect!" (55). Shortly thereafter the narrator ironically echoes Aylmer's triumphant declaration, describing the newly deceased and thus very pale Georgiana as "the now perfect woman" (56). Although this epithet registers the extent of Aylmer's folly, the ending of the story fails to indicate whether the scientist realizes that he has killed his wife in an obsessive pursuit of a delusion or remains convinced of the perfection of whiteness.

I would like to dispel a misconception the preceding paragraphs may have engendered. My intention is not to offer the definitive interpretation of "The

Birth-mark"; rather, following Morrison's lead, I contend that the story is about many things, whiteness being just one of them. People wishing to deny or minimize the relevance of race might argue that if Hawthorne's characters were black and Georgiana bore a mark deviating from this norm, the story would function in much the same way as it does in its present form. However, the fact is that the author did not make his characters black nor did he reify blackness but rather whiteness at a time when a white majority enslaved roughly one-sixth of the American population because of the visible presence of "Negro" blood. In choosing to write about a birthmark, Hawthorne encodes race into the story.

Although there is no concrete evidence that white writers connected birthmarks with African origins, in the same way that they did a bluish tinge to the fingernails, as Werner Sollors has established,[38] certainly Hawthorne knew from his study of seventeenth-century New England that birthmarks had been widely regarded as marks of the devil and thus deemed sufficient proof that the people who possessed them were witches. Moreover, it is possible that tales of conjure men and women in the South, the notorious events in the author's native Salem, and the practice of voodoo in Haiti may have suggested a link between witchcraft and African ancestry in his mind.

Further, although Hawthorne seldom depicts African American characters in his fiction,[39] and most of his comments on slavery, particularly those in his 1852 biography of Franklin Pierce and his 1862 *Atlantic Monthly* article "Chiefly about War Matters," appear hopelessly reactionary in comparison to those of his white New England literary contemporaries Emerson, Thoreau, and Melville, conflicts between intention and execution on the part of American authors are not unusual, particularly when it comes to matters of race. In four remarkable pages devoted to *Adventures of Huckleberry Finn* in *Playing in the Dark*, Morrison contends that Mark Twain, whose personal motives were antiracist, nevertheless essentially enslaves Jim in order to tell his white protagonist's story, arguing that neither Huck, nor Tom, nor Twain himself can tolerate Jim free.[40] I see a reverse situation in Hawthorne's story. As in his references to slavery in "The Old Manse," Hawthorne writes about race in "The Birth-mark" without being fully aware of it. Thus, he may have believed that the story of Aylmer and Georgiana was about a seemingly raceless subject, such as aesthetics or human duality, and he may have, on principle, taken an antiextremist stand by denouncing Aylmer's compulsion for purity. However, it is precisely because of the prevailing attitudes and policies toward African Americans during the era in which the story was written that "The Birth-mark," with its depiction of Aylmer's obsessive concern for the perfection of whiteness, is also a story about race.

If the connection between birthmarks and race in writing by white authors is not immediately apparent, the same cannot be said about their use in texts by (or attributed to) black Americans. Supposedly the verbatim account of the leader's rationale for and actions during the bloodiest slave rebellion in American history, which occurred in Southampton, Virginia, in 1831, Thomas Gray's "The Confessions of Nat Turner" includes Turner's statement that his parents bolstered his belief that he "would be a prophet" by "saying in my presence, I was intended for some great purpose, which they had always thought from certain marks on my head and breast" (413).[41] In another occult reading of a bodily marking, the presence of a small mole behind the left ear of the white baby Dodie Carteret is regarded ominously by the old black nursemaid Mammy Jane in Charles Chesnutt's *The Marrow of Tradition* (1901), a novel about a brutal race riot fomented by Dodie's father, based on events that occurred in Wilmington, North Carolina, in 1898. Other late-nineteenth- and early-twentieth-century black novels, however, present birthmarks in positive terms. In Frances E. W. Harper's *Iola Leroy, or, Shadows Uplifted* (1892), which tells the story of a family torn apart by slavery, the red spot on the temple of Robert Johnson convinces Iola that he is the brother of her mother, whom she is desperately trying to find. A pair of turn-of-the-century novels employ congenital marks as signs of royal African ancestry, birthrights that transform the lives of the characters who possess them. In Sutton E. Griggs's *Unfettered* (1902), the protagonist, Dorlan Warthell, learns from an African emissary that the mark he bears proves him to be the descendent of a long-lost prince and thus heir to a fortune that will make him one of the richest men in the world. Likewise, in Pauline Hopkins's *Of One Blood; or, The Hidden Self* (1902–3), the seemingly white main character, Reuel Briggs, discovers on an expedition to the ancient city of Meroe that the lotus lily birthmark on his breast signifies that he belongs to the Ethiopian royal family, and, as a result, he is hailed as King Ergamenes.[42]

One of the most striking black American fictional texts involving a birthmark is a little-known, two-page story by Ralph Ellison published in *New Masses* in 1940. Appearing nearly a century after Hawthorne's tale and bearing the same title, Ellison's story concerns two African American characters, Matt and Clara, who go to identify the severely battered body of their brother Willie, allegedly the victim of an automobile accident. However, when Matt searches below the navel of the corpse for Willie's birthmark, he discovers to his horror that his brother must have been lynched: "When Matt lowered his eyes he noticed the ribs had been caved in. The flesh was bruised and torn. It was just below his navel, he thought. Then he gave a start: where it should have been was only a bloody mound of torn flesh and hair. Matt felt weak. He felt as though he had been castrated himself" (16). Here, in a stinging indictment of the way in which many white Americans perceive black males, Ellison uses the word "it" in an ambiguous manner so as to conflate Willie's birthmark, the key to his identity, with his absent penis. At the conclusion of the story, the white policeman and white coroner warn Matt and Clara not to reveal what really happened to their brother or else they, too, may be hit by a car.[43] More recently, the birthmark on the eyelid of the fiercely independent title character of Morrison's *Sula* (1973), like that on Georgiana's cheek, elicits a wide range of interpretations in this novel about the lives of African American women between 1919 and 1965.[44]

Although George Schuyler's *Black No More: Being an Account of the Strange and Wonderful Workings of Science in the Land of the Free, A.D. 1933–1940* (1931) does not involve birthmarks, this satire of white and black race chauvinism, frequently categorized as a work of science fiction (like Hawthorne's tale), envisions the invention of a process that lightens skin color. No longer able to discriminate against people with darker complexions, white Americans stop reifying whiteness. In fact, because the black-no-more treatment renders black Americans somewhat lighter in color than white Americans, the latter proceed to segregate themselves from people with lighter skin. When read in the context of American racial politics, "The Birth-mark," like Schuyler's novel, portrays the imbalanced psyche that motivates and the dire consequences that result from the reification of whiteness.

As this partial survey indicates, African American writers have frequently connected birthmarks and attempts to achieve perfect whiteness with racial objectification, making explicit something implicit in Hawthorne's story and raising a question about the theory of Signifyin(g). In some cases, these black authors clearly employ the figure of the birthmark to signify on "The Birth-mark." If African American texts frequently do rewrite classic white American texts by making their racial subtexts explicit, then the question becomes what exactly is the black, Signifyin(g) difference that Gates contends functions as *the* distinguishing feature of the black American literary tradition? Indeed it might be argued that the act of seizing on the racial subtext itself constitutes the signal difference to which Gates refers; however, if so, then the questions whether and to what extent such an action differs from other forms of counter-discourse, especially that of colonized or formerly colonized people, become more pressing.

My application of Morrison's ideas about American Africanism to the relationship between Hawthorne's "The Birth-mark" and African American texts featuring birthmarks supports my argument that we would do well to consider the ways in which African American and postcolonial rewritings of dominant and dominating discourses resemble and diverge from one another. Without question, Gates's Signifyin(g) and the concept of postcolonial counter-discursiveness have been extremely valuable to critics working in postcolonial and African American studies respectively. Nevertheless, given their points of intersection, both fields would benefit from attempts to cross the disciplinary borders that have come to separate them. The next chapter examines Gilroy's black Atlantic, a theory that seeks in part to do just that.

Du Bois's travel experiences raise in the sharpest possible form
a question common to the lives of almost all these figures who
begin as African-Americans or Caribbean people and are then
changed into something else which evades those specific labels
and with them all fixed notions of nationality and national
identity. Whether their experience of exile is enforced or chosen,
temporary or permanent, these intellectuals and activists, writers,
speakers, poets, and artists repeatedly articulate a desire to escape
the restrictive bonds of ethnicity, national identification, and
sometimes even "race" itself. Some speak [...] in terms of the
rebirth that Europe offered them. Whether they dissolved their
African-American sensibility into an explicitly pan-Africanist
discourse or political commitment, their relationship to the
land of their birth and their ethnic political constituency was
absolutely transformed.

PAUL GILROY

4 The Black Atlantic

Harry Dean, Harriet Jacobs, Alice Walker

In its consideration of marginalized people's responses to a dominant discourse, Paul Gilroy's black Atlantic resembles postcolonial counter-discourse
and Henry Louis Gates's Signifyin(g). However, unlike many postcolonial critics, who choose not to examine African American cultural productions, and
Gates, who concentrates on the black American literary tradition, Gilroy takes
a major step toward moving beyond such territorialization by incorporating
elements from both postcolonial and African American studies into his theory.
One of the key arguments he puts forward in *The Black Atlantic* is that travel
abroad, particularly to the metropolitan centers of Europe, profoundly influenced the political stances of several important black American figures, as indicated by the epigraph above. Gilroy's emphasis on European travel, however,
tends to obscure the fact that direct contacts between African Americans and
Africans, including black missionary work in Africa and attendance at black

colleges and universities in the United States by Africans, date back to the nine-teenth century.[1]

Moreover, although new world slavery is the defining experience for black Atlantic peoples, with the exception of a few references to Haiti, Gilroy focuses on anglophone cultures, making no mention of Spanish- or Portuguese-speaking blacks in the Americas. This may result from his decision to privi-lege not only the English language (similar to many postcolonial critics) but also the position of England and the situation of black Britons in his black Atlantic model. As he acknowledges in *The Black Atlantic*'s third chapter, "'Jewels Brought from Bondage': Black Music and the Politics of Authenticity," the examples he provides "reflect the special position of Britain within the black Atlantic world, standing out at the apex of the semi-triangular structure which saw commodities and peoples shipped to and fro across the ocean" (88). His use of the qualifier "semi-triangular" reveals what he seems to regard as the incomplete and unequal relationship among black Britons, African Americans and black West Indians, and Africans in the black Atlantic network, suggesting that little direct contact takes place between Africa and the new world—every-thing apparently must be mediated through the British vertex. The theory thus appears to reconfigure England (and London in particular) as the metropolitan center. However, perhaps because black Britons have not produced a body of counter-discursive writing of sufficient breadth and significance to illustrate his points, Gilroy turns elsewhere for his examples.

What he concentrates on are the lives and texts of black Americans, devot-ing over one hundred pages of *The Black Atlantic* to four men: Martin Delany, Frederick Douglass, W. E. B. Du Bois, and Richard Wright.[2] In doing so, Gilroy, who decries African American exceptionalism, could be seen as engaging in a form of it himself. Although he devotes some attention to Edward Blyden and mentions Frantz Fanon and C. L. R. James, he chooses not to discuss the theo-retical texts of the latter two figures or analyze any black West Indian literature.[3] Perhaps this is because doing so would raise the question of exactly what the distinction is between the black Atlantic world and colonized peoples generally, especially given the prominence of West Indian theory and literature in postco-lonial studies. This question comes to the fore nonetheless in Gilroy's chapter on Du Bois, which ends with an extended summary of the 1928 novel *Dark Princess*. Du Bois's perspective is neither strictly black Atlantic nor exclusively Pan-African; instead, his "Romance" calls for cooperation among oppressed peoples throughout the world—African Americans, Africans, Asians, and so forth. Gilroy uses *Dark Princess* to illustrate how far Du Bois moved away from

African American exceptionalism (largely, according to Gilroy, because of his experiences in Europe). However, readers of *The Black Atlantic* may wonder, as Du Bois himself seems to have done, what ultimately the differences are between the experience of new world slavery and colonial domination;[4] they may also ask how colonized people's counter-discourse to the metropolitan center differs from black Atlantic world's "counter-narrative" of modernism.

Drawing on both postcolonial and African American theory, the black Atlantic model proves especially useful in analyzing texts featuring depictions of England, mainland Europe, and Africa by black Americans. I first use the black Atlantic to situate Dean's *The Pedro Gorino* within a geographic and historical context. Next I show that Jacobs's *Incidents in the Life of a Slave Girl* confirms the validity of Gilroy's argument that transatlantic travel significantly alters the political stances of African American writers, thereby establishing that black American women who spent time abroad underwent transformations similar to those of key male figures. Without question Gilroy raises issues of gender, cites the work of black feminists, and, in a paragraph concerning African Americans who "went to Europe and had their perceptions of America and racial domination shifted as a result of their experiences there" (18), mentions Phillis Wheatley, Ida B. Wells, Lucy Parsons, Nella Larsen, Sarah Parker Remond, Edmonia Lewis, Anna Julia Cooper, Jessie Fauset, Gwendolyn Bennett, and Lois Malliou Jones, a list that could be expanded to include female writers who traversed the Atlantic to either Europe or Africa, such as Nancy Prince, Harriet Jacobs, Shirley Graham, Eslanda Goode Robeson, Era Bell Thompson, Gwendolyn Brooks, Maya Angelou, and Alice Walker. However, in providing support for his major assertion about the effects of foreign travel on African Americans, he chooses not to examine closely the experiences or writing of women but to focus instead on the lives and texts of black American males.[5] In the final section, I raise key questions about Gilroy's theory during the course of my analysis of Walker's *Possessing the Secret of Joy,* whose African-born and American-inspired protagonist not only changes her mind about, but gives up her life to bring international scrutiny to bear on, a traditional practice that physically and mentally ravages women of all ages.

Harry Dean and the Dream of an African Empire

In *The Black Atlantic,* Gilroy asserts that in the writing of Frederick Douglass and other former slaves "a new discursive economy emerges with the refusal to subordinate the particularity of slave experience to the totalising power of universal reason held exclusively by white hands, pens, and publishing houses. Authority and autonomy emerge directly from the deliberately personal tone of this history. [...] What Richard Wright would later identify as the aesthetics of personalism flows from these narratives and shows that in the hands of slaves the particular can wear the mantle of truth and reason as readily as the universal" (69). Following World War I, black American authors, including Langston Hughes in *The Big Sea,* began to turn to autobiography in order to challenge the white historical record on Africa and the image of the continent found in white literary texts. The counter-discursive potential of the personal narrative, especially when written by an African American, was embraced by Harry Foster Dean when he endeavored to tell the idiosyncratic story of his adventures in Africa.

Almost assuming the role of the protagonist at times, the *Pedro Gorino*— the ship Dean purchased in Stavanger, Norway, in 1900, sailed to Cape Town, and used for various commercial ventures until he was forced to leave South Africa—embodies Dean's dream of founding a black African empire. By using the name of his boat as the title for the American edition of his book,[6] Dean anchors his autobiography on the chief and originary symbol Gilroy selects for his black Atlantic model. "I have settled on the image of ships in motion across the spaces between Europe, America, Africa, and the Caribbean as a central organising symbol for this enterprise and as my starting point," explains Gilroy. "The image of the ship—a living, micro-cultural, micro-political system in motion—is especially important for historical and theoretical reasons [...]. Ships immediately focus attention on the middle passage, on the various projects for redemptive return to an African homeland, on the circulation of ideas and activists as well as the movement of key cultural and political artefacts" (*Black Atlantic* 4). It would be hard to imagine a better description of the multifaceted role Dean's vessel plays in his narrative.

Subtitled *The Adventures of a Negro Sea-Captain in Africa and on the Seven Seas in His Attempts to Found an Ethiopian Empire,* Dean's autobiographical curiosity outlines his Pan-African family history, touches on his childhood in the 1860s and 1870s, and describes in detail his experiences as a sailor, businessman, and sometime secular missionary in southern Africa at the turn of the century.[7] Dean's advocacy of black American emigration to Africa links him with nineteenth-century figures such as Alexander Crummell and African Methodist Episcopal Bishop Henry McNeal Turner, and his dream of founding a black empire in Africa recalls the Ethiopianist fantasies of not only turn-of-the-century novelists such as Sutton E. Griggs and Pauline Hopkins but also

Marcus Garvey, whose ultimate objective, according to a 1924 essay, was to create "a Racial Empire upon which 'the sun shall never set'" (5). Dating back to the late eighteenth century, Ethiopianism, the teleological view of history inspired by the Psalms verse "Princes shall come out of Egypt, Ethiopia shall soon stretch forth her hands unto God" (68:31), figured prominently in sermons, pamphlets, speeches, and articles by black Americans during the nineteenth century. Because the King James Bible and classical authors used "Ethiopia" as a synonym for Africa south of Egypt generally, Ethiopianism predicted a bright future for the whole continent. It undergirded white and black efforts to Christianize and civilize Africa (which intensified in the latter half of the nineteenth century), spawned religious and political movements in West and southern Africa in the 1890s and early 1900s, pervaded early-twentieth-century Pan-Africanism and the Garvey movement, and became briefly refocused on Haile Selassie's kingdom during the Italian invasion and occupation of Ethiopia (1935–41). Although Ethiopianism's popularity steeply declined after the Second World War, it indirectly influenced a wide variety of religious, cultural, and intellectual movements, including the Nation of Islam, Black Judaism, Rastafarianism, the Black Arts movement, and Afrocentrism.[8]

Book 1 sets the tone for the rest of *The Pedro Gorino* by indicating Dean's pride in his black heritage and desire to help his race. It also portrays Dean as a romantic figure seemingly sprung from the pages of Robert Louis Stevenson. Sterling North's preface cultivates the image of Dean as a larger-than-life figure, describing him as a man who had "circumnavigated Africa eighteen times, crossed it from east to west three times and from north to south once" (*The Pedro Gorino* xi).[9] North recalls Dean telling him on their first meeting: "I look like a poor old man [...] but I am a prince in my own right back in Africa. I know things that would make the King of England tremble on his throne. I know facts that would make the imperialists of every nation blush with shame" (*The Pedro Gorino* viii). Following the opening chapter, devoted to the early Pan-Africanist Paul Cuffe, the next five chapters detail Dean's three-year journey around the world on his uncle Silas Dean's ship, a voyage that ended when he was fifteen and laid the foundation for his later efforts to forge cooperative links between new world blacks and Africans.

Ever since its original publication, Dean's book has elicited considerable skepticism. Apart from George Shepperson's helpful introduction to the 1989 reissue of the British edition of Dean's book and a 1973 M.A. thesis on Dean by John S. Burger, very little has been written about the author of *The Pedro Gorino*. Those who do comment on Dean describe him as dynamic but embittered; they also question the veracity of his autobiography. In a brief review of *The Pedro Gorino* in the *Crisis*, Du Bois recalls meeting Dean in London in 1900 at the time of the first Pan-African Conference: "Dean was bitter. He wanted to lead a black army across the straits of Gibraltar. I saw his point of view, but did not think the scheme was practical." (Dean may also be the "bitter, black American who whispered how an army of the Soudan might someday cross the Alps" that Du Bois, in "The Immortal Child," his eulogy to Samuel Coleridge Taylor in *Darkwater* [581], recalled encountering at the 1900 Pan-African Conference.) Du Bois's assessment was that the "book is the interesting and in its final chapters, fascinating story of Dean's dream. Perhaps his dream goes in some respects beyond the facts, but it is all worth reading" ("The Negro in Literature").[10] Concerned with establishing the accuracy of Dean's purported adventures in South Africa, neither Shepperson nor Burger fully investigates the first and in many ways the most important claim in Dean's book: the author's assertion that he is the great-grandson of the black sea captain and businessman Paul Cuffe (1759–1817). Burger reports that in his notebooks Dean refers to a biography he wrote about Cuffe and that Dean had transferred photographs of letters written by Cuffe onto glass plates that he used in lectures he gave about black history.[11] Indeed, the first chapter of *The Pedro Gorino* certainly shows evidence of research on Dean's part into Cuffe's life.[12] However, Dean's account of Cuffe differs greatly from those of other biographers. One of the most striking discrepancies is Dean's claim that Cuffe liberated slaves from a South Carolina plantation and transported them to Freetown in Sierra Leone. No other biography of Cuffe mentions this incident. It does serve, however, to portray Cuffe and Dean as kindred spirits—daring black sea captains prepared to strike a blow against white oppression. Moreover, Dean quotes in full a short letter written to Paul Cuffe by his "youngest son, John Cuffee," from prison in York, Pennsylvania, asking for assistance from his "father" (17–18), and Dean claims that this same "John Cuffee" was his maternal grandfather. Yet Paul Cuffe did not have a son named John, as Lamont Thomas's genealogy of the Cuffe family in his biography clearly indicates (161). Cuffe did, in fact, receive the letter Dean reprints; however, it came from a thief named Bailey who at various times had impersonated Paul Cuffe and Cuffe's brother-in-law (Sherwood 208–10, Thomas 116).[13] Dean apparently found the letter in Cuffe's papers at the New Bedford Public Library, but he must have overlooked Cuffe's reply in which he berates the impostor for betraying his race: "If the Great evil that thou hast embarked upon, were only against me as an individual [...] I should not have to lament the Cause so much. But this is a national Concern. It is a

Stain to the Whole Community of the African race. [...] The manumission of 1,500,000 Slaves depends upon the faithfulness of the few who have obtained their freedom. Yea, [...] but the Whole Community of the African race, which are according to best accounts 30,000,000" (qtd. in Thomas 116).[14]

Both questions and ironies abound. Was Dean perhaps descended from Paul Cuffe's nephew John (the son of Cuffe's older brother John), who was born in 1799?[15] If this is so, then perhaps Dean mistakenly believed that the letter to Paul Cuffe from his "youngest son, John Cuffee," in Cuffe's papers was written by his grandfather. Or did Dean fabricate the ancestral link to Paul Cuffe because he regarded the early Pan-Africanist as the perfect antecedent to his own efforts to "establish an Ethiopian Empire"?[16] In any event, by claiming to be the grandson of the "John Cuffee" who wrote a letter to his "father" from prison, Dean, an ardent black nationalist who devoted his life to assisting and defending people of African descent, unintentionally affiliates himself with a man whom Paul Cuffe himself denounced as a traitor to black people everywhere.

Whether Paul Cuffe was actually a blood ancestor of Dean's or not, he certainly served as a powerful spiritual forefather for Dean, with whom he shared not only a love for the sea but also ideas about the development of Africa, education, and black self-reliance. A builder, captain, and owner of ships, Cuffe was the wealthiest black person in America by the early 1800s and left an estate of almost twenty thousand dollars at his death (Thomas 22, 118). Cuffe's vessels had traded and whaled successfully along the African coast long before he set sail in late 1810 in his brig *Traveller* on what Thomas terms a "civilizing mission" to Sierra Leone (46). Five years later he transported thirty-eight American blacks to the British colony in the same vessel—"the first black-initiated emigration movement from the Western Hemisphere to the shores of Africa" (Thomas 100). A firm believer in education, Cuffe established a racially integrated school for children in Westport, Massachusetts, in the 1790s; personally instructed the members of his predominantly black crews, including Africans recruited in Sierra Leone; and gave lectures on Africa to black audiences in the United States. Cuffe was convinced that "black maritime trade was essential for the advancement of Africa" and, despite his concerns about the racist motivations behind white support for the back-to-Africa movement, believed that American blacks would be better off in Africa where they could "rise to be a people," as he wrote in an 1816 letter (Thomas 104, 119, 108).

As a youth on his uncle's ship, named *Traveller the Second* after Cuffe's vessel, Dean learned the rudiments of sailing, experienced Africa for the first time, and began concocting a plan for the rehabilitation of the black race. Building on the theme of family heritage introduced in the initial chapter, in the fourth chapter Dean feels "burdened with [the] great responsibility" of having been chosen by his Uncles Silas and Solomon (the latter of whom he meets in San Francisco after rounding Cape Horn) to carry on the sea life. Dean recalls that "[i]t seemed that all my seafaring ancestors were watching me from their graves on the land and in the dark sea, trying to determine if their faith had been misplaced" (43–44). After stops in Hawaii and various ports in Asia, the young Dean is delighted when the boat reaches East Africa. Demonstrating an interest in the continent's history, Dean explains that "I had always been interested in Africa because of the stories I had been told, and because it was the continent from which my ancestors had come [...]. I wanted to see for myself the remnants and ruins of its glorious past" (55).

Soon after departing from Cape Town, *Traveller the Second* stops at Saldanha Bay where Dean's uncle tells him a story that profoundly affects his attitudes toward Africans and whites. According to Silas Dean, the sailors on a Dutch ship named the *Full Moon,* who had come into Saldanha Bay to get water, kidnapped sixteen little girls and four young boys and sold them into slavery at Jamestown in 1619, thus initiating the slave trade in America.[17] Responding to the young Dean's question as to why the Hereros did not chase the Dutchmen and recapture their children, his uncle states, "Not a ship among them [... ; t]hat has been the downfall of our race" (57). From that day forward Dean commits himself to providing black people with vessels and the knowledge necessary to carry out maritime trade. When Dean reaches Liberia a short time later, its independence further fuels his dreams: "My knowledge that Liberia was the one bit of land in all Africa still held by its rightful heirs made me think of its importance as a base for operations. The dark continent held a new interest for me, and the troubles of my race had taken on a new significance. Even at that early age I was dreaming of an Ethiopian Empire" (59).

Confirming Gilroy's assertions about the effects of foreign travel on the political stances of African Americans, Dean's early experiences in Africa clearly transformed his attitudes toward both the land of his birth and his ancestral homeland. Yet, like the advocates of emigration to Africa, such as Cuffe and Crummell, and nineteenth- and turn-of-the-century black American Ethiopianists generally, Dean saw the need for African American leadership in not only the economic and but also the cultural development of Africa. Early in book 2, Dean recalls his resolve to "instigate a movement to rehabilitate Africa and found such an Ethiopian Empire as the world has never seen. [...] It would be greater than the empires of Africa's past [...] for although these kingdoms must have numbered their subjects in the hundreds of thousands, their store of knowledge was limited. I dreamed of an empire infinitely more cultured. Africa would again lift up her head. Her fleets would sail the sea. Her resources would once more enrich her own children" (69–70).

Book 2, "The Pedro Gorino," describes Dean's acquisition of a seventy-foot, two-masted vessel with which he tries to establish a black-owned and -operated shipping company based in southern Africa; it also includes his incredible account of being offered Portuguese East Africa by the colonial governor's secretary for a mere fifty thousand pounds. The story behind the name of Dean's "freak topsail schooner" is significant to Dean's nation-building project in Africa. It was originally called *Pellar Guri* after a girl of that name who rallied "all the peasants of Norway" to defeat a robber baron trying to capture the land. "From this united effort," according to a page of illuminated script affixed beneath the name, "rose the kingdom of Norway" (73). The folktale that Dean refers to actually concerns a girl named Prillar Guri, reputed to have played a role in the defeat of a group of Scottish mercenaries who were crossing Norway on their way to Sweden in the early 1600s.[18] However, a West Indian member of Dean's crew thought the name was the *Pedro Gorino* and painted this on the prow. When informed of his error, the sailor replied that *Pellar Guri* was no name for a black man's ship and so the Spanish name stuck. Thus, Dean's ship is fortuitously christened with a name that is oddly appropriate for his Quixote-like project of establishing an autonomous black African nation in the wake of Europe's Scramble for Africa.

Dean explains his decision to use Cape Town—"the most strategic point in that part of the world"—as a base for operations by depicting himself as a kind of spy in enemy country: "[W]hile awaiting my chance to help the Ethiopian race I could not do better than take up a position in the very midst of the Imperialists and learn their game firsthand" (80). Not long after establishing a lucrative shipping business, Dean to his amazement is taken for an intelligence agent of the American government by colonial officials in Lourenço Marques (now Maputo), who offer him all of Portuguese East Africa "for the ridiculously low figure of fifty thousand pounds sterling" (114). The offer, which Dean later believes was made because of Portuguese fears that the British would take over what is now Mozambique in a bold scheme to flank the Boers, triggers a manifest destiny–type fantasy for Dean: "The possibilities opened before me like a flower: Delogoa Bay, future maritime headquarters for native Africa; Lourenço Marques, a new centre of culture for the coloured race; Portuguese East Africa, a national home to which the wandering Ethiopians the world over might come and live in peace. Who could tell? With such a foothold an enterprising colony might expand until it had recaptured the whole continent" (114–15). Claiming that he wrote "[e]very prominent Ethiopian in America" requesting funds to be used to purchase the colony but was unanimously turned down, Dean hyperbolically declares, "Thus the bright bubble burst, and the greatest chance the 'negro' has ever had to rehabilitate Africa came to nothing" (122).[19] After placing much of the blame on the pernicious influences of America's climate of oppression and "false ideals," he then directly chides those African Americans who refused to heed his call to liberate Africa and themselves: "In your blindness and rustic unsophistication you reminded me of the native Somali, who, if you were to offer him a thousand bright gold sovereigns for a quart of goat's milk, would refuse, but if you were to offer him three cents worth of shell money would gladly sell it" (123). Despite his numerous refutations of white misconceptions about Africa and Africans in the book, Dean here engages in the paternalism that many earlier black American Ethiopianists exhibited toward the continent's inhabitants. Reminiscent of Othello's comparison of himself to the "base Indian [who] threw a pearl away / Richer than all his tribe" in his final speech, Dean's telling analogy seeks to point out to uncooperative African Americans the error of their ways by asserting that they are each no better than a lowly African.

In book 3, "Segow Faku, King of the Pondos," Dean recounts his efforts to build schools, unify tribes, and establish an ongoing trading concern in Pondoland, a recently subdued nation in eastern South Africa bordering the St. John River.[20] The final book, "The Net Draws Tighter," tells of Dean's work in Basutoland (now Lesotho), his efforts to establish a dialogue among the native leaders in South Africa, and his harassment by government officials that culminated in his expulsion from the country. Still hoping to raise fifty thousand pounds to buy Portuguese East Africa, Dean conceives of a plan to link Pondoland, Basutoland, and Port St. John by a system of roads that would enable the Pondos, Pondo Mesis, and Basutos to ship and receive goods to and from Cape Town and the rest of the world via the *Pedro Gorino*. Dean also believes that through his educational efforts he will succeed in sowing the seeds of unrest among these native people, stating with characteristic bravado, "Very soon now I should be in a position to do more for my race than any coloured man before me. [... My enemies] could not undermine the influence I was already gaining with the natives. They could not undo my work once I had instilled the desire for liberty in those fertile Ethiopian minds" (204).

Yet despite two attempts on his life by government agents and his earlier excoriation of "the Imperialists as [...] vulgar murderers and thieves whose egotistical, crafty, and cunning nature holds no respect for intellectual or moral values" in a letter to a friend (174), Dean underestimates the wiliness of his foes who run him into debt, destroy his property, and eventually deport him. Thus, Dean's "bright dreams" come "crash[ing] about [his] head" and he is "driven from [his] motherland by foreigners and usurpers" (255, 256). Although nostalgia pervades Dean's book, it becomes particularly acute in the final chapter. In books 2, 3, and 4, Dean mentions the need to have power installed in the *Pedro Gorino* so that it will be able to compete with motorized boats; however, he keeps putting off this modernization even though he can readily afford it. Ironically, at the time that Dean encounters intense government harassment that leads to an insurmountable financial crisis for him, his ship is in dry dock awaiting the installation of power. Even though his vessel will no doubt be confiscated to pay his debts, Dean takes some consolation in the fact that the boat will remain as it has always been. In a passage that signifies on Conrad's lament about the end of the sailing era in *An Outcast of the Islands*,[21] Dean, speaking for himself as well as his sailors, states on the final page, "we were all thinking that perhaps it was best to leave her thus, and never hear the angry rumble of an engine in her vitals, or see the wild, free spirit of her broken and surly, and the ship plunging on without regard to wind or waves. And that was the last I ever saw of the *The Pedro Gorino*" (256).

Dean's reluctance to modernize his ship, the most powerful symbol of his dream of an "Ethiopian Empire," accords perfectly with the tensions inherent in early-twentieth-century black American texts that depict Africa and reflects the double-consciousness of the black Atlantic world generally as Gilroy characterizes it. On the one hand, the authors of these texts often believed that Western and in particular American technology imported to Africa by diasporic blacks would set in motion forces that would culminate in the rehabilitation of the continent. On the other hand, these writers denounced what they regarded as the rampant and corrupting materialism of European and American culture and occasionally predicted that only a resurgent and spiritually pure Africa could redeem the West from the worldly path it had taken. Although throughout the book Dean argues that people of African descent require ships to compete globally (a position he would maintain all of his life), he apparently fears that by blindly imitating white modernization efforts blacks may be co-opted by the inauthentic ideals of the Western world, may have their "wild, free spirit[s ...] broken," and may sacrifice the lofty goals to which he has always aspired, for the sake of material gain. The threat to freedom in this passage is crucial, for, anticipating Gilroy, it serves implicitly to link modern, white Western society to the transatlantic slave trade and its legacy.

"A Visit to England" and the Shift in Purpose and Tone in *Incidents in the Life of a Slave Girl*

In the dozens of essays devoted to Harriet Jacobs's *Incidents in the Life of a Slave Girl* (1861) published in the last twenty-five years, critics have investigated a wide variety of subjects. Surprisingly, the last quarter of the book, which describes the experiences of the main character and narrator, Linda Brent, as a fugitive slave in the North and as a traveler to England, has gone relatively unanalyzed.[22] This scant critical attention can perhaps be explained by the fact that the most sensational events in the narrative, Linda's sexual harassment by her master Dr. Flint, her relationship with Mr. Sands with whom she has two children, and her seven-year confinement in an attic crawl space, occur in the first twenty-nine chapters. However, the last twelve chapters are unique in their own right, exposing the lack of freedom in the North, not only for fugitive slaves and free blacks but even for white people themselves. Chapter 37 and the strategic part it plays in Jacobs's narrative illustrate the validity of Gilroy's contentions about the effects of foreign travel on black Americans, demonstrating that African American women who journeyed abroad experienced the same kind of political transformation as their male counterparts.

Sandra Gunning's "Reading and Redemption in *Incidents in the Life of a Slave Girl*" (1996) is one of the first essays to address Jacobs's relationship with her target audience in detail, although she, like so many other critics, devotes the majority of her attention to the earlier chapters. I agree with most of Gunning's assertions about how the narrator speaks to her readers; however, where she sees Linda chiding and challenging her white northern female audience throughout the narrative, I detect a progression—or perhaps I should say a deterioration—in this relationship that can be seen, first, in the steep falling off of direct addresses to her readers after chapter 10 and, second, in a shift in purpose and tone when the narrative turns to Linda's experiences in the North in chapter 30. Linda actively cultivates a relationship with her target audience early in the narrative, informing her readers about aspects of southern slavery of which they may have no knowledge, attempting to elicit their sympathy for herself and other enslaved black women, and exhorting them to intervene politically to put an end to the peculiar institution. In chapters 30–41, however, Linda no longer bears witness to practices about which her readers can claim ignorance—many of them may in fact participate in the segregation of, discrimination toward, and prejudice against black people that take place in the North. Linda's purpose in these later chapters is to shame her readers into behaving more morally and to force them to acknowledge their role in a slave system that is not confined to the American South but rather pervades the entire nation. Having fought long and hard for a genuine freedom that still eludes her, Linda at the end of the narrative turns the tables on her readers by denying *their* freedom. Until white northerners totally divest themselves of slavery and its attendant racist ideologies, she implicitly argues, they themselves will not truly be free.

Confronted with the major binary oppositions dominating antebellum America—black versus white, slave versus free—Linda emphasizes gender, asserting the common womanhood of northern white free women and southern black slave women. Seeking, as she says in her preface, "to arouse the women of the North to a realizing sense of the condition of two millions of women at the South, still in bondage" (440), Linda, particularly in her first nine chapters, not only contends that all women should be able to preserve their chastity, fall in love, get married, raise their children, and enjoy the comforts of a home and a hearth, but also draws on her own experiences and observations to show how the institution of slavery makes it impossible for black women to do these things that white women take for granted. In her third chapter, for example, she directly entreats her readers to "contrast *your* New Year's day with that of the poor bond-woman!" (457, emphasis in original). For northern white women it is a happy day to be shared with their children; however, for the black slave woman, the day "comes laden with peculiar sorrows. She sits on her cold cabin floor, watching the children who may all be torn from her the next morning; and often does she wish that she and they might die before the day dawns" (457). Although Linda acknowledges the differences between her readers and this unfortunate black woman, she attributes them to slavery and underscores the maternal feelings shared by all women: "She may be an ignorant creature, degraded by the system that has brutalized her from childhood; but she has a mother's instincts, and is capable of feeling a mother's agonies" (457).

To my knowledge no one has commented at length on the shift in purpose and tone in the northern chapters of the book; however, several critics have noted the contrasting styles and hybrid nature of the narrative. In her introduction to the Harvard University Press edition of *Incidents* (1987), Jean Fagan Yellin, who used her discovery of Jacobs's letters to Amy Post to authenticate the slave narrative 120 years after it was first published ("Written by Herself"; see also McMillen), discusses what she describes as the book's "double tale, dramatizing the triumph of her efforts to prevent her master from raping her, to arrange her children's rescue from him, to hide, to escape, and finally to achieve freedom; and simultaneously presenting her failure to adhere to sexual standards in which she believed" (xiv). In elaborating these divergent themes, Jacobs reveals her debt to and revisions of both the African American male slave narrative and the Anglo-American female seduction novel. Nowhere are these competing discourses more pronounced than in chapter 10, "A Perilous Passage in the Slave Girl's Life."

In chapters 1–9, Linda appeals to her target audience's moral sensibilities by depicting chattel slavery as an immoral system that corrupts everyone in the South, black and white, male and female, old and young, and by presenting herself—a black woman and a former slave—as a woman with a highly developed sense of morality. In the tenth chapter, however, she must reveal to her readers that after long resisting the sexual advances of her master she became involved in a sexual relationship with another man. Apparently recognizing that certain members of Linda's target audience would be shocked by this information and possibly lose sympathy for her while others would realize that conventional morality is not applicable to slave women, Jacobs describes Linda's decision to enter into the relationship with Mr. Sands in two very different ways. For those readers for whom Linda's struggle with Dr. Flint represents an all-or-nothing battle against male oppression of women in its most extreme form, Jacobs presents Linda's thwarting of Flint's designs on her through her liaison with Mr. Sands as a carefully planned strategy: "I was determined that the master, whom I so hated and loathed, who had blighted the prospects of my youth, and made my life a desert, should not, after my long struggle with him, succeed at last in trampling his victim under his feet. I would do any thing, every thing, for the sake of defeating him. What *could* I do? I thought and thought, till I became desperate, and made a plunge into the abyss. [...] I will not try to screen myself behind the plea of compulsion from a master; for it was not so. [...] I knew what I did, and I did it with deliberate calculation" (500, emphasis in original). Almost immediately, however, concerned about appeasing her most morally exacting readers, she places the blame for her lapse on "the demon Slavery" and her extreme youth (501). Then, with another direct address to her readers, she begs for forgiveness and continued sympathy, acknowledging her moral distance from them: "I made a headlong plunge. Pity me, and pardon me, *O virtuous reader!* You never knew what it is to be a slave; to be entirely unprotected by law or custom; to have the laws reduce you to the condition of a chattel, entirely subject to the will of another. [...] I know I did wrong. No one can feel it more sensibly than I do. The painful and humiliating memory will haunt me to my dying day" (502, emphasis added). Hereafter Linda's relationship with her target audience changes significantly, most notably in the drastic decline in direct addresses to her readers: Linda addresses her readers directly fifteen times in the preface and first ten chapters; thereafter, she does so only three times.

In addition to foiling Flint's obsessive and elaborate plot to set her up as his concubine, Linda's relationship with Mr. Sands results in two children. Their advent greatly alters Linda's life and transforms *Incidents* from a story about a slave girl's battle against sexual exploitation to one concerning a slave mother's struggle to shield her children from the cruelties of the peculiar institution. Having learned that the Flints have decided to send her children Ellen and Benny to their plantation in order "to be 'broke in'" (545), Linda runs away, gambling that once Dr. Flint learns that she is gone he will sell her children in disgust and Mr. Sands will be able to buy them. Although, like her earlier and equally risky gamble on the relationship with Sands, this one eventually pays off (at least as far as her children are concerned), it will not be until Linda has endured nearly seven years in the "loophole of retreat," a cramped, stuffy crawl space in her grandmother's house, that she will finally be able to escape to the North.

Yet, in contrast to most slave narratives, Jacobs's book does not end shortly after Linda reaches the North; rather, it continues because what she finds there is *not* freedom.[23] This shift in subject matter results in another alteration in Linda's relationship to her target audience. In the chapters set in the South, Linda informs her readers of the moral outrages slave girls and slave mothers face daily. There her goals are to gain the sympathy of readers and convince them to agitate publicly for the abolition of slavery; moreover, in depicting a slave mistress risking her standing in the community to shelter Linda from Dr. Flint in chapter 18, she provides an example of a white woman on whom her readers can model their own behavior. Without question, Mrs. Bruce serves as a similar role model in the last quarter of the narrative by repeatedly shielding Linda from slave catchers in the North, as Yellin (Introduction xxxii–xxxiii) and Gunning (150) have noted; however, here Jacobs is no longer describing injustices of which her readers can disavow knowledge and for which they can disavow responsibility. This change is reflected in the new tone Jacobs employs in the final twelve chapters.

Almost immediately, Linda's description of her experiences in the North deviates from the standard portrayal of a slave's escape as a major victory. In chapter 30, she records her first view of the sun rising on "free soil" but then undercuts this by adding, "for such I *then* believed it to be" (618, emphasis in original). As she chronicles her education into the realities of city life, she simultaneously charts her disillusionment with freedom in the North. After learning that she will have to travel to New York on a Jim Crow car, Linda remarks, "This was the first chill to my enthusiasm about the Free States. Colored people were allowed to ride in a filthy box, behind white people, at the south, but there they were not required to pay for the privilege. It made me sad to find how the north aped the customs of slavery" (623).

It becomes quite clear in chapter 35, "Prejudice Against Color," that Linda regards her struggle as far from over. After describing her decision to take her meals in her room because she cannot eat in the dining room of the Pavilion Hotel in Rockaway, New York, and the subsequent protests of other black servants over what they perceive as preferential treatment, Linda boldly declares, "My answer was that the colored servants ought to be dissatisfied with *themselves,* for not having too much self-respect to submit to such treatment; that there was no difference in the board for colored and white servants, and there was no justification for difference in treatment. I staid a month after this, and finding I was resolved to stand up for my rights, they concluded to treat me well. Let every colored man and woman do this, and eventually we shall cease to be trampled under foot by our oppressors" (637, emphasis in original). Significantly, the "oppressors" are no longer southern slaveholders, but northerners like Linda's target audience. Linda is unable to address her readers directly in order to gain their sympathy, as she does in the earlier chapters of the narrative, because her readers are aware of and perhaps even participate in the oppression free blacks are subjected to and yet have apparently not displayed any compassion for those who suffer from it. Linda's encounters with segregation, discrimination, and prejudice cause her to question the putative freedom of the North; however, it is not until she travels across the Atlantic in 1845, spends ten months in Great Britain, and finally experiences real liberty that she becomes totally convinced of the bogus nature of American freedom.

The narrative's altered tone intensifies in chapter 37, "A Visit to England," in which Linda uses the international perspective she has gained from her journey abroad to shame her readers into reevaluating the degree of civilization they have achieved. By the 1850s, many Americans prided themselves on what their country had accomplished in less than one hundred years of existence. They regarded the United States as a nation founded on the ideals of freedom and justice for all and believed that it afforded greater opportunities for economic and social mobility than European countries with their rigid class structures. Linda implicitly disputes such claims. It is of England rather than the North that Linda can say, "[f]or the first time in my life I was in a place where I was treated according to my deportment, without reference to my complexion. I felt as if a great millstone had been lifted from my breast. Ensconced in a pleasant room, [...] I laid my head on my pillow, for the first time, with the delightful consciousness of pure, unadulterated freedom" (643). Significantly, it is not until she leaves the United States that she feels truly free.[24] Drawing on her own experiences in the South and the North, she compares the lives of the lowliest English peasants favorably with those of blacks in America. Although she acknowledges that "the poor are oppressed in Europe," she flatly asserts "the most ignorant and most destitute of these peasants was a thousand fold better off than the most pampered American slave" (645). Until slavery is abolished and blacks are treated fairly, Linda suggests, Americans cannot adopt a superior attitude toward other countries where such practices do not exist.

It is only after departing the land of her birth, moreover, that Linda undergoes a profound religious experience. "My visit to England is a memorable event in my life," Linda states, "from the fact of my having there received strong religious impressions" (645). Slavery so tainted Christianity in the United States that Linda rejected it: "The contemptuous manner in which the communion had been administered to colored people, in my native place; the church membership of Dr. Flint, and others like him; and the buying and selling of slaves, by professed ministers of the gospel, had given me a prejudice against the Episcopal church. The whole service seemed a mockery and a sham" (645). In England, unlike America, however, religion, like freedom, is authentic: "But my home in Steventon was in the family of a clergyman, who was a true disciple of Jesus. The beauty of his daily life inspired me with faith in the genuineness of Christian professions. Grace entered my heart, and I knelt at the communion table, I trust, in true humility of soul" (645–46). Linda's ten months abroad not only enable her to contrast America's lack of freedom with the true freedom she found in England but also arm her with the moral authority of Christianity with which she can denounce unchristian actions and attitudes in both the southern and northern United States.

Linda's tone grows even more condemnatory in the final two chapters.

Describing the passage of the Fugitive Slave Law in 1850—five years after her experience of "pure, unadulterated freedom" in England—as a "reign of terror to the colored population" (652), Linda relates how it caused her to avoid going out in the streets as much as possible and, when absolutely necessary, to take back alleys to evade detection. She decries this situation, stating, "What a disgrace to a city calling itself free, that inhabitants, guiltless of offence, and seeking to perform their duties conscientiously, should be condemned to live in such incessant fear, and have nowhere to turn for protection!" (652). Having endured numerous insults, survived "Hairbreadth Escapes" from slave hunters, and observed to her horror her daughter Ellen's virtual bondage to Mr. Sands's relations in Brooklyn, Linda comes to realize just how slight the distinction is between slavery in the South and "freedom" in the North: "I was, in fact, a slave in New York, as subject to slave laws as I had been in a Slave State. Strange incongruity in a State called free!" (655). But if Linda is indeed a slave in the North, then it is not merely the southern slaveholders who oppress her; northerners, including her readers, are complicit, too. It is left to the second Mrs. Bruce to put into words the sentiment that has been implicit in the final chapters of the narrative. Commenting on the penalty for aiding a fugitive slave—imprisonment and a thousand dollar fine—she is risking by harboring Linda, Mrs. Bruce states, "Shame on my country that it *is* so!" (656, emphasis in original).

The bold new tone reaches its peak in the description of Mrs. Bruce's purchase of Linda for three hundred dollars from Dr. Flint's daughter and son-in-law. Linda has long discouraged Mrs. Bruce from buying her from the Dodges because she does not want money to be given to the pernicious system of slavery. Thus, when she learns that the transaction has nonetheless been completed, she is dumbfounded by the news and disturbed by its implications: "'The bill of sale!' Those words struck me like a blow. So I was *sold* at last! A human being *sold* in the free city of New York! The bill of sale is on record, and future generations will learn from it that women were articles of traffic in New York, late in the nineteenth century of the Christian religion. It may hereafter prove a useful document to antiquaries, who are seeking to measure the progress of civilization in the United States" (662–63, emphasis in original). Appropriately, in a work about the sexual exploitation of black bondwomen, Linda links the peculiar institution—not merely a badge of shame for the South but rather all of the United States—and white slavery (i.e., prostitution). Building on the international perspective she used in chapter 37, Jacobs in this passage employs a historical perspective, looking ahead to an era such as ours and imagining how American slavery will be judged from that vantage point. In doing so, she draws on the faith she gained during her journey to England to point out how the selling of human beings in the largest city of the United States utterly violates the spirit of Christ's teachings.

After having long suspended the practice, Linda again uses a direct address to her readers in the narrative's penultimate paragraph, but the intimacy and poignancy of her earlier addresses have vanished. Reminding her audience that her work is a slave narrative rather than a sentimental novel, Linda states, "Reader, my story ends with freedom; not in the usual way, with marriage" (664). Then in an extraordinary passage she questions not only the legitimacy of her own freedom but also the freedom of the white people in the North (including, of course, that of her target audience): "I and my children are now free! We are as free from the power of slaveholders as are the white people of the north; and though that, according to my ideas, is not saying a great deal, it is a vast improvement in *my* condition" (664, emphasis in original). Here she no longer writes *to* northern white women, those "happy free women" she poignantly addressed earlier in the narrative, but instead writes *about* them, using her own experiences both among these women and in England to expose the limitations of *their* freedom.

In a quarter century, *Incidents in the Life of a Slave Girl* has gone from relative obscurity to one of the most widely taught and frequently analyzed African American literary texts. Certainly the critical interest in Linda's heroism and Jacobs's recasting of the slave narrative and the sentimental novel has been well deserved; however, the narrative's extended depiction of the North, portrayal of Jacobs's journey abroad, and characterization of all of antebellum America as slave territory merit attention and approbation as well. Charting the evolving relationship between Linda and her target audience, especially the shift in purpose and tone in the final twelve chapters, reveals the forcefulness of Jacobs's indictment of the northern mentality that tolerated and abetted slavery. Her experiences in England, both in terms of the freedom she enjoyed and the religious conversion she underwent there, contribute significantly to these changes.

Breaking the Silence about Female Circumcision/ Genital Mutilation in *Possessing the Secret of Joy*

Like Dean's *The Pedro Gorino*, Jacobs's *Incidents in the Life of a Slave Girl* vividly illustrates that transatlantic travel has significantly affected the worldview of African Americans—of both sexes. Adopting a different perspective, trajectory, and emphasis from Gilroy, Alice Walker in *Possessing the Secret of Joy* (1992) raises some questions about the black Atlantic model. Rather than an African American male who travels from the new world to the old, Walker's protagonist is an African woman who settles in the United States where she is strongly influenced by the nation's political and social freedoms, journeys to Europe for psychological therapy, and eventually returns to the country of her birth on a mission of vengeance and liberation. Victimized by a traditional rite that killed her sister, severely damaged her body, and destabilized her psyche, Tashi releases her repressed memories through analysis, goes back home to strike a blow against state-sponsored circumcision/mutilation, and unexpectedly comes to regard herself as an American. All but ignoring the black British vertex that Gilroy places at the heart of his black Atlantic model, Walker instead tells a story that emphasizes the idea of direct contact between the United States and Africa and counter-discursively responds to the texts of two salient European male figures, signifying in an unmotivated way on Carl Jung's *Memories, Dreams, Reflections* and in a highly motivated manner on Joseph Conrad's *Heart of Darkness*.

Possessing generated considerable controversy when it appeared because of its ringing condemnation of female circumcision/genital mutilation, also called female genital cutting, a practice dating back thousands of years that has been performed on over one hundred million women worldwide and as many as seventy million women in Africa alone. Despite accusations that as an outsider criticizing a traditional, indigenous practice she has engaged in a form of cultural imperialism in the book, Walker has continued her efforts to put an end to female circumcision/genital mutilation, using profits from her novel to finance a documentary film titled *Warrior Marks*, asserting that culture does not equal torture, and comparing the anticircumcision/mutilation campaign to nineteenth-century abolitionism. Credited with spearheading the efforts that led to the passage of a United States law outlawing the procedure and pressuring foreign governments to conduct education campaigns against female genital cutting (Boyle 73), she has also been criticized by black American and African opponents of the practice who believe she has failed to see female circumcision/genital mutilation in its proper cultural context and has been too harsh with women who perform and condone the procedure (James, Dawit and Mekuria). The novel grapples with weighty issues, among them whether there are universal values or only culturally specific ones, what the appropriate relationship between art and political activism should be, and whether it is possible to denounce practices performed in particular cultures without condemning the cultures themselves or the people who participate in the practices. Overshadowed by such contentious issues have been Walker's remarkable narrative technique and the novel's complex organization.

Possessing comprises twenty-one chapters narrated in nonlinear fashion by a chorus of thirteen distinct voices. Six of these voices belong to one character, the protagonist born with the name of Tashi in Olinkaland who later takes the name Evelyn after she moves to the United States following her marriage to Adam (the biological son of the main character Celie and the adopted son of the African American missionaries Samuel and Corrine in *The Color Purple*). The novel charts Tashi's mental problems, resulting in large part from her repressed memories of her sister's death as a result of female genital cutting, and her physical problems directly attributable to her decision to be infibulated, the most extreme form of female circumcision/genital mutilation, as a grown woman. The different voices Tashi speaks in correspond to specific stages in her mental breakdown and eventual recovery. Helping Tashi to confront her childhood memories, interpret her nightmares, and admit her pain is none other than the Swiss psychologist Carl Jung. Appearing as a character in the first third of the novel, he figures as more than that, emerging as a towering presence throughout the book, so much so that in her postscript Walker states, "I thank Carl Jung for becoming so real in my own self-therapy that I could imagine him alive and active in Tashi's treatment. My gift to him" (287).

In the first half of this section, I discuss the role played in the novel by not only Jungian psychology and therapy but also specific events in the psychologist's life and his ideas about the occult, particularly those recorded in his autobiography, *Memories, Dreams, Reflections*. In the second part, I address a series of major changes experienced or brought about by Tashi as a consequence of her decision to return to Olinka to confront the woman who killed her sister and severely damaged her own physical and mental health.

A student of Freud, Jung later broke with his mentor, expounding his own theories and methodologies, referred to variously as archetypal, analytic, or simply Jungian psychology. Like Freud, Jung believed that the psyche was composed of both conscious and unconscious parts and that the interaction between these elements shaped reality for human beings. Rather than dividing the mind into the id, ego, and superego, as Freud did in the most famous of his tripartite models, however, Jung became interested in symbol creation, eventually partitioning the human psyche into the conscious, the personal unconscious, and the collective unconscious. While the personal unconscious consists of memories and images collected during the course of an individual's life, the collective unconscious contains the accumulated knowledge, experiences, and images of the entire human race. Jung asserted that people all over the planet respond to specific myths and stories in similar ways because the memories of the human race's past dwell deep in everyone's collective unconscious. The memories in our collective unconscious take the form of archetypes, that is, recurrent patterns or images of human experience, which, according to Jung, can evoke profound and almost instinctual emotional responses. In Jungian therapy, patients are made aware of the relationship among their conscious mind, their personal unconscious, their collective unconscious, and their psychological problems.

Jung devotes an entire chapter of *Memories, Dreams, Reflections* (1963) to the subject of the original construction of and the various additions to his house in Bollingen, Switzerland. He bought the land in 1922 and the following year built a round house he called the Tower. As he explains, "I more or less had in mind an African hut where the fire [...] burns in the middle, and the whole life of the family revolves around this center. Primitive huts concretize an idea of wholeness" (223–24).[25] He kept adding to the house over the next thirty years, finally completing it after his wife died in 1955. Reflecting Walker's fascination with Jung's professional and personal life, in *Possessing* a tower is both a prominent image in Tashi's recurring nightmare and the name of the place where she begins to unlock the meaning of this dream and the repressed emotions behind it. Tashi and Adam travel to Jung's house on Lake Zurich in the hope of improving her mental condition, arriving there sometime after the completion of the Tower and before Jung's death in 1961. After a few days of working with Tashi, Mzee (Jung) shows them a movie he made in East Africa of a just-concluded ceremony. Although it is a silent picture, the end of the film depicts a fighting cock crowing vehemently. This final image causes an intense reaction in Tashi, compelling her to attempt to paint the memory it conjures within her. By the end of several hours, Tashi has drawn a twelve-foot portrait of a rooster directly onto the walls of the Tower itself. In the therapy session that follows, Tashi is able for the first time to talk about the death of her sister resulting from a female circumcision/genital mutilation ceremony. As she speaks to Mzee, the "boulder" that has been lodged in her throat "explode[s]" and she is able to see her sister's death, which she observed while hiding in the grass as a very young child, for what it really was—a "*murder*" (83). Tashi had seen a chicken gobble up a piece of flesh, presumably part of her sister Dura's body, that M'Lissa the circumciser had thrown away with her toes. The ceremony in Mzee's film, very likely a genital cutting, and the vociferous cock bring to the surface Tashi's repressed memories relating to what had been done to her sister about which she was told never to speak.

In one of his lectures in the book *Analytical Psychology: Its Theory and Practice* (1940), Jung recounts a dream about a tower he had that may also be relevant to *Possessing*. He tells the story of a patient born in Java of European parents who was very confused about her sexuality because of her experiences in the East. According to Jung, she was promiscuous and dressed provocatively. When she came to him for help, he treated her harshly, telling her she could not come to him dressed like a harlot. Soon after this Jung dreamed of her in a high tower of a castle, so far above him that it hurt his neck to look at her. This is how Jung interprets his own dream: "I woke up and instantly I thought, 'Heavens! Why does my unconscious put the girl so high up?' And immediately the thought struck me, 'I have looked down on her.' For I really thought she was bad. My dream showed me that this was a mistake, and I knew that I had been a bad doctor" (163). The next day he tells her of the dream and what he believes it means, which greatly improves their relationship: "That worked miracles, I can tell you! No trouble with the transference any more because I simply got right with her and met her on the right level" (163–64). This episode not only reveals a great deal about Jung's psychoanalytic methods but shows a man recognizing his unfair treatment of a woman, modifying it, and treating her as an equal, which certainly accords with one of the major objectives of *Possessing*.

Despite the prominence Walker accords to Jung in the novel, she does not allude to his comments about black Americans, which are scattered throughout his collected works. In a short piece titled "On the Psychology of the Negro" published in 1913, a year after he informally analyzed fifteen African American patients at St. Elizabeth's Hospital in Washington, D.C., Jung asserts that the psychoses of blacks are no different from those of whites; however, the "[i]nvestigation is complicated by the fact that the Negro does not understand what one wants of him, and besides that is ignorant [...]. He shows a great inability to look into his own thoughts" (552). In a 1930 essay originally titled "Your Negroid and Indian Behavior" but more widely known as "The Complications of American Psychology," Jung attributes "the peculiarities of the American temperament," such as the way the people of the United States walk and laugh, to "the fact that the States are pervaded by the Negro, that most striking and suggestive figure" (507). In the second of his Tavistock lectures, delivered in London in 1935, Jung uses the dream of one of the St. Elizabeth's patients as evidence of his concept of the collective unconscious. Although he "was a very uneducated Negro from the South and not particularly intelligent" (38), his dream of a man crucified on a wheel was "a repetition of the Greek mythological motif of Ixion" (40). Summing up the psychologist's attitudes toward people of color, Susan Rowland states, "On the one hand, Jung recorded his realization of the cruelty of colonization and his sense that other cultures may possess far better psychological attitudes than Western nations. On the other hand, his free use of the term 'primitive' for African and Native American peoples demonstrated a classic colonial mentality in assuming these cultures are merely far 'behind' in the Western narrative of 'progress'" (11).[26]

Nevertheless, it is apparently Jung's ability as a therapist, a white European, and a man to understand and empathize with people different from himself that attracts the novelist to him. Summing up Walker's use of the psychologist in her book, Michael Adams states, "The fictional Jung serves her as a character who exemplifies a self who cannot discover himself unless he encounters the other, a self who is not whole until he integrates that part of himself, that half of himself, that is the other. To Walker, Jung represents the attempt to reconcile and perhaps transcend all oppositions: beyond white and black, beyond male and female, beyond Eurocentrism and Afrocentrism—beyond ethnocentrism and cultural relativism and toward universalism and humanism" (176). In the one section of the novel written in his voice, which takes the form of a letter he sends to his French niece Lisette, who is Adam's mistress, Mzee expresses the profound feelings Tashi and Adam conjure in him: "They, in their indescribable suffering, are bringing me home to something in myself. I am finding myself in them. A self I have often felt was only halfway at home on the European continent. In my European skin. An ancient self that thirsts for knowledge of the experiences of its ancient kin. Needs this knowledge, and the feelings that come with it, to be whole. A self that is horrified at what was done to Evelyn [Tashi], but recognizes it as something that is also done to me. A truly universal self. That is the essence of healing that in my European, 'professional' life I frequently lost" (86).

This key passage from Walker's novel echoes a famous episode in *Memories, Dreams, Reflections* in which Jung describes an event that occurred on his 1925 journey to East Africa—presumably the same one on which he took the home movie in *Possessing*—that he believed proved the validity of his notion of the collective unconscious. While in Kenya, Jung is given the name Mzee, or "old man," the same name that Tashi and Adam use to address him when Tashi goes to Switzerland for therapy in Walker's narrative. Awakening on a train at dawn's first light, Jung observes a native man with a spear, which triggers a profound reaction in the psychologist. What follows is a passage in which Jung discusses his response to what he has seen and the significance he attaches to it: "On a jagged rock above us a slim, brownish-black figure stood motionless, leaning on a long spear, looking down at the train. Beside him towered a gigantic candelabrum cactus. I was enchanted by the sight—it was a picture of something utterly alien and outside my experience, but on the other hand a most intense *sentiment du deja vu.* I had the feeling that I had always known this world which was separated from me only by distance in time. It was as if I were this moment returning to the land of my youth, and as if I knew that dark-skinned man who had been waiting for me for five thousand years. [...] I could not guess what string within myself was plucked at the sight of that solitary hunter. I only knew that his world had been mine for countless millennia" (*Memories* 254–55). By the end of his trip to East Africa, Jung realizes he has not been on an "objective scientific" journey, as he thought he was, but rather "an intensely personal one" (273). In both Walker's passage and Jung's own, the psychologist's capacity to learn from others, to see the links between himself and them, corresponds to Walker's ideas about how people should relate to one another and the interconnectedness of the human race.

Near the end of his life, Jung came to believe that the innermost regions of the unconscious transcend the limitations of time, space, and cause and effect, making various occult phenomena possible. Walker not only clearly believes in Jung's psychological theories and methods but also shares his faith in paranormal occurrences. Readers familiar with *The Color Purple* will recall that in a postscript Walker describes herself as "author and medium." In 1950 Jung made a stone monument to express what the Tower meant to him. He carved some alchemical quotations on a piece of rock and then chiseled a circle and in the center a tiny homunculus. According to Jung, this figure "corresponds to the 'little doll' (pupilla)—yourself—which you see in the pupil of another's eye. [...] Ancient statues show him wearing a hooded cloak and carrying a lantern. At the same time he is the pointer of the way [to the gates of the sun and to the land of dreams]" (*Memories* 227). For Jung the stone, which stands just outside the Tower, served as an explanation for the edifice. Walker not only includes a photograph of herself touching this hand-carved alchemical stone in a brief essay titled "Looking for Jung: Writing *Possessing the Secret of Joy*" (1996), which describes her journey to the Tower in Bollingen in the spring of 1990, but places a drawing of Jung's stone monument, complete with the "little doll," on the cover of her book, and she refers to both dolls and pupils frequently in the novel and her other writing on female circumcision/genital mutilation.

In *Possessing the Secret of Joy,* Olinkan women clandestinely keep female dolls that are in the act of giving themselves pleasure, precisely the kind of joy or *jouissance* that female circumcision/genital mutilation seeks to curb or eliminate. Moreover, those women who have had the procedure performed on them, in particular the circumciser M'Lissa and the protagonist Tashi, are characterized by a "flatness" or deadness in the eyes. Adam immediately notices that something has gone out of Tashi's eyes when he sees her for the first time after she has been infibulated. For Walker, however, the connection between the ability to see and the capacity to experience sexual pleasure runs much deeper than this. In "Like the Pupil of an Eye: Genital Mutilation and the Sexual Blinding of Women" (1993), Walker reconsiders her own partial blinding as a girl of eight at the hands of her brother and her family's—especially her mother's—inappropriate response to it. Her injury itself was never discussed, while the incident that caused it was always referred to as "Alice's accident," as if she were to blame for her brother's deliberately shooting at her with a BB gun. Walker sees a clear link between herself and the circumcised women in Africa and elsewhere: "What I had, I realized only as a consciously feminist adult, was a patriarchal wound" (17). She makes the connection explicit in a later passage that recalls Jung's description of the figure he carved on the monument outside the Tower: "No one would think it normal to deliberately destroy the pupil of the eye. Without its pupil, the eye can never see itself, or the person possessing it, reflected in the eye of another. It is the same with the vulva. Without the clitoris and other sexual organs, a woman can never see herself reflected in the healthy intact body of another. Her sexual vision is impaired, and only the most devoted lover will be sexually 'seen.' And even then, never completely" (19). In an essay that identifies Walker as one of her personal heroines and expresses her delight that the author has "become so publicly supportive of ongoing struggles to eradicate these harmful practices" (1031) yet voices concerns about the "outrage" Walker directs toward those women who take part in and condone female circumcision/genital mutilation, Stanlie M. James finds the comparison between the writer's blinding and female genital cutting problematic. "While little boys with BB guns are emblematic of violent patriarchal societies," states James, "the logic of the analogy suggests that boys shooting and blinding their sisters is a traditional ceremonial practice sanctioned by this society in much the same fashion as female circumcision is in other societies. Although

Walker is certainly imbued with a sympathetic perspective, centering her own story within this international struggle for women's rights seems to have the unintentional consequence of 'othering' or marginalizing the very people she wishes to support" (1031–32).

The act of creating the stone monument put Jung in touch with his forebears. While working on it he "became aware of the fateful links between me and my ancestors," believing that he "had to answer questions which fate had posed to my forefathers, and which had not been answered, or as if I had to complete, or perhaps continue, things which previous ages had left unfinished" (*Memories* 233). Eventually the Tower itself became a monument to and an environment for Jung's ancestors. At the end of his chapter about the Tower, Jung writes, "my ancestors' souls are sustained by the atmosphere of the house, since I answer for them questions that their lives once left behind. I carve out rough answers as best I can. I have even drawn them on the walls" (*Memories* 237), as Tashi does in *Possessing*.

Walker has a similar sense of her ancestors' presence in her life and the responsibility she owes to them, believing that they passed things on to her for her to write about, complete, solve. Without question slavery and its legacy (including African complicity in the slave trade) and female genital cutting are subjects that Walker feels compelled to address in her works. In a 1992 interview, Paula Giddings asked the author whether she has the right as an outsider to judge and intervene in traditional African practices. Walker explained that she believes she has the right because "Slavery intervened" (60). The thought of her "great-great-great-great-great grandmother" enduring not just capture, the Middle Passage, the auction block, the loss of her children, and rape but also female circumcision/genital mutilation outrages her: "I can't stand it! I would go nuts if this part of her story were not factored in. Imagine if men came from Africa with their penises removed. Believe me, we would have many a tale about it" (60). In "The Light That Shines on Me," Walker revisits "In Search of Our Mothers' Gardens" (1974), her famous paean to her female ancestors (particularly her mother) for keeping the creative spirit alive and passing it on to succeeding generations of African American women despite oppressive conditions. In this 1993 essay, she states her belief that she has a responsibility to tell Tashi's story and to denounce female genital cutting, regarding this as her own legacy to future generations: "To write a book such as this, about a woman such as Tashi, about a subject such as genital mutilation, is in fact, as far as I am concerned, the reason for my education" (25). If her book saves at least one girl from circumcision/mutilation, then it will be successful because "in this one instance, at least, the pen will prove mightier than the circumciser's knife. Her little beloved face will be the light that shines on me" (25). We should be no more surprised that Walker, the contemporary, highly successful black American woman writer, attempts to forge a link with an unknown baby girl in an unspecified location in Africa or Asia (or Europe or America) than we should be that she draws inspiration from the ideas, methods, *Weltanschauung,* and experiences of a white male European psychologist who was born in 1875. Faith in such synchronicity (or meaningful coincidence) is at the core of both Jung's and Walker's personal belief systems.

Charting a different route from Gilroy, who emphasizes how European travel changes the political stances of key African American men, Walker depicts an African woman significantly revising her ideas about the traditional practices of her native continent as a result of her experiences in the United States. And, in contrast to Naipaul, who signifies in an unmotivated way on Conrad in *A Bend in the River* (discussed in chapter 2), Walker constructs a motivated counter-discourse to *Heart of Darkness* in *Possessing.*[27] Like Marlow, who journeys to a remote African location to remove a falsely revered compatriot engaged in the exploitation of the local people under the guise of civilization and progress, Tashi returns to her African homeland to eliminate an honored compatriot who tyrannizes over the Olinka in the name of purity and authenticity. Walker, however, concentrates on a traditional African practice that affects the lives of millions of African women. Whereas Marlow, a male outsider, reclaims another male outsider on behalf of the European colonizing mission and returns to Europe where he perpetuates the lie about Kurtz's civilization, Tashi rises up against a fellow African woman, sacrificing herself in an effort to liberate girls from state-sponsored torture and falsity.

Possessing's dedication and three epigraphs work together to adumbrate the book's major themes and Tashi's striking transformations. Walker begins by announcing that she has written her book with "Tenderness and Respect" for the sake of the "Blameless Vulva." Somewhat complicating matters, the first epigraph appears in two different versions: in the hardcover edition, Walker quotes a passage from *African Saga* (1982) by Mirella Ricciardi, a European settler in Africa, containing the assertion that "Black people are natural, they possess the secret of joy, which is why they can survive the suffering and humiliation inflicted upon them"; meanwhile, in the paperback she opts for an uncredited paraphrase: "There are those who believe Black people possess the secret of joy and that it is this that will sustain them through any moral or spiritual devastation." The lengthy second epigraph comes from Walker's own novel, *The Color Purple* (1982). In it, Nettie, an African American missionary living in the fictional West African nation of Olinka, writes to her sister Celie back home in the American South about Celie's children, Olivia and Adam, and Tashi, a close Olinkan friend who has been Adam's lover. With much regret, Nettie reports that Tashi has decided to have her face scarred and undergo the "female initiation ceremony" even though she is already a grown woman. Walker identifies a "Bumper sticker" as the source for her final epigraph: "When the axe came to the forest, the trees said the handle is one of us."

Immediately focusing attention on the part of the female anatomy that is partially or fully excised in female circumcision/genital mutilation ceremonies, Walker's dedication states unequivocally that such procedures are brutal and totally without justification, thereby raising the question of *why* this practice continues to take place on a massive scale in Africa and other parts of the world. The trio of passages that follow provide the multifaceted answer. Walker most likely changed the first epigraph in the softcover edition to shift attention away from Ricciardi and onto the statement itself, which, when seen within the context of her novel, Walker clearly believes to be a lie that has been used to reduce the culpability of those who have inflicted horrors on people of African descent, whether they be Africans and Europeans responsible for slavery, Europeans responsible for colonialism, or Africans responsible for female circumcision/ genital mutilation. If outsiders like Ricciardi can convince themselves that blacks have the capacity to tolerate more pain and suffering than other peoples, then the crimes directed against them in the past appear less heinous and the devastations visited on them in the present, in the form of civil wars, circumcision/mutilation, and the AIDS epidemic, do not necessitate immediate intervention. Thus, before the book proper begins, Walker introduces the Conradian theme of willful falsification.

If Ricciardi's self-deluding and self-exonerating untruth explains why outsiders have frequently turned a blind eye to atrocities in which people of African descent are the victims, the second and third epigraphs suggest why Africans have at times allowed their own people to cruelly mistreat them. The quotation from *The Color Purple* pinpoints the legacy of colonialism and imperialism as the reason why Africans have embraced traditional practices, occasionally at the expense of their own health and welfare. According to Nettie, Olivia reports that Tashi is "happy that the initiation ceremony isn't done in Europe or America" because this makes it "even more valuable to her," and other passages from this earlier novel describing the forced relocation of the Olinka by the British and the consequent destruction of the Olinka's sacred roofleaf (a plant with which they had traditionally covered their houses) explain how Tashi comes to view female circumcision/genital mutilation as an authentic and therefore anticolonial rite. In *Possessing*, however, Walker strives to demonstrate, in excruciating detail, just how misguided this belief is. The final epigraph likewise warns against danger from within. In the context of *The Color Purple*, the handle of the axe could be seen to represent African American missionaries, like Samuel, Corrine, Nettle, Adam, and Olivia, who in that novel Walker depicts as attempting to impose their own distorted and alienating religion on spiritually contented Africans and in the process unwittingly abetting the European domination of the continent.[28] However, given the role that female circumcision/genital mutilation plays in *Possessing* and the fact that the primary function of an axe, like a circumciser's knife, stone, rusty razor, or tin can lid, is to sever something from something else, clearly the helve refers to *tsungas* (to use Walker's term) such as M'Lissa, who, though women themselves, nevertheless perform countless circumcisions/mutilations of young girls all in the name of tradition.

Over the course of the novel, the protagonist undergoes or effects four striking metamorphoses. First, Tashi recovers her repressed memories of Dura's death, breaks her silence about it, and by the end of the book succeeds in putting the taboo surrounding female circumcision/genital mutilation in Olinka and other societies on trial. Second, through her confrontation with M'Lissa, Tashi converts the old *tsunga* from a national treasure into a symbol of the state-sponsored torture of girls and forces her to acknowledge the horror of her own existence. Third, Tashi transforms herself from the Western stereotype of the long-suffering black female to the founder of an African women's resistance movement. Finally, as a result of returning to Africa, Tashi stops considering herself an outsider in the United States and comes to see herself as an American.

Walker clearly links the efforts to forbid the young Tashi from talking about or crying over her sister during the colonial period to postindependence Olinkan society's refusal to allow any discussion of female circumcision/genital mutilation. In describing her trial, Evelyn (Tashi) points out that "How did your mother die? [...] is a taboo question in Olinka. One never asks for fear of the answer" (161), presumably referring to women who have died in childbirth as a result of complications from genital cutting. Similarly, the protagonist recounts the effort to muzzle Adam as he gives testimony about the effects that infibulation has had on her: "As soon as he utters the word 'ritual' there is a furor in the court. Male voices and female voices, calling for Adam's silence. Shut up, shut up, you disgraceful American! the voices cry. This is our business you would put into the streets! We cannot publicly discuss this taboo" (162–63). Even though Olinka women face being beaten with clubs or riddled with stones if they demonstrate their support for Tashi, they nevertheless find a covert way to express their solidarity with her and their opposition to circumcision/mutilation, holding aloft girl babies and exposing their unaltered genitals on the day of Tashi's execution (280).

Throughout the novel Walker takes pains to establish the falsity of the language used in connection with female circumcision/genital mutilation, and, when Tashi learns that M'Lissa not only is still alive but also has been embraced as a national heroine, she decides to return to Olinka and put an end to the old woman's "lying life" (208). Words such as "bathing," "cleansing," and "purifying" rather than "cutting" are used to describe the procedure; in the rebel camp, M'Lissa refers to Tashi's excised genital area "not as a wound but as a healing" (63); and Tashi herself has been led to believe that cutting off part of her body will make her "whole": "Completely woman. Completely African. Completely Olinka" (24, 64). Like Marlow in search of Kurtz, Tashi travels first to the country's capital (Ombere) and then on to M'Lissa's isolated place of residence, and just as Marlow's presence causes Kurtz to recognize the "horror" of the life he has led, M'Lissa's lengthy discussions with Tashi cause the *tsunga* to see herself for what she really is: "Dragging my half-body wherever half a body was needed. In service to tradition, to what makes us a people. In service to the country and what makes us who we are. But what are we but torturers of children?" (226). Later, when Mbati, M'Lissa's former caretaker who has become a close friend of Tashi, learns the history of female circumcision/genital mutilation from Pierre (the son of Adam and Lisette), Tashi uses Kurtz's final, self-incriminating word to describe the younger woman's expression: "Her lovely face is filled with horror" (235). The word appears again when a dying AIDS patient reveals to Adam that he worked for a Western pharmaceutical company whose contaminated polio vaccine led to the AIDS epidemic: "As Hartford's voice became barely audible [...], an unbidden glimpse of what he was describing invaded my mind. I closed my eyes tightly to banish the sight. It was too late. I felt as if a whole other world of grief and disaster had just been dropped on my soul. I groaned in agony, almost as he had done. The sound of my own sorrow was shocking to me. But, surprisingly, my sorrow made Hartford look, finally, *released. Father, thank you for hearing my confession,* he said, savoring my pained expression [...]. As if he'd waited until certain that he had transmitted the full horror of his existence to someone who could still feel, Hartford began to breathe the shallow, rustling wheeze everyone on the AIDS floor knew so well" (266, emphasis in original). In contrast to Marlow, however, who suppresses the truth, telling the Belgian woman to whom Kurtz was betrothed that his dying words were her name, Tashi seeks to expose the falsehoods that undergird female circumcision/genital mutilation. On her way to kill M'Lissa, Tashi stops at a stationery store to compose a sign warning women against self-delusion: "If you lie to yourself about your pain, you will be killed by those who will claim you enjoyed it" (108).

In *Possessing*'s final sections, Walker addresses the "secret of joy" referred to in the novel's title. One of the floors in the building where Tashi is imprisoned has been taken over by people infected with AIDS, and Walker through Tashi asserts that female circumcision/genital mutilation has hastened the spread of the disease, especially among women (251–52). In an echo of the initial epigraph, Olivia reports that Tashi becomes infuriated while working with the patients: "No one has any idea why he or she is sick. That's the most difficult thing. Witnessing their incomprehension. Their dumb patience, as they wait for death. It is their animal-like ignorance that most angers Tashi, perhaps because she is reminded of herself. She calls it, scornfully, the assigned role of the African: to suffer, to die, and not to know why" (250). However, Tashi has already made the decision to suffer in silence no longer, intending to sacrifice her life to spare girls and women from her pain. Falling somewhere between the hardcover and softcover versions of the first epigraph by quoting from Ricciardi's book but not mentioning her by name, part 21 relates how Mbati reads to the condemned woman "from the book of a white colonialist author who has lived among Africans and failed to see them as human beings who can be destroyed by suffering. 'Black people are natural,' she writes, 'they possess the secret of joy, which is why they can survive the suffering and humiliation inflicted upon them'" (271). In response to this passage, Tashi says to Mbati, "These settler cannibals. Why don't they just steal our land, mine our gold, chop down our forests, pollute our rivers, enslave us to work on their farms, fuck us, devour our flesh and leave us alone? Why must they also write about how much joy we possess?" (272). Making good on her promise to let Tashi know the "*definitive* secret of joy" before she dies, Mbati unfurls a banner a moment before the firing squad's bullets penetrate Tashi's body that reads "RESISTANCE IS THE SECRET OF JOY!" (281). Thus, in the novel as a whole, as in the front matter, Walker refutes sentiments such as Ricciardi's and William Faulkner's "They endured" (from the appendix to *The Sound and the Fury*), replacing them with something on the order of "We resisted."

In addition to signifying in a motivated way on Conrad (and Ricciardi and

Faulkner), Walker in *Possessing* steers clear of England, which Gilroy places at the center of the black Atlantic model, creating a fictional world in which direct links between the United States and Africa are forged. This process culminates in Tashi's realization that *she* epitomizes what it means to be an American. Although frequently institutionalized in the United States and the object of the medical staff's incredulity as a result of her infibulated genitals during her only successful labor, Tashi vehemently expresses her "love" for America (38, 55), coming to identify more with Old Glory than with the Olinkan flag (107). However, she has never considered herself an American even though the fight for freedom of speech and the struggle for freedom from oppression that she brings to Olinka reflect the ideals on which the United States was founded. It is none other than M'Lissa, in an attempt to distract Tashi from her murderous quest, who causes Tashi to reassess her relationship to her adopted country. After providing countless descriptions of other people in response to the *tsunga*'s question "What does an American look like?" Tashi, to her surprise, comes to understand why she loves the United States so much: "[A]n American looks like a wounded person whose wound is hidden from others, and sometimes from herself. An American looks like me" (213). For years memories of Dura's death were buried in Tashi's psyche and she consciously hid her physical wounds from other people. After recovering her repressed memories and coming to see female circumcision/genital mutilation for what it really is, Tashi is inspired by the years she has spent in the United States to cut down the woman who has been elevated to the status of a national treasure for her butchery of Olinka women in order to break the taboo surrounding the procedure.[29]

Unlike Gilroy, who chooses to use the lives and texts of black American males to illustrate his major points and assigns a privileged, mediating position to Britain in his black Atlantic model, Walker makes an African woman the protagonist of her novel, depicts direct connections between the United States and Africa, and stresses how Tashi's experiences in America inspire her to strike a blow against an Olinkan national icon. Although *Possessing* contains many harrowing scenes, culminating in Tashi's execution, in the final analysis Walker provides an upbeat message through the main character's ultimately successful efforts to change her own life and the lives of other women.[30] In doing so, she counter-discursively responds to both Jung's autobiography and Conrad's *Heart of Darkness*, signifying on the former in an unmotivated and the latter in a motivated way.

My analysis of Walker's woman-centered exploration of cultural, political, and social issues Gilroy has chosen not to address has allowed me to pose questions about the configuration and the emphases of the black Atlantic. This in turn adds weight to my argument that further attempts to navigate, traverse, and plot the intersections of postcolonial theory, African American literary criticism, and the black Alantic are needed.

[I]ndeed a survey of the civilized world at the end of the 19th
century but confirms the proposition with which I started—the
world problem of the 20th century is the Problem of the
Color line—the question of the relation of the advanced races
of men who happen to be white to the great majority of the
underdeveloped or half developed nations of mankind who
happen to be yellow, brown, or black....

W. E. B. DU BOIS

Conclusion

The preceding passage from "The Present Outlook for the Dark Races
of Mankind," a speech W. E. B. Du Bois presented at the third annual meeting of the American Negro Academy in Washington, D.C., in March 1900,
demonstrates that he (along with several other late-nineteenth- and early-
twentieth-century black American intellectuals) was concerned about many
of the same issues being addressed by writers and theorists designated as postcolonial today. At a time when the United States was implementing what he
calls a "new imperial policy" (53) as a result of the Asian and Caribbean pos-
sessions it had recently acquired from Spain, Du Bois unequivocally links the
situation of African Americans not only to other diasporic blacks and Africans
but also colonized peoples throughout the world. Over the course of his long
life, Du Bois, the father of Pan-Africanism as well as an ardent and consistent
critic of colonialism, came to question and later abandoned his early belief that
African Americans were the people most qualified to lead the black world into
a new era of freedom and ascendancy. In "The Conservation of Races" (1897),
he refers to black Americans as "the advanced guard of the Negro people" (42)

and in "The Present Outlook" argues that their actions will shape the future for people in both America's newly acquired territories and Europe's colonies: "We must remember that the twentieth century will find nearly twenty millions of brown and black people under the protection of the American flag, a third of the nation, and that on the success and efficiency of the nine millions of our own number depends the ultimate destiny of Filipinos, Porto [sic] Ricans, Indians, Hawaiians, and that on us too depends in large degree the attitude of Europe toward the teeming millions of Asia and Africa" (53). Disillusioned with the lack of progress made by African Americans and disheartened by the imminent Italian conquest of Ethiopia, however, in a piece published in the *Pittsburgh Courier* in 1936, Du Bois connects the freedom of black Americans to that of Africans, asserting that the former will never achieve their rights as full citizens as long as Europe continues to exploit the latter (Frederickson 151). In "American Negroes and Africa's Rise to Freedom," which appeared in print two years before his life came to an end in Ghana in 1963, he completely reverses his earlier position, stating, "Indeed, it now seems that Africans may have to show American Negroes the way to freedom" (337).

Twenty years after Du Bois's death, Salman Rushdie published "'Commonwealth Literature' Does Not Exist," in which he anticipates postcolonialism and seeks to move beyond the boundaries that some critics would come to establish for the field, including a reluctance to engage fully with the experiences and cultural productions of African Americans. In this essay, composed before commonwealth studies would transform into postcolonial studies, Rushdie remarks, "'Commonwealth literature,' it appears, is that body of writing created, I think, in the English language, by persons who are not themselves white Britons, or Irish, or citizens of the United States of America. I don't know whether black Americans are citizens of this bizarre Commonwealth or not. Probably not. [...] By now 'Commonwealth literature' was sounding very unlikeable indeed. Not only was it a ghetto, but it was actually an exclusive ghetto" (63). Later in the essay, he envisions a deterritorialized literary critical approach: "It is possible, I think, to begin to theorize common factors between writers from these societies—poor countries, or deprived minorities in powerful countries—and to say that much of what is new in world literature comes from this group. This seems to me to be 'real' theory, bounded by frontiers which are neither political nor linguistic but imaginative" (69).

Here Rushdie appears to adumbrate Homi Bhabha's assertion over a decade later that "[p]ostcolonial perspectives emerge from the colonial testimony of Third World countries and the discourses of 'minorities' within the geographical divisions of East and West, North and South" (*Location* 171). As I noted in chapter 1, some critics have objected strongly to Bhabha's inclusive conception of postcolonialism, especially as it relates to the United States. Faulting Bhabha for failing to account for the differences between racial minorities in Europe, a direct consequence of colonialism, and those in America, whose history is more "heterogeneous," Jenny Sharpe in "Is the United States Postcolonial? Transnationalism, Immigration, and Race" (1995) warns that "[t]he refashioning of postcolonial studies as minority discourse has not only moved us far afield from the early objectives of colonial discourse analysis but also risks playing into a liberal multiculturalism that obfuscates the category of race" (104, 108). In contrast to Bhabha, she offers a sharply focused delineation of postcolonialism as it relates to America: "I want to propose that the postcolonial be theorized as the point at which internal social relations intersect with global capitalism and the division of labor. In other words, I want to define the 'after' to colonialism as the neocolonial relations into which the United States entered with decolonized nations" (106). I wholeheartedly agree with Sharpe that simply conflating postcolonial and ethnic American (including African American) studies would be more detrimental than beneficial. We should never lose sight of the fact that the texts and contexts of black Americans and those of colonized or formerly colonized persons differ significantly. In institutional terms, because each of these disciplines has its own history and traditions, a professor specializing in postcolonial studies cannot and should not be expected to be able to teach African American studies competently without acquiring the proper background—and vice versa. This does not mean, however, that we should hesitate to map out and explore the confluences of these fields. Nor (to change the metaphor) does it preclude the possibility of cross-pollination between postcolonial theory and African American literary studies.

Although postcolonial studies seems new because the term itself is of recent coinage, Rushdie's essay serves as a reminder that postcolonialism had a different name just a few years ago. What is missing from his discussion (and from Bhabha's when read in isolation)—and often from other postcolonial theory and criticism—is a comprehensive engagement with the history of anticolonial struggles, a history that ought to take account of African American experience and cultural productions but must not minimize the extent to which these diverge from those of colonized and formerly colonized people. When we examine the writings of Du Bois, Harriet Jacobs, Pauline Hopkins, Harry Dean, and many others, we see that black Americans and those people now categorized as postcolonial have shared experiences and goals and grappled with and theorized about several of the same issues. Unfortunately the rubric "postcolonial"—perhaps in part because of its apparent newness—has sometimes resulted in critical, disciplinary, and theoretical barriers that have served to isolate postcolonial and African American literary studies. Just as the rapprochement of poststructuralist theory and African American studies bore fruit for Henry Louis Gates Jr., Houston Baker, and others in the 1980s, applying postcolonial theoretical concepts to black American literature can likewise be extremely productive, as Paul Gilroy's readings of Delany, Douglass, Du Bois, and Wright in *The Black Atlantic* amply document.

Through *Confluences'* analyses of texts by Rushdie, Jean Rhys, V. S. Naipaul, Walter Mosley, Hopkins, Toni Morrison, Dean, Jacobs, and Alice Walker, I have sought in a modest and preliminary way to demonstrate the strengths and extend the range of, as well as raise some questions about, postcolonial counter-discourse, Gates's Signifyin(g), and Gilroy's black Atlantic. With certain texts using one of these theoretical models in isolation works well; however, with others a combination of two or all three of the theories can produce sounder, more profound, and more densely textured readings. I therefore urge both postcolonial and African American critics to emulate, expand on, and, where appropriate, emend Gilroy's bold attempt to bridge postcolonial and African American studies, embracing the black Atlantic's stress on movement through space and intercultural connections. Additionally, I hope that people working in these fields will consider addressing some of the explicit and implicit questions posed by this book, including but not limited to the following: Exactly what is the relationship between postcolonial theory and transatlantic slavery (and the black diaspora it engendered)? Can counter-discursive rewritings of canonical texts avoid reinforcing the dominant discourse they seek to unsettle? At what point, if ever, does a writer's metropolitan politics and lifestyle outweigh his or her postcolonial origins? To what degree does African American literary revisionism resemble postcolonial counter-discourse? Must England serve as the anchor for the black Atlantic nexus or can connections among peoples affected by the slave trade be routed differently? And, in sum, where do the experiences and the counter-discursive responses of African Americans flow together with those of colonized or formerly colonized people and where do they branch off into separate channels?

Notes

Chapter One. An Overview: The Black Atlantic as a Bridge between
Postcolonial and African American Literary Studies

1   There has been considerable debate over whether "postcolonial" or "post-colonial" should be the proper spelling for this term. See, for example, Ashcroft, Griffiths, and Tiffin, *Empire* 193–99; Mishra and Hodge; and McLeod. In this book, I use the former, more commonly accepted spelling. In addition, I use African American (without a hyphen) to refer to people of African descent in what would become or what is now the United States and as a synonym for black American.

2   The Morrison passage comes from an essay titled "Black Matter(s)" (1991), which appeared in slightly altered form the following year in *Playing in the Dark.*

3   Bhabha also discusses the *unheimlich* in "DissemiNation: Time, Narrative, and the Margins of the Modern Nation" (1990).

4   See *Post-Colonial Literatures: Expanding the Canon,* edited by Deborah L. Madsen (1999); *Postcolonial America,* edited by C. Richard King (2000); *Postcolonial Theory and the United States: Race, Ethnicity, and Literature,* edited by Amritjit Singh and Peter Schmidt (2000). I will return to objections to Bhabha's broad definition of postcolonialism in the conclusion.

5 In "Postcolonialism after W. E. B. Du Bois" (2000), Kenneth Mostern makes the case that *The Souls of Black Folk* anticipates in several specific ways the postcolonial critique Bhabha offers in *The Location of Culture*.

6 More recently, near the end of the introduction to *Signifying with a Vengeance: Theories, Literatures, Storytellers* (2002), Mustapha Marrouchi asks, along with several other questions, "Is the African-American writer and her narrative a site for and the space in which voices of subaltern consciousness are constantly made anew?" (43). His fifth chapter, "Fear of the *Other*, Loathing the Similar," devoted largely to Toni Morrison, strongly suggests that the answer is yes.

7 Page references in this book will be to the second edition of *Empire*.

8 These are by no means the only subjects discussed in *The Empire Writes Back*, which strives to codify the field by making connections among and imposing order on a wide variety of postcolonial theories.

9 Although a few African American literary critics are included, their selections are devoted to theory and colonial discourse, not black American literature.

10 See Senghor's "Negritude: A Humanism of the Twentieth Century," a speech he presented at the first Festival of African Arts in Dakar in 1966. In yet another cross-cultural interaction, the African Personality movement associated with Edward Blyden and Majola Agbegi in turn influenced the African American journalist, historian, and Garveyite John E. Bruce (1856–1924), the author of an early serial novel, *The Black Sleuth* (1907–9), whose West African protagonist studies in the United States and becomes a highly effective detective in Europe. See also Hughes's "The Twenties" (1966) where he claims, "Had the word *negritude* been in use in Harlem in the twenties, Cullen, as well as McKay, Johnson, Toomer, and I, might have been called poets of *negritude*" (32).

11 Gates distinguishes the thrust of his two books as follows: "In [. . .] *Figures* [. . .], I sought to chart one noncanonical critic's experiments with [. . .] theories of criticism, which I drew on to read black texts, as if on safari through the jungle of criticism. This gesture has been crucial to the development of my thinking about the 'proper work' for black criticism: to define itself with—and against—other theoretical activities. While this sort of criticism has helped to demonstrate that distinct literary canons need not necessarily segregate critics—indeed, that shared critical approaches can define a canon of criticism—I believe it necessary to draw on the black tradition to define a theory of its nature and function" (*Signifying* xxiv). Because *Confluences* argues for critical deterritorialization, it is somewhat more sympathetic to *Figures* than it is to *Signifying*, although it makes ample references to both texts.

12 In addition to Baker's *Long Black Song* and Gayle's *The Way of the New World*, which I discuss below, Gates devotes three and a half pages to Stephen Henderson's *Understanding the New Black Poetry* (1972).

13 Gates not only rejects Baker's repudiative theory and the Black Aesthetic, but also, like the authors of *Empire*, Negritude, which he sees as possessing the flaws of both: "To think of oneself as free simply because one can claim—one can utter—the negation of an assertion is not to think deeply enough. *Negritude* already constituted such a claim of blackness as a transcendent signified, of full and sufficient presence; but to make such a claim, to feel the need to make such a claim, is already to reveal too much about perceived absence and desire" (*Figures* 53).

14 By concentrating on the Africanist presence in classic American literature in *Playing in the Dark,* Morrison devotes her attention to what Gates calls the "discourse of the black"; however, as I will argue in chapter 3, the implications of her assertions about American Africanism call into question Gates's claim that Signifyin(g) is a thoroughly nonrepudiative theory of African American literature.

15 Marrouchi defines signifying as "imitation with a mocking difference" and "*improvising with difference*" (10, 32).

16 Despite Gilroy's frequently expressed opposition to African American exceptionalism, his preference for African American literary texts can be seen as perpetuating it. For a discussion of African American exceptionalism, see my *Black on Black: Twentieth-Century African American Writing about Africa* (2000), especially 13–14.

Chapter Two. Postcolonial Counter-discourse: Salman Rushdie, Jean Rhys, V. S. Naipaul

1 Numerous critics, myself included, have discussed the pervasive and distorting effect that Conrad's novella has had on Western portrayals of Africa. See, for example, Chinua Achebe's "An Image of Africa" (1977) and chapter 4 of Rob Nixon's *London Calling: V. S. Naipaul, Postcolonial Mandarin* (1992).

2 See, for example, Kwame Anthony Appiah's "The Postcolonial and the Postmodern," chapter 7 of *In My Father's House* (1992).

3 King's definition, "the contest for hegemony [. . .] between Britain and Russia," echoes David Fromkin's use of the phrase to "describe the whole of the Anglo-Russian quarrel about the fate of Asia" (936) in an essay titled "The Great Game in Asia" (1980).

4 M. E. Yapp's lecture "The Legend of the Great Game" (2000) exemplifies the seeming inability of historians and critics to agree on a single definition. Early on he discusses the Game as an "abstract concept," representing "life and action," which Kipling "juxtapose[s]" to the Lama's "Way"; however, he later connects it to British colonial rule through his reference to "the game of policing the empire."

5 See also Rushdie's "Dynasty" (1985).

6 In *To Begin the World Anew: The Genius and Ambiguities of the American Founders* (2003), Bernard Bailyn argues that it was the provincial (or peripheral) status of the

founders of the American republic that enabled them to challenge European ideas about government and create a wholly original nation through a combination of idealism and realism.

7   Although clearly patterned on the master of Thornfield Hall in *Jane Eyre,* Rhys never names Antoinette's husband. On the significance of this decision, see Rody 219 and Spivak 271. For the sake of convenience, however, I will refer to this character as Rochester.

8   Octave Mannoni's *Prospero and Caliban* (1956) is an early example; the list also encompasses Stephen Greenblatt's well-known essay "Learning to Curse: Aspects of Linguistic Colonialism in the Sixteenth Century" (1990).

9   For a discussion of the role that Daniel and Alexander Cosway play in Rhys's novel, see Peter Hulme's "The Locked Heart: The Creole Family Romance of *Wide Sargasso Sea*" (1994).

10 Stressing the novel's revisionary feminism over its revisionary postcoloniality, Caroline Rody states, "I want to claim the rebellious heroine Antoinette/Bertha as our greatest figure for the resisting female reader—a prophetic figure for Rhys to create in 1966, just before so many female readers began to reject their marginalized relationships to writing and, inspired by a visionary impulse, to reenter the big house of English literature with a flame" (218).

11 Iago recognizes this apparent power, stating in his soliloquy at the end of act 2 that "His soul is so enfettered to her love / That she may make, unmake, do what she list, / Even as her appetite shall play the god / With his weak function" (2.3.339–42).

12 My reading of Antoinette's transformation may appear to run directly counter to Spivak's argument that, in contrast to Brontë's animalistic portrayal of Bertha Mason, Rhys depicts Antoinette's humanity and sanity throughout the novel (268–69). However, although we differ on the question of the protagonist's mental state, I am otherwise in agreement with Spivak's reading of the scene in part 3 in which Antoinette attacks her stepbrother, as I indicate at the end of this section. My point here is not so much that Antoinette does in fact become monstrous or bestial but rather that she is perceived this way first by Rochester and later by other (English)men in positions of power.

13 Commenting on this scene, Arnold Davidson remarks, "it requires no great perspicacity to see that this dispossessed, disconsolate, lost boy is a stand-in for Rochester himself; is, indeed, the Rochester whom that same character, with his pose of domination and control, would hide from all eyes, especially his own, and, as such, the child weeps for everything, everything" (38).

14 Only in the first trial scene, the lone one to take place in Venice, and the last, which occurs after the deaths of four characters, does the justice system work properly. In act 1, scene 3, the defendant is openly accused in a courtroomlike setting, and the duke, acting as the judge, allows the accuser (Brabantio) and Othello the opportunity to make their arguments and call witnesses. Based on the testimony

Desdemona provides, the duke renders a fair and impartial decision. When the setting moves to Cyprus, however, Iago is able to exploit the peculiarities of the colonial setting to undermine the justice system profoundly. In act 2, scene 3, he choreographs the revels that inebriate Cassio and the brawl that results in the lieutenant's dismissal. Othello, acting as judge, renders a verdict that is tainted by the fact that Cassio is either too befuddled or too humbled to speak, and Iago acts as the sole witness, dooming Cassio despite his protestations of love for him. Beginning in act 3, scene 3, Iago accuses Desdemona of being unfaithful to Othello, offering a string of lies and specious "proofs" to a very emotional Othello who nevertheless sits in judgment of his wife. Unlike Othello and Cassio in the previous trial scenes, Desdemona is never openly accused nor is she given a fair chance to defend herself or call witnesses in her defense. Othello has already determined to kill Desdemona when in act 5, scene 2 he finally informs her of her supposed crime. Again, an overwrought and far from impartial Othello acts as judge, jury, and executioner when he accuses himself of being a "Turk" later in the same scene. It is only in the final moments of the play that the justice system functions properly once more. After being openly charged with villainy, hearing the evidence of his crimes from various characters, and admitting his guilt, Iago is condemned to be tortured for his perfidy. (This reading of *Othello* as a series of trial scenes is an expansion of that offered by David Bevington, who limits his discussion to the first three.)

15 Carl Plasa, who looks first at Tia and Christophine and then at Annette as the protagonist's doubles, observes, "*Wide Sargasso Sea* recovers the prehistory of the Bertha of *Jane Eyre* as the story of Antoinette, and in so doing provides a powerful counter-statement to Rochester's representation of his West Indian experiences in the earlier text. At the same time, however, the narrative liberated from *Jane Eyre* claims its space by means of the marginalization of the very slave history with which it seeks alignment" (86).

16 In *Conrad and the Nineteenth Century* (1979), Ian Watt traces the development of the phrase "going native." In English the original term was "going fantee," and it arose in connection with contact between Europeans and West Africans. According to Watt, "*Heart of Darkness* is unique in being the first [text] to connect the process of 'going fantee' with an even more general consequence of the colonial situation: the fact that the individual colonialist's power, combined with the lack of any effective control, was an open invitation to every kind of cruelty and abuse" (145).

17 In *A Congo Diary* (1980), a text clearly inspired by and patterned after the journal Conrad kept during his sojourn in the Congo, Naipaul declares, "History has disappeared. Even the Belgian colonial past. And no one, African, Asian, European, has heard of Conrad or *Heart of Darkness*" (13). To a certain extent, then, Naipaul in *A Bend in the River* can be seen as rewriting Conrad's novella for the postindependence era.

18 This argument echoes Naipaul's assessment of the continent in "A New King for

the Congo": "The past has vanished. Facts in a book cannot by themselves give people a sense of history. Where so little has changed, where bush and river are so overwhelming, another past is accessible, better answering African bewilderment and African religious beliefs: the past as *le bon vieux temps de nos ancetres*" (205).

19   Lynda Prescott and Mustapha Marrouchi contend that the European linguist, educator, priest, and anthropologist Huismans plays a role in Naipaul's book similar to that of Kurtz in *Heart of Darkness*. In contrast, Fawzia Mustafa links Salim to the two main characters of Conrad's narrative: "Naipaul's narrator tells his story with the self-consciousness of a Marlow, but finally exits like a latter-day Kurtz, to take refuge in a union with his 'Intended,' the daughter of Nazruddin, who lives, of course, on Gloucester Road in London" (152). However, as I argue in the paragraphs to follow, Naipaul, from the beginning, patterns Salim's decline on Kurtz's.

20   Like the servant whom the English protagonist Scobie betrays near the conclusion of Graham Greene's *The Heart of the Matter* (1948), Metty was known as Ali on the coast.

21   As Nixon puts it, "A clear rift separates his reputation in the United States and Britain, on the one side, from his standing in what I shall provisionally call (with all the customary reservations) the Third World, on the other" (3).

Chapter Three. Signifyin(g): Walter Mosley, Pauline Hopkins, Toni Morrison

1   *The Norton Anthology of African American Literature* (1997), which Gates edited along with Nellie McKay, might be seen as the culmination of this project. For Gates's thoughts on the challenges and ironies of this landmark work, see "Canon-Formation, Literary History, and the Afro-American Tradition: From the Seen to the Told" (1994).

2   In a nearly identical passage about Fortune's poem in *Figures*, Gates uses the word "content" instead of "context" (242).

3   Perhaps more than any other writer, Ishmael Reed has recognized that the detective story—like the hoodoo religion, the basic gumbo recipe, and the city of New Orleans—accommodates a variety of disparate elements and can be manipulated to suit a wide range of purposes. Replete with photographs, drawings, cartoons, dictionary definitions, and a bibliography, *Mumbo Jumbo* (1972) expands the boundaries of the novel. Ostensibly a mystery set in New Orleans in the 1920s that features the hoodoo detective Papa La Bas, Reed's most famous book also provides a bitingly comic, postmodern critique of race prejudice, Western imperialism, and African American and Anglo American literature.

4   The first black female sleuth created by an African American novelist since Hopkins's Venus Johnson in *Hagar's Daughter*, the title character of Dolores Komo's *Clio Browne: Private Investigator* (1988) runs the Browne Bureau of

Investigation in St. Louis. The middle-aged widow of a cop and the daughter of the founder of the first black detective agency in the country, Clio receives the often-unsolicited assistance of her secretary, her mother, and her elderly female neighbor in solving the murders of young women who work on a Mississippi riverboat restaurant. The heroine of Eleanor Taylor Bland's Marti MacAlister novels, which began appearing annually with *Dead Time* in 1992, is also the widow of a policeman. However, she too wears a shield, having worked ten years on the force in Chicago before joining the department in suburban Lincoln Prairie (based on Waukegan, Illinois) as a homicide detective after her husband Johnny died on duty under mysterious circumstances. These circumstances eventually bring her back to Chicago to solve Johnny's murder in the fourth installment of the series, *Done Wrong*. Valerie Wilson Wesley's savvy black private eye and fiercely protective single mother, Tamara Hayle, is a survivor like her hometown of Newark, New Jersey. The seven novels of the series, which began with *When Death Comes Stealing* in 1994, provide readers with historical information about the Garden State's beleaguered largest city. In contrast to other writers, Barbara Neely has not tied her middle-aged detective, Blanche White, to a specific location. However, whether it is North Carolina, Maine, or Boston, setting plays a major role in the series (which began with *Blanche on the Lam* in 1992), in part because the heroine is a domestic worker (like Hopkins's Venus) who gains intimate knowledge about the places where she cooks and cleans and learns the secrets of the people for whom she works.

5 In *Fear of the Dark* published in 1988, two years before the first Easy Rawlins novel, *Devil in a Blue Dress,* Gar Anthony Haywood uses contemporary Los Angeles as the setting. Haywood's detective, Aaron Gunner, finds himself at the flash point of a potential national racial conflagration when he is hired to investigate the murder of a leading member of a black militant organization by a psychotic white racist. Despite the decades that separate them, Mosley and Haywood's detectives are both war veterans who prefer the dangerous autonomy of private investigation to the more sedate life and steady income of conventional employment. To an even greater extent than Haywood's Gunner series, Gary Phillips's Ivan Monk novels underscore the racial tensions in the City of Angels in the 1990s. Set in the wake of the violence following the nationally televised beating of Rodney King by white policemen, the first novel in the series, *Violent Spring,* which appeared in 1994, begins with the discovery of the body of a Korean merchant at the site of a memorial erected in memory of those killed in the 1992 riots. Although, like Haywood, Phillips uses contemporary Los Angeles as the location for his novels, like Mosley, he typically constructs plots that revisit significant events in the country's racial past, such as the 1965 Watts riots and the institution of the Negro baseball leagues.

6 For a widely cited discussion of hard-boiled detective fiction and its conventions, see Cawelti.

7   In *Little Scarlet,* set in 1965 in the wake of the Watts riots, things in Los Angeles have changed so drastically that the police ask Easy to help them solve the murder of a black woman and, at the end of the novel, officially recognize him as a private investigator.

8   Mosley may be alluding to James Ellroy's *The Black Dahlia* (1987), a police procedural based on real-life events that is set, like *Devil,* in Los Angeles in the late 1940s and emphasizes the era's racial and ethnic tensions.

9   It has long been my pet theory that the first name of Mosley's hero derives from the twelve-year-old title character of Rudolph Fisher's stories "Ezekiel" (1932) and "Ezekiel Learns" (1933). Ezekiel is a wide-eyed but clever young boy newly arrived in Harlem from the South and born within a year of Easy Rawlins, who in the latter story witnesses a petty crime and stealthily intervenes to ensure that justice is done. However, given the major role played by Signifyin(g) in Mosley's mysteries, the similarity between the names Easy and Esu, the Yoruba god of interpretation whose African American manifestation, according to Gates, is the Signifying Monkey, is intriguing.

10 As I discuss in the body of the text, although Mosley will violate this rule in *White Butterfly,* the failure of Easy's marriage to Regina ultimately serves to vindicate Chandler.

11 Easy minimizes the differences between himself and Primo, observing that the events in *Devil* occurred in 1948 "before Mexicans and black people started hating each other. Back then, before ancestry had been discovered, a Mexican and a Negro considered themselves the same. That is to say, just a couple of unlucky stiffs left holding the short end of the stick" (177).

12 In *A Little Yellow Dog,* set in 1963, Mouse has begun to change. He has learned to read, takes a steady job, stops carrying a gun, and starts talking about finding religion. It may, in fact, be precisely these changes that are responsible for the formerly invincible Mouse's nearly fatal wounding in this book, which is pervaded by disillusionment about the future and the prospect of change, a disillusionment typified by the Kennedy assassination.

13 Evidence that Mouse's argument has a profound effect on Easy surfaces late in the novel when, after being knocked out by Joppy and Albright, Easy has a dream about a great naval battle in which Mouse pulls him away from the line and yells, "We gotta get outta here, man. Ain't no reason t'die in no white man's war" (194).

14 The literary legacy of the *Creole* revolt does not end with "A Dash for Liberty." The rebellion is also the subject of Theodore Ward's four-act musical *Madison* (1956), based on Douglass's "The Heroic Slave."

15 Even today many of the facts relating to the *Creole* rebellion and its aftermath remain sketchy or unknown. Before 1970 the only detailed description of the revolt was an 1842 account in the *Senate Documents* consisting of depositions taken from

white sailors and passengers involved in the incident, and this remains the single most important source of information about the uprising. Since 1970, four articles on the *Creole* episode have appeared that have helped to bring the major events of the rebellion into somewhat clearer focus. See Clinton Johnson, Jones, Jervey and Huber, and Bernier "Arms." The summary that follows is taken from these essays and *Senate Documents*.

16   In contrast to the documented reports of the rebels being freed in Jones and in Jervey and Huber, Clinton Johnson makes the undocumented assertion that the nineteen participants in the revolt were charged with piracy and murder and an unspecified number of them were tried, convicted, and executed (249).

17   See Douglass's "American Prejudice Against Color: An Address Delivered in Cork, Ireland, 23 October 1845," "American and Scottish Prejudice Against the Slave: An Address Delivered in Edinburgh, Scotland, on 1 May 1846," "Farewell to the British People: An Address Delivered in London, England, on 30 March 1847," and "Slavery, the Slumbering Volcano: An Address Delivered in New York, New York, on April 23, 1849," in *The Frederick Douglass Papers*. Five months prior to publishing "Madison Washington: Another Chapter in His History," the *Liberator* ran an article, on 7 January 1842, titled "The Creoles—Strike for Liberty—The Hero Mutineers." In the interim, on 28 April 1842, the *National Anti-Slavery Standard* published a brief article titled "Madison Washington," which reads in part as follows: "Madison had been some time in Canada—long enough to love and rejoice in British liberty. But he loved his wife who was left a slave in Virginia still more. At length Madison resolved on rescuing her from slavery. Although strongly dissuaded by his friends from making the attempt in person, he would not listen, but crossed the line into this State [i.e., New York . . .]. So strong was Madison's determination, that at this time he assured his friends he would have his wife or lose his life." The piece goes on to speculate "whether [Washington's unnamed wife] was on board the Creole."

18   Curiously, given the mystery surrounding Washington's life before and after the *Creole* affair, in the only sentence of Brown's "Madison Washington" (1863) not to be included in his "Slave Revolt at Sea" (1867) we are told, "Not many months since, an American ship went ashore at Nassau, and among the first to render assistance to the crew was Madison Washington" (85).

19   Bernier reports that Douglass printed a new version of his novella during the Civil War, probably in 1863, under the title *The Heroic Slave, a Thrilling Narrative of the Adventures of Madison Washington, in Pursuit of Liberty* ("Arms" 105). See also her essay "A Comparative Exploration of Narrative Ambiguities in Frederick Douglass's Two Versions of *The Heroic Slave* (1853, 1863?)" (2001).

20   On this subject Yarborough states, "It must be noted that there are several instances where Brown, Child, and Hopkins employ remarkably similar phrasing. Brown had appropriated material from Child before, in the first edition of *Clotel*. There

is evidence of extensive borrowing here as well—either by Brown from an earlier version of Child's sketch or by Child from Brown's in *The Black Man,* or by both Brown and Child from an earlier text by another writer" (186).

21 James McPherson emphasizes the didactic purpose of the *Freedmen's Book* in his foreword to the 1968 reprint: "Because many of the pupils in freedmen's schools were adults whose experiences in slavery had provided little training for the responsibilities of freedom, Mrs. Child sprinkled the book with advice on home economics, the raising of children, rules of good health, habits of industry and morality, and the like."

22 Born in Maine in 1859, Hopkins was neither a survivor of slavery like Douglass or Brown (both of whom actively resisted the "peculiar institution" by escaping to the North) nor a contemporary witness to it like Child. As a magazine editor and a literary artist—and a woman—who was most active during the period known as the "nadir" during which African Americans faced the worst postbellum conditions, Hopkins necessarily approached the *Creole* revolt as a historically significant event with particular relevance for her turn-of-the-century black readers. A number of critics, including Claudia Tate and Mary Helen Washington, have addressed the issue of authorial control of history during the 1890s and early 1900s.

23 Discussions of Hopkins's editorial responsibilities and the role politics played in the purchase and subsequent demise of the *Colored American Magazine* can be found in Braithwaite; Du Bois, "The Colored"; Johnson and Johnson; Charles Johnson; and Meier.

24 On the subject of naming and unnaming in African American literature and culture, see Ellison, "Hidden," Stuckey 193–244, and Benston. Benston claims that "For the Afro-American [. . .] self-creation and reformation of a fragmented familial past are endlessly interwoven: naming is inevitably genealogical revisionism. All of Afro-American literature may be seen as one vast genealogical poem that attempts to restore continuity to the ruptures or discontinuities imposed by the history of black presence in America" (152).

25 Robert Stepto, for example, has shown the importance of the protagonist's last name to the opening and closing paragraphs as well as the very structure of Douglass's "The Heroic Slave."

26 Here I am using "fictive" both as it is generally understood and in the more specific sense of the term William Andrews employs in his essay on "The Heroic Slave": "The marginal world of the earliest black American novels may be usefully termed a fictive world, in the special sense that Barbara Herrnstein Smith applies 'fictive' to the subjects and objects of representation in various 'mimetic artforms' like poetry, the novel, or the drama. What is re-presented in these types of literary discourse are not 'existing objects or events' but 'fictive member[s] of an identifiable class of natural ("real") objects or events'" (26).

27 Throughout this section, I will provide parenthetical references to both the more accessible reprint of Hopkins's story in *Short Fiction by Black Women, 1900–1920* (which will be listed first) and the story as it originally appeared in the *Colored American Magazine*.

28 I do not mean to suggest that Hopkins was averse to depicting heroes in her stories and sketches or that Madison Monroe is less than heroic in "A Dash for Liberty." My argument is that Hopkins supplements (rather than supplants) the notion of the individual hero with the notion of community.

29 This presentation of the black woman's right to control her own body recalls Harriet Jacobs's vivid and effective treatment of the same theme in *Incidents in the Life of a Slave Girl* (1861), which is itself a deliberately fictionalized depiction of the author's own life as a slave, a fugitive, and a free woman.

30 Susan's ancestry resembles that of the title character of Brown's novel *Clotel; or, The President's Daughter* (1853), who is the mixed-race daughter of Thomas Jefferson.

31 It is worth noting that this union of the light-skinned Susan and the "unmixed African," Madison Monroe, epitomizes the racial solidarity that Hopkins argues for in the story.

32 An essay collection on race in Poe, the title of which, *Romancing the Shadow*, derives from the second chapter of Morrison's book, appeared in 2001.

33 There are some intriguing similarities between *Playing in the Dark* and D. H. Lawrence's references to race in relation to white American writing in *Studies in Classic American Literature* (1923).

34 In a 1999 American Literature Association Conference session devoted to Hawthorne and race, organized by Elizabeth Ammons, I advanced many of the arguments to be found in the body of the text in a paper that provoked the most extreme responses any of my work has ever elicited. Immediately after the paper, two people approached me about publishing it. One of these offers, tendered by the associate editor of a journal devoted to nineteenth-century American literature, was quickly withdrawn when the editor in chief read the paper and took an intense dislike to it. Somewhat embarrassed, the associate editor sent me her colleague's comments and encouraged me to send the essay to a journal specializing in Hawthorne, which I did after expanding the paper to address the objections that had been passed on to me. The response was two dismissive, even brutal, reader's reports. At this point it occurred to me that these intensely negative reactions derived not so much from the essay's quality (or lack thereof) but from an impatience with, fear of, or disdain for explorations of the relationship between race and literature generally and Toni Morrison's arguments about classic American literature in particular.

35 In contrast to Sharon Cameron, who in *The Corporeal Self: Allegories of the Body in Melville and Hawthorne* (1981) asserts, "If in 'Prophetic Pictures' the emblem

is distanced from the body, and if in 'The Minister's Black Veil' the emblem lies directly outside the body, 'The Birth-mark' affixes the emblem to the body, making the two inseparable" (84), I want to emphasize that Georgiana's birthmark is not an emblem fastened *to* her body but, as the story demonstrates, an integral part *of* it.

36 I will not make the assertion that the birthmark indicates that Georgiana possesses some amount of African blood and thus, given her eventual fate, should be seen as a tragic mulatta; nor will I contend that Aminadab, who addresses Aylmer as "master" and is characterized by "his vast strength, his shaggy hair, his smoky aspect, and the indescribable earthiness that incrusted him" (43), should be read as a black person. Instead, I want to concentrate on Aylmer's and later Georgiana's own extreme responses to her birthmark and suggest that they can be read usefully in the context of American racial politics.

37 See Melville's *Moby Dick; or, The White Whale:* "not yet have we solved the incantation of this whiteness, and learned why it appeals with such power to the soul; and more strange and far more portentous—why, as we have seen, it is at once the most meaning symbol of spiritual things, nay, the very veil of the Christian's Deity; and yet should be as it is, the intensifying agent in things the most appalling to mankind" (196).

38 In his extensive study of interracial literature, *Neither Black nor White yet Both: Thematic Explorations of Interracial Literature* (1999), Sollors has established that in European and American literature written prior to and in the years following the initial publication of Hawthorne's "The Birth-mark" a bluish tinge to the fingernails was frequently used as a sign of mixed-race origins. Two major French writers with whom Hawthorne was familiar, Victor Hugo and Eugène Sue, published stories in which the *sang mêlé* of a character is established by the stretching forth of the hand to reveal the presence of a darkish hue to the fingernails. While my argument in the body of the text is in no way dependent on whether Hawthorne knew of this convention when he wrote "The Birth-mark," the fact that he depicts Georgiana's nevus as a crimson *hand* is suggestive.

39 One example of an African American character in Hawthorne's fiction that does come to mind is Roderick Elliston's servant Scipio in "Egotism; or, The Bosom Serpent."

40 See *Playing* 54–57. Morrison has written about Twain's novel at greater length in other essays. See, for example, her introduction to *Adventures of Huckleberry Finn*, reprinted as "This Amazing, Troubling Book."

41 For an excellent discussion of the dubious nature of Gray's text, see Sundquist *To Wake* 36–83. Gray attempts to undermine Turner's statement by referring to the birthmarks parenthetically as "a parcel of excrescences which I believe are not at all uncommon, particularly among negroes, as I have seen several with the same. In this case he has either cut them off or they have nearly disappeared" (413). For

the link between birthmarks and special status in African societies, see Gayraud Wilmore 64 and Mechal Sobel 44, 162.

42 For extended discussions of *Unfettered* and *Of One Blood,* see Gruesser, *Black on Black* 23–32 and 34–40.

43 For a reading of Ellison's story that makes reference to Hawthorne's tale, see Robyn Wiegman "The Anatomy of Lynching" (1993).

44 Several critics (e.g., Barbara Christian, Melvin Dixon, and Patrick Bryce Bjork) have discussed Sula's birthmark and the various responses it provokes. In *A World of Difference: An Inter-Cultural Study of Toni Morrison's Novels* (1994), Wendy Harding and Jacky Martin foreground a reading of bodily markings in Morrison, including Sula's birthmark, by making reference to Hawthorne's "The Birth-mark" (21–23).

Chapter Four. The Black Atlantic: Harry Dean, Harriet Jacobs, Alice Walker

1 Booker T. Washington's *The Man Farthest Down: A Record of Observation and Study in Europe* (1912) provides an example of an African American who clearly was *not* politically transformed by his European experiences. Instead, Washington uses his second trip to the continent to bolster his ideas about the position of black Americans in the United States. For a useful discussion of this travel book, see Dickson Bruce. I am grateful to Ira Dworkin for bringing Washington's text to my attention.

2 Delany receives eleven pages, Douglass fourteen, Du Bois thirty-five, and Wright forty-one. In a later essay, "Route Work," Gilroy does include a three-page discussion of Phillis Wheatley, who, he asserts, "represents something like the start of black Atlantic crossing" (23). However, she does not really serve to confirm Gilroy's assertion about the transforming effects of European travel. Although Wheatley journeyed to London to have her poems published, she wrote them in America; thus, their politics could not have been influenced by her experiences in England.

3 Gilroy does not claim to be offering comprehensive proof for his theory in *The Black Atlantic:* "I have said virtually nothing about the lives, theories, and political activities of Frantz Fanon and C. L. R. James, the two best-known black Atlantic thinkers. Their lives fit readily into the pattern of movement, transformation, and relocation I have described. But they are already well known if not as widely read as they should be, and other people have begun the labour of introducing their writings into contemporary critical theory" (xi).

4 As discussed in chapter 1, the authors of *The Empire Writes Back* raise but fail to engage this question fully in "Rethinking the Post-colonial," a new chapter included in the second edition of their book.

5   Gilroy briefly analyzes Toni Morrison's *Beloved* (along with Sherley Anne Williams's *Dessa Rose,* David Bradley's *The Chaneysville Incident,* and Charles Johnson's *Oxherding Tale* and *Middle Passage*) in the final six pages of the book to illustrate how contemporary black novelists utilize history and social memory.

6   Both the American and British edition were published in 1929. The British edition of the book is titled *Umbala* ("it is true").

7   There are at least two differences between the American and British editions of Dean's book. Book 1 is titled "I Go to Sea at the Age of Twelve" in the American and "My First Voyage" in the British edition. Interestingly, there is also a negative comment about Cecil Rhodes that appears only in the American edition. After describing Rhodes's giant cement crypt in Matabeleland, Dean remarks, "Thus his body might never be removed from the country he had conquered, and his iron spirit might continue to subdue the Ethiopian race even after he was gone. This was the last grandiose gesture of an African conqueror whose cruelty was only equaled by that of Henry the Navigator" (*The Pedro Gorino* 202).

8   For more information on Ethiopianism, see Drake, Moses, Sundquist, and chapter 1 of my book *Black on Black.*

9   North's claims about Dean's travels around and within Africa closely resemble those in the undated three-page "Biography" by and about Dean in Dean's papers. The 1989 Pluto Press reissue of the British version of the book does not contain North's preface, which provides information about Dean and the composition of the book. Quotations from Dean's autobiography are taken from the reprint of the British edition unless indicated otherwise.

10 North (who cowrote the book with the indigent and ailing sixty-four-year-old Dean and would later write *Rascal*) echoes Du Bois in a letter written thirty-six years after the publication of *The Pedro Gorino:* "Dean was a colorful and attractive figure. The fact that he wouldn't show me his diaries and letters [while they were writing the book together] may have meant that he was slightly romanticizing his past. His dreams may have surpassed his c[a]pacities. But I remember him kindly" (Letter to Dr. Robert I. Rotberg). Shepperson likewise admits that when he first read Dean's autobiography he had "an uneasy suspicion that there was more fiction than fact in his book" (vii). Reconsidering the narrative almost forty years later, Shepperson expresses more confidence in Dean's truthfulness because in the interim some of the author's assertions about South Africa at the beginning of the century had been confirmed. Although Burger found it impossible to verify many of Dean's claims, he concurs with Shepperson on the veracity of *The Pedro Gorino* in his thesis, "An Introduction to Harry Dean[,] Pan-Negro-Nationalist," which Shepperson relies heavily on and praises in his introduction. Drawing liberally on Dean's diaries and notebooks at the DuSable Museum of African American History in Chicago, Burger not only provides dates for some of the events mentioned in Dean's book but also recounts the author's life after the period covered in *The Pedro*

Gorino. He describes Dean's activities in Liberia between 1909 and 1914, his two periods in Chicago (1914–20 and 1927–35), his unsuccessful efforts in the 1920s to purchase a ship to conduct trade between California and Liberia, his founding of a nautical college for blacks in Alameda, California, in 1924, his lectures on Africa and black history, and his efforts to establish black agricultural communities in Washington state in the 1930s. In 1998, I was able to confirm some of Burger's assertions about Dean's activities in California in the early 1920s. The 1924 Oakland city directory includes a "Dean, Harry," with the occupation of "mstr mar" (presumably master mariner), residing at 1530 Lincoln Avenue in Alameda (624). In addition, "Capt. Harry Dean" published two articles in the *San Francisco Chronicle* in 1923—"Liberian Development Possibilities" and "Ship Deal Discrimination Charge." In the former, which is accompanied by a portrait of Dean, he claims the "wonderful country" of Liberia holds the key to the "Solution of the Negro Problem" and mentions his nautical school. The people Dean wrote about were in South Africa when he claimed they were, but Burger found no mention of him in their writings (although Burger speculates that they may not have named Dean in order to protect him from government censure). Echoing Shepperson, North, and Du Bois, Burger suggests that Dean's memory may have failed him at times and that he may have "embellished" many of the incidents in the book "for the sake of interest and readability" (10). In his final assessment, however, Burger gives Dean the benefit of the doubt: "In so far as the validity of general information available is concerned, it is the author's opinion that much is true but requires further verification" (10). Burger was apparently unaware of a letter to the editor published in the *Colored American Magazine* in 1903 written by A. Kirkland Soga, a South African editor whom Dean mentions in *The Pedro Gorino,* that not only proves Dean was in South Africa at that time but indicates that Dean was both familiar with and deeply impressed by Pauline Hopkins's work ("Editorial and Publishers Announcements" 467). Although Soga's letter does not explicitly state that Dean was familiar with Hopkins's *Of One Blood,* it seems likely that Dean read this Ethiopianist serial in the magazine.

11   Dean was not the only descendent of Paul Cuffe—if in fact he was a descendent as I discuss in the body of the text—to write a biography of his ancestor. Henry Noble Sherwood reports that "Horatio P. Howard, a great grandson of Captain Cuffe, wrote a short biography of his grandsire [in 1913] and erected a monument in his memory [in Westport, Massachusetts, in 1913]" (225). Howard also established the Captain Paul Cuffe Scholarships at Tuskegee Institute (226).

12   In an anonymous essay in the New Bedford Public Library's Paul Cuffe Collection titled "Uncle John's Burying Place" that probably dates from the 1970s, Dean is described as "a man who claims descent, and I think must have looked into the Cuffe papers and then let his truly inspired imagination flow freely." Although the library's record of researchers who have used the Cuffe Collection does not go back

as far as the 1920s, the glass plates with Cuffe's letters in Dean's papers (which he used in lectures he gave on black history) indicate that at some point he must have had access to the Cuffe papers. Moreover, his inclusion in *The Pedro Gorino* of a story concerning the origins of Paul Cuffe's father that has been refuted by Cuffe's biographers suggests that he may have contacted Cuffe's descendants and/or their neighbors in the New Bedford area at the time he consulted the library's Cuffe materials. Dean's account in his first chapter of a young boy named Said Kafu who nursed the Scottish pirate McKinnon Paige back to health and accompanied him to Massachusetts where they took the names of Cuffe and Slocum respectively closely resembles the "family tradition" about Paul Cuffe's father that was repeated in a 1930 *Boston Globe* article titled "The Story of Paul Cuffee," which briefly mentions Dean's book. I am grateful to Paul Cyr of the New Bedford Free Public Library for bringing both "Uncle John's Burying Place" and "The Story of Paul Cuffee" to my attention.

13 Dean dates the letter from "John Cuffee" 13 January 1818. The actual date was exactly one year earlier (Thomas 157).

14 Paul Cuffe discusses his repudiation of his "son John Cuffe" in a 1 March 1817 letter to James Forten (qtd. in Harris 249). This letter was written in response to a 25 January 1817 letter by Forten in which Forten mentions the impostor.

15 This is a possibility that Lamont Thomas suggested to me in a 24 May 1993 phone conversation.

16 John S. Burger told me in a 10 June 1993 phone conversation that he did not recall Celestine T. Fulchon, a member of Dean's family with some knowledge of its genealogy, being able to confirm Dean's claim that he was descended from Paul Cuffe.

17 Although Dean cannot be held responsible for any inaccuracies in his uncle's story, and its veracity is of course less important than its effect on Dean, the tale of the *Full Moon* is hard to verify. A Dutch man-of-war commanded by a Captain Jope did land the first black people in the English colonies near Jamestown in August of 1619; however, Wesley Frank Craven states that a letter by John Rolfe, the source of all later accounts of the episode, including that of John Smith, "clearly indicates that the Negroes had been acquired in the West Indies and such a conclusion is reinforced by unmistakable evidence of [. . . the] number of the Spanish names among the few Negroes listed by name in the census of 1625" (81). Rolfe does not mention the name of the Dutch vessel. In his notes to *The Libretto for the Republic of Liberia*, Melvin Tolson states that the name of the ship that landed near Jamestown was the *Jesus*. See also Bennett 29–30.

18 The story is well known in Norway, and thus it is quite possible that Dean may have purchased a ship named after this girl. I am grateful to Styrk Fjose for this information.

19 Throughout his book Dean puts the word "negro" in quotation marks. North explains in his preface to *The Pedro Gorino* that "Captain Dean feels that the word

'negro' is of false derivation, undescriptive, and in every way unfit for the position it fills in our language. He claims there is no 'negro' race, only many African races" (*The Pedro Gorino* xii).

20 For a brief discussion of Dean's missionary work in South Africa, see Campbell 201.

21 I have in mind the long first paragraph of the second chapter of Conrad's novel, which concludes: "The sea of the past was an incomparably beautiful mistress, with inscrutable face, with cruel and promising eyes. The sea of to-day is a used-up drudge, wrinkled and defaced by the churned-up wakes of brutal propellers, robbed of the enslaving charm of its vastness, stripped of its beauty, of its mystery and of its promise" (*An Outcast of the Islands* 25).

22 None of the critical essays in Deborah Garfield and Rafia Zafar's collection *Harriet Jacobs and Incidents in the Life of a Slave Girl: New Critical Essays* (1996) or Nellie McKay and Frances Smith Foster's Norton Critical Edition of *Incidents* (2001) is devoted primarily to the chapters of the narrative set in the North.

23 Frederick Douglass, whose 1845 *Narrative* served as the prototype for the African American (male) slave narrative, provided the model in *My Bondage and My Freedom* (1855) that Jacobs would emulate and expand in her narrative. Douglass devotes the first twenty-one chapters of his second autobiography to his enslavement and the final four to his life thereafter. Chapters 1–29 of *Incidents* are set in the South; 30–41 take place in the North and England.

24 Both Jacobs and Douglass were fugitive slaves in England in 1845. Douglass crossed the Atlantic shortly after Jacobs because it was feared that the publication of his *Narrative* would result in his capture and reenslavement if he remained in the United States. His sojourn in the United Kingdom lasted twenty-one months, during which time his freedom was purchased by British abolitionists. Jacobs traveled as a nurse to Imogen Willis, whose mother, Mary Stacie Willis, died in March 1845, and she remained in Great Britain for ten months (Yellin, *Harriet* 84–87). Her assertions about the lack of prejudice she encountered while abroad signify in an unmotivated way on statements by Douglass, such as the following, which he made in a letter to William Lloyd Garrison, that is reprinted in *My Bondage and My Freedom:* "The truth is, the people here know nothing of the republican negro hate prevalent in our glorious land. They measure and esteem men according to their moral and intellectual worth, and not according to the color of their skin. Whatever may be said of the aristocracies here, there is none based on the color of a man's skin. This species of aristocracy belongs preeminently to 'the land of the free, and the home of the brave.' I have never found it abroad, in any but Americans" (372). Yellin reports that Jacobs made two other journeys to England, one in a fruitless attempt to secure a British publisher for *Incidents* and another in the late 1860s to raise funds for her efforts on behalf of African Americans in Savannah, Georgia (*Harriet* 137–39, 212–17).

25 The similarities between Jung's Tower and Shug's round house in *The Color Purple* are striking.

26 For an in-depth discussion of Jung's ideas about race, see Adams.

27 Lorraine Hansberry signifies on *Heart of Darkness* in a motivated way in *Les Blancs*. For a reading of Hansberry's final play as a rewriting of Conrad's novella, see *Black on Black* 144–50.

28 Walker develops her ideas about religion most fully in her essay "The Only Reason You Want to Go to Heaven. . . ." For a reading of the African American missionaries in *The Color Purple* in the light of this essay, see *Black on Black* 151–57.

29 Although there is no question that M'Lissa has died, exactly how she met her fate remains uncertain. Tashi offers two different versions of her role in the *tsunga's* death, at first telling Olivia she did not do it (254–55) but later asserting that she was responsible (276). Even the cause of death is not definitively established. The prosecutors believe that Tashi killed M'Lissa with the cutting implements she brought expressively for that purpose. Tashi, however, claims that she smothered the old woman. Because a fire destroys M'Lissa's house and burns her body, the truth is not known.

30 Similar to Rhys's protagonist in *Wide Sargasso Sea* (discussed in chapter 2), Tashi dies rebelling against the forces of oppression; however, unlike the largely delusional Antoinette who sets fire to Thornfield Hall, Tashi assassinates M'Lissa in a state of mental clarity.

Works Cited

Achebe, Chinua. "An Image of Africa." 1977. *Falling into Theory: Conflicting Views on Reading Literature.* 2nd ed. Ed. David H. Richter. Boston: Bedford, 2000. 323–33.

Adams, Michael Vannoy. *The Multicultural Imagination: "Race," Color, and the Unconscious.* London: Routledge, 1996.

Adell, Sandra. *Double-Consciousness/Double Bind: Theoretical Issues in Twentieth-Century Black Literature.* Urbana: University of Illinois Press, 1994.

Ammon, Henry. *James Monroe: The Quest for National Identity.* New York: McGraw, 1971.

Ammons, Elizabeth. Introduction. *Short Fiction by Black Women, 1900–1920.* Ed. Elizabeth Ammons. New York: Oxford University Press, 1991. 3–20.

Andrews, William L. "The Novelization of Voice in Early African American Literature." *PMLA* 105 (Jan. 1990): 23–34.

Appiah, Kwame Anthony. *In My Father's House: Africa in the Philosophy of Culture.* New York: Oxford University Press, 1992.

Ashcroft, Bill, Gareth Griffiths, and Helen Tiffin. *The Empire Writes Back: Theory and Practice in Post-colonial Literatures.* 2nd ed. New York: Routledge, 2002.

———. *Key Concepts in Post-colonial Studies.* New York: Routledge, 1998.

————, eds. *The Post-colonial Studies Reader.* New York: Routledge, 1995.

Babener, Liahna K. "Raymond Chandler's City of Lies." Fine 127–49.

Bailyn, Bernard. *To Begin the World Anew: The Genius and Ambiguities of the American Founders.* New York: Knopf, 2003.

Baker, Houston A. *Long Black Song: Essays in Black American Literature and Culture.* Charlottesville: University Press of Virginia, 1972.

Baucom, Ian. "The Survey of India." Sullivan 351–58.

Baym, Nina, et al., eds. *The Norton Anthology of American Literature.* Vol. 1. 4th ed. New York: Norton, 1998. 2 vols.

Bennett, Lerone, Jr. *Before the Mayflower: A History of Black America.* 1961. Chicago: Johnson, 1969.

Benston, Kimberly W. "'I Yam What I Yam: The Topos of Unnaming in Afro-American Literature." *Black Literature and Literary Theory.* Ed. Henry Louis Gates Jr. New York: Methuen, 1984. 151–72.

Bernier, Celeste-Marie. "'Arms Like Polished Iron': The Black Slave Body in the Narratives of a Slave Ship Revolt." *Slavery and Abolition* 23 (Aug. 2002): 91–106.

————. "A Comparative Exploration of Narrative Ambiguities in Frederick Douglass's Two Versions of *The Heroic Slave* (1853, 1863?)." *Slavery and Abolition* 22 (Aug. 2001): 64–86.

Bevington, David. Introduction. *Othello.* By William Shakespeare. New York: Bantam, 1988. xix–xxxi.

Bhabha, Homi K. "DissemiNation: Time, Narrative, and the Margins of the Modern Nation." *Nation and Narration.* Ed. Homi K. Bhabha. London: Routledge, 1990. 291–322.

————. *The Location of Culture.* London: Routledge, 1994

"Birthmark." *Compton's Interactive Encyclopedia.* 1998 ed.

Bjork, Patrick Bryce. *The Novels of Toni Morrison: The Search for Self and Place within the Community.* New York: Lang, 1992.

Bland, Eleanor Taylor. *Dead Time.* New York: St. Martin's, 1992.

————. *Done Wrong.* New York: St. Martin's 1995.

Boyle, Elizabeth Heger. *Female Genital Cutting: Cultured Conflict in the Global Community.* Baltimore: Johns Hopkins University Press, 2002.

Braithwaite, William Stanley. "Negro America's First Magazine." *Negro Digest* 6.2 (1947): 21–26.

Brontë, Charlotte. *Jane Eyre.* 1847. Ed. Beth Newman. Boston: Bedford, 1996.

Brown, William Wells. *Clotel; or, The President's Daughter.* 1853. New York: Macmillian, 1970.

————. "Madison Washington." *The Black Man, His Antecedents, His Genius, and His Achievements.* 1863. New York: Arno, 1969. 75–85.

————. *The Negro in the American Rebellion: His Heroism and His Fidelity.* Boston: Lee, 1867.

Bruce, Dickson D. "Booker T. Washington's *The Man Farthest Down* and the Transformation of Race." *Mississippi Quarterly* 48 (Spring 1995): 239–53.

Bruce, John E. *The Black Sleuth.* 1907–9. Ed. John Cullen Gruesser. Boston: Northeastern University Press, 2002.

Burger, John S. "An Introduction to Harry Dean Pan-Negro-Nationalist." M.A. Thesis. Roosevelt University, 1973.

Cameron, Sharon. *The Corporeal Self: Allegories of the Body in Melville and Hawthorne.* Baltimore: Johns Hopkins University Press, 1981.

Campbell, James T. *Songs of Zion: The African Methodist Episcopal Church in the United States and Africa.* New York: Oxford University Press, 1995.

Carby, Hazel. Introduction. *The Magazine Novels of Pauline Hopkins.* New York: Oxford University Press, 1988. xxix–l.

Cawelti, John G. *Adventure, Mystery, and Romance: Formula Stories as Art and Popular Culture.* Chicago: University of Chicago Press, 1976.

Chandler, Raymond. *The Big Sleep.* 1939. *The Raymond Chandler Omnibus.* New York: Modern Library, 1975. 1–139.

———. "Casual Notes on the Mystery Novel." *Raymond Chandler Speaking.* Ed. Dorothy Gardiner and Katherine Sorley Walker. Boston: Houghton, 1977. 63–70.

———. "Twelve Notes on the Mystery Story." 1977. *Hardboiled Mystery Writers: Raymond Chandler, Dashiell Hammett, Ross MacDonald.* Ed. Matthew J. Bruccoli and Richard Layman. Dictionary of Literary Biography Documentary Ser. Vol. 6. Detroit: Gale, 1989. 56–61.

Chesnutt, Charles. *The Marrow of Tradition.* 1901. Ann Arbor: University of Michigan Press, 1969.

Child, Lydia Maria. "Madison Washington." *The Freedmen's Book.* 1865. New York: Arno, 1968. 147–53.

Christian, Barbara. *Black Women Novelists: The Development of a Tradition, 1892–1976.* Westport, Conn.: Greenwood, 1990.

Coffin, Joshua. *An Account of Some of the Principal Slave Insurrections: And Others, which Have Occurred, or Been Attempted, in the United States and Elsewhere during the Last Two Centuries. With Various Remarks.* New York: American Anti-Slavery Society, 1860.

Conrad, Joseph. *Heart of Darkness.* 1899. 3rd ed. Ed. Robert Kimbrough. New York: Norton, 1987.

———. *An Outcast of the Islands.* 1896. *An Outcast of the Islands/Almayer's Folly.* London: Collins, 1955.

Cooke, Michael G. "Naming, Being, and Black Experience." *Yale Review* 67.2 (1978): 167–86.

Craven, Wesley Frank. *White, Red, and Black: The Seventeenth Century Virginian.* Charlottesville: University of Virginia Press, 1971.

Cudjoe, Selwyn R. *V. S. Naipaul: A Materialist Reading*. Amherst: University of Massachusetts Press, 1988.

Davidson, Arnold E. *Jean Rhys*. New York: Ungar, 1985.

Dawit, Seble, and Salem Mekuria. "The West Just Doesn't Get It." *New York Times* 7 Dec. 1993: A 27.

Dean, Harry. "Biography [of Dean]." Harry Dean Collection. DuSable Museum of African American History, Chicago.

———. "Liberian Development Possibilities." *San Francisco Chronicle* 8 July 1923.

———. *The Pedro Gorino: The Adventures of a Negro Sea-Captain in Africa and on the Seven Seas in His Attempts to Found an Ethiopian Empire*. Boston: Houghton, 1929.

———. "Ship Deal Discrimination Charge." *San Francisco Chronicle* 8 Dec. 1923.

———. *Umbala: The Adventures of a Negro Sea Captain in Africa and on the Seven Seas in His Attempts to Found an Ethiopian Empire*. 1929. London: Pluto, 1989.

Dixon, Melvin. *Ride Out the Wilderness: Geography and Identity in Afro-American Literature*. Urbana: University of Illinois Press, 1987.

Douglass, Frederick. *The Frederick Douglass Papers. Series One: Speeches, Debates, and Interviews*. 5 vols. Ed. John W. Blassingame, et al. New Haven, Conn.: Yale University Press, 1979–92.

———. "The Heroic Slave." *The Life and Writings of Frederick Douglass*. Vol. 5. Ed. Philip S. Foner. New York: International, 1950–75. 5 vols. 473–505.

———. *My Bondage and My Freedom*. 1855. New York: Dover, 1969.

Drake, St. Clair. *The Redemption of Africa and Black Religion*. Chicago: Third World, 1970.

Du Bois, W. E. B. "American Negroes and Africa's Rise to Freedom." 1961. *The World and Africa*. Millwood, N.Y.: Kraus-Thomson, 1976. 334–38.

———. "The Colored Magazine in America." *Crisis* Nov. 1912: 33–35.

———. "The Conservation of Races." 1897. *The Oxford W. E. B. Du Bois Reader*. Ed. Eric J. Sundquist. New York: Oxford University Press, 1996. 38–47.

———. *Darkwater*. 1920. *The Oxford W. E. B. Du Bois Reader*. Ed. Eric J. Sundquist. New York: Oxford University Press, 1996. 481–623.

———. "The Negro in Literature." *Crisis* Nov. 1929: 376.

———. "The Present Outlook for the Dark Races of Mankind." 1900. *The Oxford W. E. B. Du Bois Reader*. Ed. Eric J. Sundquist. New York: Oxford University Press, 1996. 47–54.

duCille, Ann. "Postcolonialism and Afrocentricity: Discourse and Dat Course." *The Black Columbiad: Defining Moments in African American Literature and Culture*. Ed. Werner Sollors and Maria Diedrich. Cambridge, Mass.: Harvard University Press, 1994. 28–41.

"Editorial and Publisher's Announcements." *Colored American Magazine* 6 (May/June 1903): 466–67.

Ellison, Ralph. "The Birthmark." *New Masses* 2 July 1940: 16–17.

———. "Hidden Name and Complex Fate." *Shadow and Act.* New York: Signet, 1966. 148–68.

Ellroy, James. *The Black Dahlia.* New York: Mysterious, 1987.

Farrison, William. *William Wells Brown: Author and Reformer.* Chicago: University of Chicago Press, 1969.

Faulkner, William. *The Sound and the Fury.* 1929. 2nd ed. Ed. David Minter. New York: Norton, 1994.

Fine, David, ed. *Los Angeles in Fiction: A Collection of Essays.* Rev. ed. Albuquerque: University of New Mexico Press, 1995.

Fisher, Rudolph. *The Conjure-Man Dies.* 1932. New York: Arno, 1971.

———. "Ezekiel." 1932. *The City of Refuge: The Collected Stories of Rudolph Fisher.* Ed. John McCluskey Jr. Columbia: University of Missouri Press, 1987. 40–43.

———. "Ezekiel Learns." 1933. *The City of Refuge: The Collected Stories of Rudolph Fisher.* Ed. John McCluskey Jr. Columbia: University of Missouri Press, 1987. 44–47.

———. "John Archer's Nose." 1935. *The City of Refuge: The Collected Stories of Rudolph Fisher.* Ed. John McCluskey Jr. Columbia: University of Missouri Press, 1987. 158–94.

Frederickson, George M. *Black Liberation: A Comparative History of Black Ideologies in the United States and South Africa.* New York: Oxford University Press, 1995.

Fromkin, David. "The Great Game in Asia." *Foreign Affairs* 58.4 (Spring 1980): 936–51.

Garnet, Henry Highland. "An Address to the Slaves of the United States." 1848. *Walker's Appeal in Four Articles and an Address to the Slaves of the United States.* By David Walker and Garnet. New York: Arno, 1969.

Garvey, Marcus. "African Fundamentalism." 1924. *African Fundamentalism: A Literary and Cultural Anthology of Garvey's Harlem Renaissance.* Ed. Tony Martin. Dover: Majority, 1991. 4–6.

Gates, Henry Louis, Jr. "Canon-Formation, Literary History, and the Afro-American Tradition: From the Seen to the Told." *Falling into Theory: Conflicting Views on Reading Literature.* Ed. David H. Richter. Boston: Bedford, 1994. 172–80.

———. *Figures in Black: Words, Signs, and the "Racial" Self.* 1987. New York: Oxford University Press, 1989.

———. *The Signifying Monkey: A Theory of Afro-American Literary Criticism.* New York: Oxford University Press, 1988.

———, ed. *"Race," Writing, and Difference.* Spec. issue of *Critical Inquiry* 12.1 (1985): 1–299.

Gates, Henry Louis, Jr., and Nellie Y. McKay, eds. *The Norton Anthology of African American Literature.* New York: Norton, 1997.

Gayle, Addison. *The Way of the New World: The Black Novel in America.* Garden City, N.Y.: Anchor, 1975.

Giddings, Paula. "Alice Walker's Appeal." *Essence* July 1992: 59–62, 102.

Gilroy, Paul. *The Black Atlantic: Modernity and Double Consciousness.* Cambridge, Mass.: Harvard University Press, 1993.

———. "Cultural Studies and Ethnic Absolutism." *Cultural Studies.* Ed. Lawrence Grossberg, Cary Nelson, and Paula A. Treichler. New York: Routledge, 1992. 187–98.

———. "A Dialogue with Bell Hooks." *Small Acts* 208–36.

———. "It Ain't Where You're from, It's Where You're At." *Small Acts* 120–45.

———. "Route Work: The Black Atlantic and the Politics of Exile." *The Post-Colonial Question: Common Skies, Divided Horizons.* Ed. Iain Chambers and Lidia Curti. New York: Routledge, 1996. 17–29.

———. *Small Acts: Thoughts on the Politics of Black Culture.* New York: Serpent's Tail, 1993.

Gray, Thomas R., ed. "The Confessions of Nat Turner." 1831. *The Return of Nat Turner: History, Literature, and Cultural Politics in Sixties America.* By Albert E. Stone. Athens: University of Georgia Press, 1992. 407–29.

Greenblatt, Stephen. "Learning to Curse: Aspects of Linguistic Colonialism in the Sixteenth Century." *Learning to Curse: Essays in Early Modern Culture.* New York: Routledge, 1990. 16–39.

Greene, Graham. *The Heart of the Matter.* 1948. New York: Penguin, 1978.

Griggs, Sutton E. *Unfettered.* 1902. New York: AMS, 1971.

Gruesser, John Cullen. *Black on Black: Twentieth-Century African American Writing about Africa.* Lexington: University Press of Kentucky, 2000.

———. "Ligeia and Orientalism." *Studies in Short Fiction* 26.2 (Spring 1989): 145–49.

———. *White on Black: Contemporary Literature about Africa.* Urbana: University of Illinois Press, 1992.

Gunning, Sandra. "Reading and Redemption in *Incidents in the Life of a Slave Girl.*" *Harriet Jacobs and Incidents in the Life of a Slave Girl: New Critical Essays.* Ed. Deborah M. Garfield and Rafia Zafar. New York: Cambridge University Press, 1996. 131–155.

Hansberry, Lorraine. *Les Blancs.* 1973. *The Collected Last Plays.* Ed. Robert Nemiroff. New York: NAL, 1983.

Harding, Wendy, and Jacky Martin. *A World of Difference: An Inter-Cultural Study of Toni Morrison's Novels.* Westport, Conn.: Greenwood, 1994.

Harper, Frances E. W. *Iola Leroy, or, Shadows Uplifted.* Philadelphia: Garrigues, 1892.

Harris, Sheldon H. *Paul Cuffe: Black Americans and the African Return.* New York: Simon, 1972.

Hawthorne, Nathaniel. "The Birth-mark." *Mosses* 36–56.

———. "Chiefly about War Matters." 1862. *Tales, Sketches, and Other Papers. The Complete Works of Nathaniel Hawthorne.* Vol. 12. Boston: Houghton, 1887. 299–345.

———. "Egotism; or, The Bosom-Serpent." *Mosses* 268–83.

———. *The Life of Franklin Pierce.* Boston: Ticknor, 1852.

———. "The Minister's Black Veil." Baym 1252–61.

———. *Mosses from an Old Manse. The Centenary Edition of the Works of Nathaniel Hawthorne.* Vol. 10. Columbus: Ohio State University Press, 1974.

———. "The Old Manse." *Mosses* 3–35.

———. *The Scarlet Letter.* Baym 1306–1447.

Hayford, J. E. Casely. *Ethiopia Unbound: Studies in Race Emancipation.* 1911. London: Cass, 1969.

Haywood, Gar Anthony. *Fear of the Dark.* New York: St. Martin's, 1988.

Himes, Chester. *A Rage in Harlem.* 1957. New York: Vintage, 1989.

Hopkins, Pauline. *Contending Forces: A Romance Illustrative of Negro Life North and South.* 1900. New York: Oxford University Press, 1988.

———. "A Dash for Liberty." *Colored American Magazine* Aug. 1901: 243–47. Rpt. in *Short Fiction by Black Women, 1900–1920.* Ed. Elizabeth Ammons. New York: Oxford University Press, 1991. 89–98.

———. *Hagar's Daughter: A Story of Southern Caste Prejudice.* 1901–2. *The Magazine Novels of Pauline Hopkins.* New York: Oxford University Press, 1988. 1–284.

———. *Of One Blood; Or, the Hidden Self. The Magazine Novels of Pauline Hopkins.* New York: Oxford University Press, 1988. 439–621.

———. *A Primer of Facts Pertaining to the Early Greatness of the African Race and the Possibility of Restoration by Its Descendants—with Epilogue.* Cambridge, Mass.: P. E. Hopkins, 1905.

———. "Talma Gordon." 1900. *Spooks, Spies, and Private Eyes: Black Mystery, Crime, and Suspense Fiction.* Ed. Paula L. Woods. New York: Doubleday, 1995. 3–18.

Hughes, Langston. *The Big Sea.* 1940. New York: Hill, 1963.

———. "The Twenties: Harlem and Its Negritude." *Langston Hughes Review* 4 (Spring 1985): 29–36.

Hulme, Peter. "The Locked Heart: The Creole Family Romance in *Wide Sargasso Sea.*" *Colonial Discourse/Postcolonial Theory.* Ed. Francis Barker, Peter Hulme, and Margaret Iverson. Manchester, U.K.: Manchester University Press, 1994. 72–88.

Jacobs, Harriet. *Incidents in the Life of a Slave Girl.* 1861. *The Classic Slave Narratives.* Ed. Henry Louis Gates Jr. New York: NAL, 2002. 437–668.

James, Stanlie M. "Shades of Othering: Reflections on Female Circumcision/Genital Mutilation." *Signs: Journal of Women in Culture and Society* 23 (Summer 1998): 1031–48.

Jervey, Edward D., and C. Harold Huber. "The *Creole* Affair." *Journal of Negro History* 65.3 (1980): 196–211.

Johnson, Abby Arthur, and Ronald Maberry Johnson. *Propaganda and Aesthetics: The Literary Politics of Afro-American Magazines in the Twentieth Century.* Amherst: University of Massachusetts Press, 1979.

Johnson, Charles S. "The Rise of the Negro Magazine." *Journal of Negro History* 13 (Jan. 1928): 7–21.

Johnson, Clinton H. "The *Creole* Affair." *Crisis* Oct. 1971: 248–50.

Jones, Howard. "The Peculiar Institution and National Honor: The Case of the *Creole* Slave Revolt." *Civil War History* 21 (Mar. 1975): 28–50.

Jung, Carl. *Analytical Psychology: Its Theory and Practice.* New York: Pantheon, 1968.

———. "The Complications of American Psychology." *Civilization in Transition. The Collected Works of C. G. Jung.* Vol. 10. Ed. Sir Herbert Read, Michael Fordham, and Gerhard Adler. New York: Pantheon, 1964. 21 vols. 502–14.

———. *Memories, Dreams, Reflections.* Trans. Richard and Clara Winston. Ed. Aniela Jaffe. New York: Pantheon, 1963.

———. "On the Psychology of the Negro." *The Symbolic Life: Miscellaneous Writings. The Collected Works of C. G. Jung.* Vol. 18. Trans. R. F. C. Hull. Ed. Sir Herbert Read, Michael Fordham, and Gerhard Adler. Princeton, N.J.: Princeton University Press, 1976. 21 vols. 552.

———. "The Tavistock Lectures: Lecture II." *The Symbolic Life: Miscellaneous Writings. The Collected Works of C. G. Jung.* Vol. 18. Trans. R. F. C. Hull. Ed. Sir Herbert Read, Michael Fordham, and Gerhard Adler. Princeton, N.J.: Princeton University Press, 1976. 21 vols. 36–56.

Kelly, Philippa. "'The Cannibals That Eat Each Other': *Othello* and Postcolonial Appropriation." *SPAN: Journal of the South Pacific Association for Commonwealth Literature and Language Studies* 36 (1993): 1–7. <http://wwwmcc.murdoch.edu.au/ReadingRoom/listserv/SPAN/36/Kelly.html>.

Kennedy, J. Gerald, and Liliane Weissberg, eds. *Romancing the Shadow: Poe and Race.* New York: Oxford University Press, 2001.

King, C. Richard, ed. *Postcolonial America.* Urbana: University of Illinois Press, 2000.

Kipling, Rudyard. "The Ballad of East and West." *Ballads and Barrack-Room Ballads.* New ed. New York: Macmillan, 1898. 3–11.

———. *Kim.* 1901. Sullivan 3–240.

———. "The White Man's Burden." 1899. Sullivan 260–61.

Kling, Blair B. "*Kim* in Historical Context." Sullivan 297–309.

Komo, Dolores. *Clio Browne: Private Investigator.* Freedom, Calif.: Crossing, 1988.

Lawrence, D. H. *Studies in Classic American Literature.* 1923. New York: Penguin, 1972.

"Madison Washington." *National Anti-Slavery Standard.* 28 Apr. 1842.

"Madison Washington: Another Chapter in His History." *Liberator* 10 June 1842: 1.

Madsen, Deborah L. *Post-Colonial Literatures: Expanding the Canon.* London: Pluto, 1999.

Mannoni, Octave. *Prospero and Caliban.* New York: Praeger, 1956.

Marrouchi, Mustapha. *Signifying with a Vengeance: Theories, Literatures, Storytellers.* Albany: SUNY Press, 2002.

McClintock, Anne. "The Angel of Progress: Pitfalls of the Term Post-colonialism." Williams and Chrisman 291–304.

McKay, Nellie Y., and Frances Smith Foster, eds. *Incidents in the Life of a Slave Girl.* By Harriet Jacobs. New York: Norton, 2001.

McLeod, John. *Beginning Postcolonialism.* Manchester, U.K.: Manchester University Press, 2000.

McMillen, Liz. "A Slave Girl's Authentic Life." *Chronicle of Higher Education* 8 Dec. 1993: A 9, A 15.

Meier, August. "Booker T. Washington and the Negro Press with Special Reference to the *Colored American Magazine.*" *Journal of Negro History* 38 (Jan. 1953): 67–90.

Melville, Herman. *Moby-Dick: or, The Whale.* 1851. New York: NAL, 1980.

Miller, Christopher L. *Blank Darkness: Africanist Discourse in French.* Chicago: University of Chicago Press, 1985.

Mishra, Vijay, and Bob Hodge. "What Is Post(-)colonialism?" Williams and Chrisman 276–90.

Morrison, Toni. "Black Matter(s)." *Falling into Theory: Conflicting Views on Reading Literature.* 2nd ed. Ed. David H. Richter. Boston: Bedford, 2000. 310–22.

———. *Playing in the Dark: Whiteness and the Literary Imagination.* New York: Vintage, 1993.

———. *Sula.* New York: Knopf, 1973.

———. "This Amazing, Troubling Book." *Adventures of Huckleberry Finn.* By Mark Twain. 3rd ed. Ed. Thomas Cooley. New York: Norton, 1999. 385–92.

———. "Unspeakable Things Unspoken: The Afro-American Presence in American Literature." 1989. *Toni Morrison: Modern Critical Views.* Ed. Harold Bloom. New York: Chelsea, 1990. 201–30.

Moses, Wilson J. *The Golden Age of Black Nationalism, 1850–1925.* 1978. New York: Oxford University Press, 1988.

Mosley, Walter. *Bad Boy Brawly Brown.* Boston: Little, 2002.

———. *Black Betty.* New York: Norton, 1994.

———. *Devil in a Blue Dress.* 1990. New York: Pocket, 1991.

———. *Gone Fishin'.* New York: Pocket, 1998.

———. *Little Scarlet.* New York: Little, 2004.

———. *A Little Yellow Dog.* New York: Norton, 1996.

———. *A Red Death.* 1991. New York: Pocket, 1992.

———. *Six Easy Pieces.* New York: Atria, 2003.

———. *White Butterfly.* New York: Norton, 1992.

Mostern, Keith. "Postcolonialism after W. E. B. Du Bois." Singh and Schmidt 259–76.

Muller, Gilbert H. "Double Agent: The Los Angeles Crime Cycle of Walter Mosley." Fine 287–301.

Mustafa, Fawzia. *V. S. Naipaul.* New York: Cambridge, 1995.

Naipaul, V. S. *A Bend in the River.* New York: Vintage, 1980.

————. *A Congo Diary.* Los Angeles: Sylvester, 1980.

————. "Conrad's Darkness." 1974. *The Return of Eva Peron with the Killings in Trinidad.* New York: Vintage, 1981. 221–45.

————. "A New King for the Congo: Mobutu and the Nihilism of Africa." 1975. *The Return of Eva Peron with the Killings in Trinidad.* New York: Vintage, 1981. 183–219.

Neely, Barbara. *Blanche on the Lam.* New York: Penguin, 1993.

Nixon, Rob. *London Calling: V. S. Naipaul, Postcolonial Mandarin.* New York: Oxford University Press, 1992.

North, Sterling. Letter to Dr. Robert I. Rotberg. 5 June 1965. Harry Dean Collection. DuSable Museum of African American History, Chicago.

————. Preface. Dean, *The Pedro Gorino* vii–xiv.

Oakland, Berkeley, Alameda City Directory. Oakland: Post-Husted, 1924.

Parry, Ann. "Recovering the Connection Between *Kim* and Contemporary History." Sullivan 309–20.

Parry, Benita. "Two Native Voices in *Wide Sargasso Sea.*" Rhys 247–50.

"Pauline E. Hopkins." *Colored American Magazine* Jan. 1901: 218–19.

Phillips, Gary. *Violent Spring.* 1994. New York: Berkley, 1997.

Plasa, Carl. *Textual Politics from Slavery to Postcolonialism: Race and Identification.* New York: Macmillan, 2000.

Posner, Richard. *Public Intellectuals: A Study in Decline.* Cambridge, Mass.: Harvard University Press, 2002.

Prescott, Lynda. "Past and Present Darkness: Sources for V. S. Naipaul's *A Bend in the River.*" *Modern Fiction Studies* 30 (Autumn 1984): 547–59.

Reed, Ishmael. *Mumbo Jumbo.* 1972. New York: Atheneum, 1988.

Rhys, Jean. *Wide Sargasso Sea.* 1966. Ed. Judith L. Raiskin. New York: Norton, 1999.

Rody, Caroline. "Burning Down the House: The Revisionary Paradigm of Jean Rhys's *Wide Sargasso Sea.*" Rhys 217–25.

Rothstein, Edward. "Kipling Knew What the U.S. May Now Learn." *New York Times* 26 Jan. 2002: B 7, B 9.

Rowland, Susan. *Jung: A Feminist Revision.* Malden, Mass.: Blackwell, 2002.

Rushdie, Salman. "America and Anti-Americans." *New York Times* 4 Feb. 2002: A23. Rpt. as "February 2002." *Step across This Line: Collected Nonfiction 1992–2002.* New York: Random, 2002. 341–44.

————. "The Assassination of Indira Gandhi." 1984. *Imaginary Homelands* 41–46.

————. "Chekov and Zulu." *East, West.* New York: Pantheon, 1994. 147–71.

————. "'Commonwealth Literature' Does Not Exist." 1983. *Imaginary Homelands* 61–70.

————. "Dynasty." 1985. *Imaginary Homelands* 47–52.

————. *East, West: Stories.* New York: Pantheon, 1994.

————. "The Empire Writes Back with a Vengeance." [London] *Times* 3 July 1982: 8.

————. *Imaginary Homelands: Essays and Criticism 1981–1991.* New York: Viking, 1991.

————. "Kipling." 1990. *Imaginary Homelands* 74–80.

————. *Midnight's Children.* 1980. New York: Penguin, 1995.

Said, Edward. *Culture and Imperialism.* New York: Vintage, 1994.

————. *Orientalism.* New York: Vintage, 1979.

Schuyler, George. *Black No More: Being an Account of the Strange and Wonderful Workings of Science in the Land of the Free, A.D. 1933–1940.* 1931. College Park, Md.: McGrath, 1969.

————. *The Ethiopian Murder Mystery: A Story of Love and International Intrigue.* 1935–36. *Ethiopian Stories.* Ed. Robert A. Hill. Boston: Northeastern University Press, 1994. 51–122.

Senghor, Leopold. "Negritude: A Humanism of the Twentieth Century." Williams and Chrisman 27–35.

Shakespeare, William. *Othello.* Ed. David Bevington. New York: Bantam, 1988.

Sharpe, Jenny. "Is the United States Postcolonial? Transnationalism, Immigration, and Race." King 103–21.

Shepperson, George. Introduction. *Umbala.* By Harry Dean. vii–xxiii.

Sherwood, Henry Noble. "Paul Cuffe." *Journal of Negro History* 8 (Apr. 1923): 153–229.

Singh, Amritjit, and Peter Schmidt, eds. *Postcolonial Theory and the United States: Race, Ethnicity, and Literature.* Jackson: University of Mississippi Press, 2000.

Sobel, Mechal. *Trabelin' On: The Slave Journey to an Afro-Baptist Faith.* 1979. Princeton, N.J.: Princeton University Press, 1988.

Sollors, Werner. *Neither Black nor White yet Both: Thematic Explorations of Interracial Literature.* Cambridge, Mass.: Harvard University Press, 1999.

Spivak, Gayatri Chakravorty. "Three Women's Texts and a Critique of Imperialism." *"Race," Writing, and Difference.* Ed. Henry Louis Gates Jr. Chicago: University of Chicago Press, 1986. 262–80.

Stepto, Robert. "Storytelling in Early Afro-American Fiction: Frederick Douglass's 'The Heroic Slave.'" *Georgia Review* 36 (1982): 355–68.

"The Story of Paul Cuffee." *New Bedford Sunday Standard* 5 Jan. 1930.

Stuckey, Sterling. *Slave Culture: Nationalist Theory and the Foundations of Black America.* New York: Oxford University Press, 1987.

Sullivan, Zohreh, ed. *Kim.* By Rudyard Kipling. New York: Norton, 2002.

Sundquist, Eric J. *To Wake the Nations: Race in the Making of American Literature.* Cambridge, Mass.: Harvard University Press, 1993.

Tate, Claudia. *Domestic Allegories of Political Desire: The Black Heroine's Text at the Turn of the Century.* New York: Oxford University Press, 1992.

Thomas, Lamont D. *Paul Cuffe: Black Entrepreneur and Pan-Africanist.* 1986. Urbana: University of Illinois Press, 1988.

Tiffin, Helen. "Post-colonial Literatures and Counter-discourse." Ashcroft, Griffiths, and Tiffin, eds. 95–98.

Tolson, Melvin B. *Libretto for the Republic of Liberia.* New York: Twayne, 1953.

"Uncle John's Burying Place." Paul Cuffe Manuscript Collection. New Bedford Free Public Library, New Bedford, Massachusetts.

United States Senate. *Senate Documents.* 27th Cong., 2nd Sess., No. 51. 1841–42. 1–46.

Walker, Alice. *The Color Purple.* New York: Washington Square, 1983.

———. "In Search of Our Mothers' Gardens." 1974. *"Everyday Use."* Ed. Barbara T. Christian. New Brunswick, N.J.: Rutgers University Press, 1994. 39–49.

———. "The Light That Shines on Me." Walker and Parmar 20–26.

———. "Like the Pupil of an Eye: Genital Mutilation and the Sexual Blinding of Women." Walker and Parmar 15–19.

———. "Looking for Jung: Writing *Possessing the Secret of Joy." Anything We Love Can Be Saved: A Writer's Activism.* New York: Random, 1996. 122–26.

———. "The Only Reason You Want to Go to Heaven Is That You Have Been Driven out of Your Mind (off Your Land and out of Your Lover's Arms): Clear Seeing Inherited Religion and Reclaiming the Pagan Self." *Anything We Love Can Be Saved: A Writer's Activism.* New York: Random, 1996. 3–27.

———. *Possessing the Secret of Joy.* New York: Pocket, 1993.

Walker, Alice, and Pratibha Parmar. *Warrior Marks: Female Genital Mutilation and the Sexual Blinding of Women.* New York: Harcourt, 1993.

Ward, Theodore. "Madison." Hatch-Billops Archives, New York.

Washington, Booker T., and Robert E. Park. *The Man Farthest Down: A Record of Observation and Study in Europe.* 1912. New Brunswick, N.J.: Transaction, 1984.

Washington, Mary Helen. *Invented Lives: Narratives of Black Women, 1860–1960.* Garden City, N.Y.: Anchor, 1987.

Watt, Ian. *Conrad in the Nineteenth Century.* Berkeley: University of California Press, 1979.

Wesley, Valerie Wilson. *When Death Comes Stealing.* New York: Avon, 1995.

Wiegman, Robyn. "The Anatomy of Lynching." *Journal of the History of Sexuality* 3.3 (1993): 445–67.

Williams, Patrick, and Laura Chrisman, eds. *Colonial Discourse and Post-colonial Theory: A Reader.* New York: Columbia University Press, 1994.

Wilmore, Gayraud S. *Black Religion and Black Radicalism: An Interpretation of the Religious History of Afro-American People.* 2nd ed. Maryknoll, N.Y.: Orbis, 1984.

Yapp, M. E. "The Legend of the Great Game." *The British Academy Review.* "Lectures and Conferences." Jan.–July 2000. <http://www.britac.ac.uk/news/review/03-00a/10-yapp.html>.

Yarborough, Richard. "Race, Violence, and Manhood: The Masculine Ideal in Frederick Douglass's 'The Heroic Slave.'" *Frederick Douglass: New Literary and Historical Essays.* Ed. Eric J. Sundquist. New York: Cambridge University Press, 1990. 166–88.

Yellin, Jean Fagan. *Harriet Jacobs: A Life*. New York: Basic, 2004.

———. Introduction. *Incidents in the Life of a Slave Girl*. By Harriet Jacobs. 1861. Ed. Jean Fagan Yellin. Cambridge, Mass.: Harvard University Press, 1987. xiii–xxxiv.

———. "Written by Herself: Harriet Jacobs' Slave Narrative." *American Literature* 53 (Nov. 1981): 479–86.

Index

African American literary theory (*cont.*) theory, 2–3. *See also* counter-discourse; postcolonialism; Signifyin(g)

African American literature: birthmarks in, 93–95, 146–47 (n. 41); challenges white historical record, 72–73, 99; Ethiopianism in, 100; relationship of, to white literary theory, 12–13

African Personality movement, 10, 136 (n. 10)

Africans: in detective fiction, 59–60; portrayed as primitive in *A Bend in the River*, 46. *See also* African American detectives in fiction

African Saga (Ricciardi), 123

Afrocentrism: essentialism of, 12, 17; impact of Ethiopianism on, 100; marginalization of, in academy, 4

AIDS, 124, 126–27

American Africanism, 87–88

American Colonization Society, 78. *See also* back-to-Africa movement

"American Negroes and Africa's Rise to Freedom" (Du Bois), 131

Ammons, Elizabeth, 77

Analytical Psychology (Jung), 118

Anderson, Benedict, 4

Andrews, William, 75, 79

"Angel of Progress, The" (McClintock), 23

Angelou, Maya, 98

Anglo-American Claims Commission, 74

anti-Negro propaganda, and Signifyin(g), 15

Ashcroft, Bill, 6–10, 25

Ashcroft, Bill, works of (with Griffiths and Tiffin): *The Empire Writes Back*, 6–10, 12, 14; *Key Concepts in Post-colonial Studies*, 6; *The Post-colonial Studies Reader*, 6–7, 9

autobiography, 99–101, 116, 128

Babener, Liahna, 61

back-to-Africa movement, 79, 102–3; and American Colonization Society, 78; and Crummell, 99, 103; and Garvey, 100; and Liberia, 74, 78–79, 103, 149 (n. 10); and Sierra Leone, 17, 101–2; and Turner, 99

Bad Boy Brawly Brown (Mosley), 60

Baker, Houston, 10, 12–14, 133; *Long Black Song*, 13–14

Baldwin, James, 9, 14

Baucom, Ian, 27

Behn, Aphra, 15

Bend in the River, A (Naipaul), 20, 24–25, 45–53

Benjamin, Walter, 4

Bennett, Gwendolyn, 98

Bernier, Celeste-Marie, 73

Bhabha, Homi, 6–7; definition of postcolonialism by, 4, 131–33

Bhabha, Homi, works of: "DissemiNation," 4; *The Location of Culture*, 3–4

Big Sea, The (Hughes), 99

Big Sleep, The (Chandler), 61

"Birth-mark, The" (Hawthorne), 21, 57–58, 87–93, 146 (nn. 36, 38)

birthmarks: in African American literature, 93, 147 (n. 44); associated with African royalty, 93, 146–47 (n. 41); associated with witchcraft, 92; as code for race, 92–93

Black Aesthetic, 12, 14, 137 (n. 13). *See also* Black Arts movement

Black Arts movement: essentialism of, 12; impact of Ethiopianism on, 100; impact of Marxism on, 13; impact of structuralism on, 10. *See also* Black Aesthetic

black Atlantic: and cross-cultural interactions, 16–17, 20, 57, 97; and double-consciousness, 106; and maritime travel, 18–19, 96; and postcolonial theory, 4–5, 20; Walker's work questions Gilroy's model of, 115, 123, 129, 133. *See also* diaspora; Gilroy, Paul

Black Atlantic, The (Gilroy), 4, 17–19, 96–98, 133

Black Betty (Mosley), 60, 67

Black Boy (Wright), 16

black Britons, 17, 97

Black Judaism, 100

Black Man, The (W. W. Brown), 80

"Black Man's Burden, The" (Fortune), 56

black missionaries to Africa, 96, 100, 116, 124–25

Black No More (Schuyler), 94

Black Sleuth, The (Bruce), 59

black West Indians: in black Atlantic network, 97; as colonized peoples, 57; displacement of, 20; literature of, 97

Blyden, Edward, 97

Boer War, 104

Britain: abolition in colonies of, 86; Gilroy's emphasis on, in *The Black Atlantic*, 97; Jacobs travels to, 111–13; and postcolonial theory, 9; religious freedom of, 112; views of slavery in, 74

Brontë, Charlotte, 12, 20, 32; *Jane Eyre*, 12, 20, 24, 31–32, 36

Brooks, Gwendolyn, 98

Brown, Charles Brockden, 8

Brown, William Wells, 73–76, 79–80, 84–85, 143–44 (n. 20)

Brown, William Wells, works of: *The Black Man*, 80; "Madison Washington," 73, 76; "Slave Revolt at Sea," 73, 76

Bruce, John Edward, 58, 136 (n. 10); *The Black Sleuth*, 59

Burger, John S., 100–101

Carby, Hazel, 77

center-periphery theory, 7. *See also* metropolitan center

Césaire, Aimé, 10

Chandler, Raymond, 57, 60–61, 69; *The Big Sleep*, 61

Channing, Ellery, 88

"Chekov and Zulu" (Rushdie), 20, 24–26, 28, 30

Chesnutt, Charles, 93

Child, Lydia Maria, 73–76, 79, 84, 143–44 (n. 20)

Child, Lydia Maria, works of: *Freedmen's Book*, 76, 144 (n. 21); "Madison Washington," 73, 76

Chrisman, Laura, 6

Coetzee, J. M., 12

Coffin, Joshua, 75

Coleridge, Samuel Taylor, 101

Colonial Discourse and Post-colonial Theory (Williams and Chrisman), 6

colonization: of African Americans, 10; of black West Indians, 57; Jung's views on, 119; in *Wide Sargasso Sea*, 37, 41–44

Colored American Magazine, 77–79, 84, 144 (n. 23), 145 (n. 27), 149 (n. 10)

Color Purple, The (Walker), 16, 56, 116, 120, 124–25

"'Commonwealth Literature' Does Not Exist" (Rushdie), 131

Commonwealth studies, 5

"Complications of American Psychology, The" (Jung), 118

"Confessions of Nat Turner, The" (Gray), 93

Congress Party (India), 26, 28–31

Conjure-Man Dies, The (Fisher), 59

Conrad, Joseph, 47; *An Outcast of the Islands*, 106. See also *Heart of Darkness* (Conrad)

"Conrad's Darkness" (Naipaul), 45

"Conservation of Races, The" (Du Bois), 130

Contending Forces (Hopkins), 72, 77, 79, 84

Cooke, Michael G., 78

Cooper, Anna Julia, 98

counter-discourse: and African American writing, 12, 19; in *The Black Atlantic*, 96; and modernity, 18; in *Possessing the Secret of Joy*, 128; and postcolonialism, 11–12; and racial dynamics in texts, 24; reservations about, 44; as response to metropolitan center, 11; in *Wide Sargasso Sea*, 20, 43. *See also* Signifyin(g)

Creole rebellion: Hopkins signifies on white historical record about, 21, 57; and need for black community action, 73; and sexual vulnerability of women in slavery, 81; and Washington, Madison, 73–81; writing about, 80–86, 142–43 (n. 15)

creoles, in *Wide Sargasso Sea*, 33–34, 39, 43. *See also* "Dash for Liberty, A" (Hopkins)

creolization, 7, 19–20

Crummell, Alexander, 99, 103. *See also* back-to-Africa movement; Ethiopianism

Cuffe, John, 102, 150 (n. 14)

Cuffe, Paul, 100–103, 149 (n. 11), 150 (n. 14)

Cuffee, John, 101–2

"Cultural Studies and Ethnic Absolutism" (Gilroy), 4, 19

Culture and Imperialism (Said), 32, 87

Dark Princess (Du Bois), 97

Darkwater (Du Bois), 101

"Dash for Liberty, A," (Hopkins), 21, 57, 72–73, 77–82, 86

Dean, Harry Foster: African American exceptionalism of, 105; connection of, to postcoloniality, 132; counter-discourse of, 99; desire of, to undermine imperialism, 104, 106; Pan-Africanism of, 102; *The Pedro Gorino*, 98–107; plans of, for rehabilitation of black race, 102–4; veracity of, questioned, 101

Defoe, Daniel, 12

Delany, Martin, 97, 133

Derrida, Jacques, 3–4, 57

Devil in a Blue Dress (Mosley), 21, 57–58, 62, 68, 71–72

diaspora, 9–10, 13, 17–20. *See also* black Atlantic; Pan-Africanism

discourse analysis, 10

disenfranchisement of African Americans, 72, 77, 84, 86

displacement, 3, 7, 18, 20, 42

"DissemiNation" (Bhabha), 4

doll symbolism, in *Possessing the Secret of Joy*, 120–21

double-consciousness, 8, 19, 106; and twoness, 17

Douglass, Frederick: in *The Black Atlantic*, 97, 133; counter-discourse of, 98–99; as fugitive slave in England, 151 (n. 24); "The Heroic Slave," 73, 75–76, 79, 85, 143 (n. 20); and the *Liberator*, 74–75, 143 (n. 17); speaks of Washington, Madison, 75, 143 (n. 17)

Du Bois, W. E. B.: in *The Black Atlantic*, 97; and concept of twoness, 17; diasporic perspective of, 19, 97; opposes ideas of Washington, Booker T., 79; and postcolonialism, 4, 132–33; recalls meeting Dean, 101; rejects African American exceptionalism, 19, 130

Du Bois, W. E. B, works of: "American Negroes and Africa's Rise to Freedom," 131; "The Conservation of Races," 130; *Dark Princess*, 97; *Darkwater*, 101; "The

Present Outlook for the Dark Races of Mankind," 130–31; *The Souls of Black Folk*, 19, 136 (n. 5)

duCille, Ann, 4

Dunbar, Paul Laurence, 16

East, West (Rushdie), 25. *See also* "Chekov and Zulu" (Rushdie)

Eliot, T. S., 8, 14, 16

Ellison, Ralph: discusses signifying, 12; *Invisible Man*, 14, 16; Reed signifies on, 15; and use of birthmark, 93–94

Emerson, Ralph Waldo, 88, 92

Empire Writes Back, The (Ashcroft, Griffiths, and Tiffin), 6–10, 12, 14; excludes African American writing from postcolonialism, 8; rejects "Black writing" model, 9

English language: Gilroy's privileging of, in *The Black Atlantic*, 97; use of, by marginalized authors, 9, 15, 62–63; use of, by settlers, 8

essentialism: and Black Aesthetic, 14; Gates rejects, 12, 17, 55; and Negritude, 10

Esu-Elegbara, 13, 14, 16

Ethiopianism: origins of, 99–100; paternalism of, 103, 105; scholarly writing about, 148 (n. 8)

Ethiopian Murder Mystery, The (Schuyler), 59

Fanon, Frantz, 97, 147 (n. 3)

Fauset, Jessie, 98

female genital mutilation, 21, 115–16, 121–28

female seduction novel, 109

Figures in Black (Gates), 11, 13, 54, 87

Fisher, Rudolph, 142 (n. 9); *The Conjure-Man Dies*, 59; "John Archer's Nose," 59

Flaubert, Gustave, 15

Foe (Coetzee), 12

For the Love of Imabelle (Himes), 60

Fortune, T. Thomas, 56

Foucault, Michel, 4–5

Freedmen's Book (Child), 76, 144 (n. 21)

Freud, Sigmund, 4, 116

Fugitive Slave Law, 113, 151 (n. 24); and fugitive slaves in North, 107, 113

Gandhi, Indira, 26, 28–29

Gandhi, Rajiv, 26, 29–30

Garnet, Henry Highland, 75

Garvey, Marcus, 100

Gates, Henry Louis, Jr., 94–95; and African American literary criticism, 12–14; connects poststructuralism with African American studies, 133; imposes limits on theory of Signifyin(g), 54, 86–87; and postcolonialism, 3, 10–11, 20; rejects essentialism, 14, 55

Gates, Henry Louis, Jr., works of: *Figures in Black*, 11, 13, 54, 87; *"Race," Writing, and Difference*, 3; *The Signifying Monkey*, 11, 13, 15, 54, 56

Gayle, Addison, 12, 55; *The Way of the New World*, 14

Giddings, Paula, 122

Gilroy, Paul, 107, 115, 123, 129; merges postcolonialism and African American studies, 4–5, 19, 96, 133; theorizes on impact of transatlantic travel on African American political thought, 17, 98

Gilroy, Paul, works of: *The Black Atlantic*, 4, 17–19, 96–98, 133; "Cultural Studies and Ethnic Absolutism," 4, 19; "Route Work," 5; *Small Acts*, 4–5

going native, 45, 50, 52, 139 (n. 16)

Gone Fishin' (Mosley), 60

Gordimer, Nadine, 3

Graham, Shirley, 98

Mishra, Vijay, 6

Missouri Compromise, 78

Mitchell-Kernan, Claudia, 12

Mobutu Sese Seko (Big Man; *A Bend in the River*), 45, 47, 50

Moby Dick (Melville), 88

modernism: connections of, to slavery, 18; contradictions of, 47; counter-discourse to, 18, 98, 106

Monroe, James, 79

Morrison, Toni: and Africanist presence in American literature, 1–2, 21, 87, 92; and American Africanism, 87–88; birthmarks in writings of, 87; displacement in writings of, 3

Morrison, Toni, works of: *Playing in the Dark*, 1–2, 21, 87, 145 (n. 33); *Sula*, 21, 87, 94, 147 (n. 44); "Unspeakable Things Unspoken," 2, 88

Mosley, Walter: alludes to Signifying Monkey, 62; signifies on detective genre, 21, 60, 64, 72; uses Los Angeles as setting, 61

Mosley, Walter, works of: *Bad Boy Brawly Brown*, 60; *Black Betty*, 60, 67; *Devil in a Blue Dress*, 21, 57–58, 62, 68, 71–72; *Little Scarlet*, 60, 142 (n. 7); *A Little Yellow Dog*, 60, 67, 142 (n. 12); *A Red Death*, 60, 67, 72; *Six Easy Pieces*, 60; *White Butterfly*, 60, 67. *See also* Rawlins, Easy

motivated signifying: associated with parody, 15; of Fortune, on "White Man's Burden," 56; of Hansberry, on *Heart of Darkness*, 152 (n. 27); of Morrison, in *Playing in the Dark*, 87; of Mosley, on detective genre, 20–21; of Rhys, on *Jane Eyre* and *Othello*, 53; of Rushdie, on *Kim*, 53; of Walker, on *Heart of Darkness*, 115, 123, 128; on white historical narrative, 55

Mukherjee, Arun, 23

Mumbo Jumbo (Reed), 15, 140 (n. 3)

Naipaul, V. S., 139 (n. 17)

Naipaul, V. S., works of: *A Bend in the River*, 20, 24–25, 45–53; "Conrad's Darkness," 45; "A New King for the Congo," 45

naming, significance of, 79, 144 (nn. 24–25)

Narrative of Arthur Gordon Pym, The (Poe), 88

Nation of Islam, 100

Native Son (Wright), 16

Negritude movement: and "Black writing" model, 9; essentialism of, 10, 12, 17, 55; Gates rejects, 137 (n. 13); limitations of, 11

Nehru, Jawaharlal, 28

"New King for the Congo, A" (Naipaul), 45

Nixon, Rob, 53, 137 (n. 1)

North, lack of freedom in, 107–8, 110–11, 113–14

Of One Blood (Hopkins), 93

"Old Manse, The" (Hawthorne), 92

"On the Psychology of the Negro" (Jung), 118

Orientalism (Said), 1, 5–6

Oronooko (Behn), 15

Othello (Shakespeare), 20, 24, 31–33, 35–38, 43–44, 105

Outcast of the Islands, An (Conrad), 106

Pan-Africanism: and Dean, 99, 101–2; and Du Bois, 17, 97, 130–31; and Ethiopianism, 100; and transatlantic travel, 19

Parry, Ann, 27

Parry, Benita, 43

Parsons, Lucy, 98

of African American women, 98, 107, 111–13, 123. *See also* *Black Atlantic, The* (Gilroy); Dean, Harry Foster; Du Bois, W. E. B.; Jacobs, Harriet

trickster, 13–14. *See also* Rawlins, Easy; Signifyin(g)

Turner, Henry McNeal, 99

Twain, Mark, 8

twoness, 17

unmotivated signifying, 15, 20–21, 53, 115, 128

unnaming, 79, 144 (n. 24)

"Unspeakable Things Unspoken" (Morrison), 2, 88

Vesey, Denmark, 80–81

Walker, Alice: connection of, to ancestors, 122; and the fight against female genital mutilation, 115, 121, 124; and Gates's literary theory, 56; modifies Gilroy's model of black Atlantic, 21, 115, 123; motivated signifying of, on Conrad, 128; transformation of views of, through transatlantic travel, 98; unmotivated signifying of, on Hurston, 16; unmotivated signifying of, on Jung, 128; use of Jung by, in *Possessing the Secret of Joy*, 116–20, 122

Walker, Alice, works of: *The Color Purple*, 16, 56, 116, 120, 124–25; "In Search of Our Mothers' Gardens," 122; "The Light That Shines on Me," 122; "Like the Pupil of an Eye," 121; "Looking for Jung," 120; *Possessing the Secret of Joy*, 21, 114–29

Warrior Marks (Walker and Parmar), 115

Washington, Booker T., 79, 84, 147 (n. 1)

Washington, Madison, 73–81

Way of the New World, The (Gayle), 14

Webster-Ashburton Treaty, 74

Wells, Ida B., 98

West Indies: and black Atlantic, 17, 72, 97; and *Creole* rebellion, 21; and *Wide Sargasso Sea*, 31, 33, 37–38, 42, 44

"What Is Post(-)colonialism?" (Mishra and Hodge), 6

Wheatley, Phillis, 14–15, 98

white American literature: black presence in, 1–2, 87–88

White Butterfly (Mosley), 60, 67

"White Man's Burden, The" (Kipling), 30, 56

whiteness, obsession with: in "The Birth-mark," 89, 91–93, 146 (nn. 36, 38); mocked in African American literature, 94

white people: historical record of, challenged by African American authors, 72–73, 99; and lack of freedom under slavery, 107, 114; as missionaries to Africa, 100; use of slavery by, to highlight white freedom, 88; and women's assistance to slave women, 110

Wide Sargasso Sea (Rhys), 12, 20, 24, 31–44

Williams, Patrick, 6

women, sexual exploitation of: after slavery, 84, 86; during slavery, 77, 81–82, 85, 107, 109–10, 145 (n. 29). *See also* Jacobs, Harriet; rape

Woolf, Virginia, 15

Wright, Richard: in *The Black Atlantic*, 97, 133; Ellison signifies on, 16; and personalism, 99; Reed signifies on, 15; and Senghor, 10

Yarborough, Richard, 73, 75–76, 80, 82

Yellin, Jean Fagan, 109–10

"Your Negroid and Indian Behavior" (Jung), 118